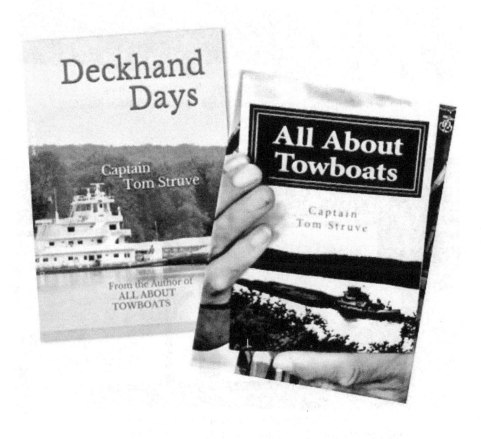

Pilothouse view of towboat downbound approaching
the Fort Madision, Iowa, raiload bridge on the Mississppi River.

Pilothouse view of towboat upbound approaching
the Fort Madision, Iowa, raiload bridge on the Mississppi River.

Best Regards,

Tom Struve

:)

PILOTHOUSE DAYS

Stories from

My Years

as a

Towboat Captain

By

Captain Tom Struve

Pilothouse Days

BookworQs.com

August 2020

PILOTHOUSE DAYS

Copyright © 2020 by Tom Struve

First Printing: 2020

ISBN 9781796308891

BookworQs, LLC

This book is available in digital and print formats at
Amazon.com:books

Also available at the authors web site

bookworQs.com

Special discounts may be available on quantity purchases
by corporations, associations, educators, and others.
For details, contact the author.

U.S. trade bookstores and wholesalers,
please contact the author Tom Struve at
Tom.struve.17@gmail.com

Pilothouse Days

Dedication

Every day,
twenty-four hours a day,
all over America,
towboat professionals are at work
moving commodities
that enable us to enjoy lower costs on almost everything.

One loaded barge weighs 1,400 tons.
Fifteen of them and a towboat weigh close to 22,000 tons!
A fifteen-barge tow covers 126,000 square feet,
more than the size of two football fields end to end.

Towboat professionals are warriors,
and I dedicate this book to all of them, but
especially to those
with whom I had the pleasure to serve.

A very special **Thank You**
to

Captain Larry Hetrick ("Sudsy")
for trusting me with those very important first lessons.

*Full sails and
following winds
to all of you.*

Salute!

A huge thank you
to our marvelous editor,
Julie
at Free Range Editorial
FreeRangeEditorial.com

I continue to be grateful
to all who allow me to use their photos.
Thank you
Richard E. (Dick) Dunbar,
Dick's Towboat Gallery
towboatgallery.com

and
Kyle Pfenning
veteran river captain
Hundreds of awesome towboat videos at
youtube.com/user/marktwained

Excerpt from Chapter 11

"Morning, Jimmy! Did you git a good sleep?" I had just pulled the ship ups back to half ahead as we made our final approach down into Lock 11 at Dubuque, Iowa, when Jimmy walked in. He came and stood beside me, hoping I would hand over the controls to start a new southbound towboatin' day. "You ready to go ta work?" I asked as a I slid over and let him stand at the controls.

"Had a good night's sleep, did a small load of laundry, played a little cribbage with John, got some coffee," he explained. "I'm ready."

Bill and Charlie stepped carefully onto the stern of the load we were faced up to. Charlie, always a comedian, pretended to slide a bit on the few tiny snowflakes that had collected on the lee side of each of the barge fittings. I smiled at them, grabbed the microphone, and re-minded them, "Boys, you gotta be extra, extra careful out there not to slip. Promise me you are taking your time and watching every step you take. 'Specially because you are on opposite corners with no way to git to one another quickly. You gotta be super careful, please!"

Both men waved without turning back. Far over to our starboard side, tall plumes of steam sliced through the cold air out of dozens of tiny stacks above the massive John Deere plant.

I cautioned Jimmy just a bit. "You got just a bit of a west wind blowing you off the wall, so once you get down on the wall don't hes-itate to stop and get your tow flat on the wall. He nodded and pulled the throttles back to dead slow, watching his headway closely, glancing frequently out the starboard pilothouse windows. He *held a nice little point* as before and just prior to the end of the long wall, he steered to port when Bill waved, indicating he was clear of the end of the wall.

"The *Captain Newt* to the *Mallard*. I'm down below here up-

held a nice little point – This is when a captain steers past the position needed and holds the tow in that position before letting the tow come back to a straight line.

bound with a construction crane barge. I'll stay out away from the wall till you go by. See you on the one whistle, if that's OK."

I reached past Jimmy and keyed the mic without picking it up. "Ten-four, Captain. One whistle."

A few moments later, Charlie waved his arm indicating the port bow of the tow had cleared the short bullnose. About twenty minutes later, the lockman sounded the horn indicating we could be on our way. Both deckhands waved the all gone signal, and Jimmy moved the throttles to one-half ahead, starting us moving out of the lock chamber.

"You get down around the corner, you'll see the railroad bridge," I explained. "This one is almost a copy of the Hastings Railroad Bridge. 'Bout a hundred forty-five feet each span, but it's out in the middle of the river. *Shape it*, back up, do whatever you feel good about."

Jimmy backed and killed out our headway then leaned the starboard bow of our tow against the long wall once he cleared the short wall bullnose. He twisted the stern out into the channel.

Once he *shipped the engines forward*, I grabbed the radio microphone. "The *Mallard* is downbound departing Lock Twelve."

Jimmy came full ahead and headed out into the channel.

"I got the railroad bridge open for ya, Captain. Bring her on down," came the reply from the railroad bridge tender.

shape it – slang for steering a tow deep in the turn, "shaping" a turn
shipped the engines forward – move the ship up controls forward, engaging the transmissions and beginning forward propulsion

Table of Contents

Excerpt from Chapter 11

Pilothouse Days

MV *Julie White*, formerly MV *Lindholm*.
Sister and copy of MV *Mallard*.
Telescopic pilothouse. Twin screw, 2,000 horsepower.

1. Getting Ready to Go Around

"I think they are gonna pass by *on the one*."

We were completing our overnight *orders*, moving one loaded barge down to Twin City's barge fleets near South St. Paul. We'd left the ADM (Archer Daniels Midland) barge-loading facility minutes before and were traveling downbound just upstream from downtown St. Paul, Minnesota, on the Mississippi River. Most of the lovely bright yellow and orange leaves on the softwood trees lining the Mississippi had already succumbed to October freezes and subsequent windy rainstorms. Bald eagle sightings are frequent along this leisurely stretch of the river, with a state park on the *right bank* and an old industrial riverfront on the *left bank*.

My *steersman*, Jimmy Svoboda, was leaning forward, watching intently over the pilothouse console on the *Mallard*. The approach or position

orders – slang expression describing direction given to the boat crews by dispatchers. Typically, each morning and afternoon, company officials (most commonly called "dispatchers") provide a list of "orders" or directions about what barges to move and/or where to go.
right bank – The right bank is always the right side of a river, moving downstream. This important designation helps to communicate where something is located or where boats might travel or pass one another.
left bank – The left bank is always the left side of a river, moving downstream.
steersman – a person learning how to steer a towboat

of any *pleasure craft* forward of your tow always merits some concern. I seldom got too worked up about it. I was enjoying sitting on the rear bench of the pilothouse in the love seat-type arrangement with a pillow behind my lower back and a big glass of ice water next to me.

"You know, I used to work with a pilot named Whitey Fleshman. He had serious concerns about pleasure boats passing near our tow. I really felt sorry for him. He musta run somebody over somewhere along the way. Whenever a pleasure boat came into view, even a long way off, he would jump out of his chair, lean over the sticks, pull back the throttles, and just agonize.

"Which way you think they're gonna go?' he'd shout. He did that every time a boat came on the horizon in front of him. Canoe, cabin cruiser. Didn't make any difference. He was a super nice guy. I wish I'd asked him why he was so anxious all the time. Just seemed a shame."

"Should I blow them a whistle?" Jimmy asked.

"I wouldn't unless you get in a really tight spot with them. I can't tell you how many times I tried when I started out as a pilot to follow the Rules of the Road and blow a whistle when a pleasure craft was coming at me. Almost without exception, Jimmy, all it does is screw them up. The moment they hear that whistle, they seem to assume they must be doing something wrong, and frankly, too many dang times they change course, most times dangerously. You try it if you want. You see if I'm not right. Too many times they do something really stupid."

The Rules of the Road are the official guidelines governing every boat on the water. Raft or canoe to the biggest tow or ship around. There is a rule or two for every passing or encounter. The rules include who has the *right of way* and who is *burdened*.

"Jimmy, do you have all the rules memorized yet?"

pleasure craft – motorboats, canoes, sailboats used for recreation
right of way – When passing or overtaking another vessel, one of the vessels has priority and selects how passing or overtaking will occur.
burdened – In a right of way scenario, the burdened vessel has the least ability to maneuver. Example, a sailboat is almost always the burdened vessel in contrast to any boat that has propulsion.

"Yeah. Pretty much. It took me the longest time to git *one whistle* or *two whistle* and *ascending* or *descending* straight. Jist like when I was first deckin'. Trying to get the red and green running lights straight. I always had to look back from the head of the tow to see the lights on the top outside corners of the pilothouse, and then I'd see which way to put 'em."

Jimmy was a good steersman. Not the best pilot I had the opportunity to train, but not the worst. Southern Minnesota farm boy. Giant hands callused from years of hard work. Modest dresser. Always in a plaid long sleeve shirt. Mutton chop sideburns, mostly unkempt. Brown hair, bright blue eyes, prominent German nose, lots of nose hair. About six foot two, same as me, but a lot more muscle. Hailed from Kenyon, Minnesota, a town of about 1,800 on the Zumbro River. His dad managed the co-op feed store there, and Jimmy was throwing bags of feed and fertilizer into the beds of pickups before he could see up inside the box. He came from a family of ten kids. Seven brothers, two sisters. Big family reunion each fall, held at the Lutheran church cemetery, coinciding with the annual Kenyon Rose Fest.

Most of his classmates opted for trade schools after high school or became working partners on the family farm. Jimmy met a guy named Steamboat Bill at a bar while staying with his cousin over the 4th of July in Newport, Minnesota. His new pal worked on the river and told him how jobs were easy to get, and the work was OK. Jimmy stopped at the address Bill gave him, and they hired him on the spot. He drove home to Kenyon, grabbed his work clothes, and said goodbye to very concerned parents.

"You be damn sure to always have clean underwear on, case you gotta go to the hospital," his mother warned.

"Do they give you a life vest?" his dad asked.

Drove me crazy that he refused to buy a decent pair of sunglasses. "Jimmy, I am gonna git pissed if you don't listen to me about this. There might not be a more hostile environment for that one set of eyeballs that you own than staring out onto the water from this pilothouse day after day. I can't see a dang thing out of your sunglasses because they have so many scratches! What in the world are you thinking, man!?" I was teasing, but in fact, I was very concerned.

one whistle – overtaking with the other boat to your left
two whistle – overtaking with the other boat to your right
ascending – traveling upstream
descending – traveling downstream

"I know. I know. Next time I git uptown, I'm gonna git me some good ones. Maybe some of them polarized jobs."

I felt honored that Twin City Barge repeatedly put steersmen with me. Many of these pilots in training were enthusiastic and wanted to learn, listen, and do well. Occasionally, despite their intense desire, some student pilots simply lacked the natural ability and skill to succeed. They could learn, but it would never come easy or be very pretty. Trying to teach folks who lacked natural ability could be trying.

I liked working with Jimmy. He was about midway between really skilled and sort of skilled. But he reeeally wanted to learn. He had a great attitude, always a friendly smile, and a huge, easy laugh. He'd gotten on the *Mallard* two days earlier. They put him with us, knowing that we were ***going around***, over to Chicago, and thought that seeing the entire Upper Mississippi all the way to St. Louis downstream from St. Paul and then the entire Illinois River going upstream to our Chicago area fleet and office would be good for him. Jimmy would show glimpses of true natural skill and ability from time to time. I had a good feeling about that young man. He was grateful to be aboard and clearly understood the value of this opportunity.

The natural ability part of being a towboat pilot can be explained like this: With a bit of common sense and some time around towboats and barges, most people can get ***between the sticks*** and get up or down the river. What differentiates good pilots and captains from average or not so good is the ability to see yourself getting into trouble before you are too far gone to recover. It is just that simple.

Here's another way to explain it. Folks in towboat pilothouses with great natural ability have an inherent sense (born with it — you either have it or you don't) of spatial geometry. Whether navigating upstream or down, you are constantly envisioning ***your tow*** in the space immediately ahead of you

going around – Twin City Barge had operations in both the St. Paul and Chicago Harbors. In the spring and fall they would shift towboats from one location to the other. We called it "going around" because you would travel the Mississippi to St. Louis and then go up the Illinois or the reverse.

between the sticks – Towboats do not have steering wheels. The captain steers with levers called "sticks" mounted on the console in the pilothouse. There is a set of sticks for each set of rudders, steering rudders and backing rudders. Steering rudders are used going forward, and backing rudders are used to steer in reverse.

your tow – one or a group of barges, steered from behind and lots of times you need to steer in a way that gives you room to get the tow through that next space.

Not long after I became a pilot at Twin City Barge, the management there recognized my natural aptitude and leadership gifts and arranged whenever possible for me to be a captain on their towboats. I ran a good towboat. I was an accomplished and personable pilot, and it wasn't long before I gained a reputation among my fellow captains and the deck crews of being fun, fair, and highly skilled. On towboats where I was captain, everyone enjoyed working hard, and we got a lot done. We did things rapidly and efficiently and earned a healthy respect from other crews. It was one of my first major lessons in managing people. I saw over and over that people love being on the winning team. People love being part of the most successful group. People thrive when challenged to do better than average and love to be recognized as the best. The varsity team.

***

Towboat season in St. Paul was about to end. November brings seriously cold temperatures at night and stretches of chilly, silver-sky days when farmers hurry to get the last of the row crops gathered from fields and into storage. Every barge company rolls the dice to get one more tow downbound out of St. Paul just in the nick of time to avoid getting frozen in. The massive grain depots where barges are loaded work around the clock during those fall harvest months, making that last big push.

"We are not getting out of here one day too soon, Jimmy. S'posed to dip down to five degrees tonight. The deckhands have been super careful not to get lines wet for days now 'cause they're no good when it freezes overnight. Wet, frozen line is too stiff to tie up a barge."

Jimmy looked back at me. "This is about the time they always take their boats around, right?"

I nodded. "Everybody says you need to be southbound no later than Thanksgiving. A cool, wet fall causing the water temps to dip and a robust early winter storm with subzero temps for only a day or two will lock up Lake Pepin bad. Two years ago an ADM tow got stuck in Lake Pepin. They hammered and hammered, determined to get through. Punched a bunch of holes in the lead barges and finally gave up. They had crews up here all winter long tending to pumps. Didn't get the barges out of the middle of the lake till spring."

"Holy crap. I didn't know that. Well, I can't wait to get headed south.

Pilothouse Days

If we git a lot of ice, won't some of the buoys git moved out of place? I am really hoping when I'm steering to see them all where they're s'posed to be, so I can make good notes in my *river charts.*"

"We should be OK, Jimmy. Comin' back upriver in the spring is when you see all the buoys moved or missing because of the winter ice. That is when it pays to have been back and forth here enough times that you know where to run without buoys. I've made the upbound spring trip for Twin City for the past six years, and we always seem to pass the northbound *buoy tender* down around Hannibal or somewhere like that. From there, all the way to St. Paul, you just feel your way along. Worse than buoys being missing is that lots of them have been moved *off station* by the ice. You gotta watch super careful with your charts to be sure where you are running. You almost gotta pretend that the buoys you see aren't there."

***

The day before, we were in at the *wharf barge* taking on fuel. Upon a large old flat-deck construction barge, Twin City Barge had constructed a metal warehouse with a machine shop and mechanics' area inside the up-stream half. There were lockers for equipment and storage accessible with a forklift on the other half. The floor was seasoned blacktop, and rolls of line and spools of flexible steel cable were stacked opposite the locked door of the storage area that held sundry supplies like bedding, towels, batteries, mops, brooms, and the like for their towboats. The wharf barge was held in place by long sloping steel tubes on each end and the wood-planked truck-access ramp. These movable connections to shore allowed the entire stationary floating unit to move up and down, depending on *the stage of the river*.

I walked up the ramp, which smelled of *creosote* and fuel and every-thing spilled on it over the years. Just past the modest parking area at the edge

river charts – In the days before technology-augmented mapping, captains and pilots used river charts like we used to use road maps. They often made personal notes in the charts about nav-igating in challenging areas, which others would find valuable. Photo on page 20.
buoy tender – The US Coast Guard operates special towboat-barge units complete with a crane. They carry lots of navigation buoys and equipment and travel along rivers fixing navigation aids that need attention. Photo on page 20.
off station – a river buoy that has gotten moved from where it is supposed to be
wharf barge – a barge secured to the bank of a river that serves as a mooring station, supply depot, repair shop, etc.
stage of the river – "Stage" is the water level above some arbitrary point, usually with the zero height being near the river bed. "Flood stage," for instance, is the stage at which a river will overflow its banks.
creosote – an acrid solution used to treat timbers and wooden poles like pilings and telephone poles to keep them from rotting; banned as a carcinogen around 2005.

of this man-made levee, I entered the nearest of the Twin City Barge offices to say hi to the dispatchers. Ed Williams, John Schwab, and the head dispatcher, Bob Jorgens. The dispatch center was one big room with fluorescent lights and multiple magnetic whiteboards covered with dozens of one-inch-by-two-inch magnets. Each magnet had a crayon-applied number and represented a barge in one ofthe many fleets. It was fun to see that office environment, phones ringing and men in shirts and ties. So different from the on-the-water-aboard-the-towboat working portion of this business. The dispatchers liked me, and I liked them. I like to think I was one of their favorites.

"I gotta tell ya, Jimmy, I was tickled when Bob told me about our tow. They're giving us two loads and six empties for this trip going around. What a breeze. And then the empties turned out to be *hoppers* — no stacked covers. Man! And, I think Bob said we go all the way through to St. Louis with this tow. Somebody here is living right, I can tell you that!

"Yer gonna like steering the way we arranged our tow, Jimmy. Way better than if we woulda made it a *knockout single*. We'll be so much closer to the head of the tow, and the two loads made up as a *unit tow* will let us scoot right along. This is gonna be a nice trip."

It was 11:30 a.m. We had just arrived at one of Twin City's *lower fleets*, and we *topped the loaded barge around* before placing it in the *starboard* bow corner location, finishing off a tow of fifteen loads for the waiting *line-haul towboat* called the MV *American Beauty*.

"The *Beauty* to the *Mallard*, come in on channel seven."

"Go ahead there, Captain," I responded after switching marine radio channels.

hoppers – open container barges without covers used to haul materials not needing protection from weather
knockout single - the tow can be locked in one single locking if you unfasten the towboat from the tow and move it into the notch in the tow.
a unit tow – a group of barges arranged with rakes (round, sloping ends) on each end so you can go faster
lower fleets – In the St. Paul/Minneapolis Harbor these were the fleets farthest downstream. "Fleets" are spaces along the river with moorings along the shore where barges are temporarily stored.
topped the barge around – turn the barge 180 degrees and go the other direction
starboard – the right side of the boat or the tow
line-haul towboat – A line-haul towboat is typically larger (between two and ten-thousand horsepower). Most are live-aboard and tow larger numbers of barges long distances, St. Louis to St. Paul, for instance. Photo on page 21.

Pilothouse Days

"Man! We ain't gittin' outta here one minute too soon! I don't know how you all put up with this cold. I can't stop shiverin'!"

"I hear ya. We are gonna be right behind you guys southbound in a couple days, headin' over to Chicago. Hopefully, we all will make it through these larger *pools* on the upper end without too much ice!"

"Well, maybe we'll see you down the line. Thanks for bringin' us this last barge. We'll be southbound as soon as they turn me loose."

"Ten-four. Good luck to you. If we don't talk on the way out, we'll see you up here next year." I hung the microphone back on the console. It was close to lunch and an afternoon nap. Frank Rhymer was our pilot and about to come up and take over the helm of the *Mallard*.

"Are you gonna steer for Frank too, Jimmy?" I asked.

"Heck, yes! All I can. He said he would be happy for me to steer some for him. I hope to grab just a quick catnap late in the day and git some good night running experience with both of you if you'll let me."

"Frank is really good, Jimmy. Pay close attention to what he shares with you. He used to work over on line-haul towboats for Mobil Oil. Unit tows all over the place. He is one of the best I have ever seen."

As captain on the *Mallard*, I was on the **forward watch**. Frank Rhymer, our pilot, worked the **after watch**. Frank and I really liked each other and worked together occasionally. I loved working on Twin City's towboats with him. Frank had a great Southern sense of humor and loved to visit. Stories, stories, and more stories.

The pilothouse, mounted on **telescopic slides**, moved a bit as Frank, with his perpetual toothpick in his mouth, walked up the port stairway. "Good morning, Tommy! How you doin', Jimmy? Staying outta trouble?" Jimmy slid out of the pilothouse chair, and Frank moved in front of the controls.

pools – When the Army Corps of Engineers installs locks and dams on a river, the water that backs up behind them is called a "pool." In some areas the pools are very wide, extending bank to bank.
forward watch – 6 a.m. to noon, and 6 p.m. till midnight
after watch – noon till 6 p.m. and midnight to 6 a.m.
telescopic slides – Some towboats are built so the pilothouse can move up and down utilizing a hydraulic hoist. These boats can navigate under low bridges.

"I am finer than frog's hair, Frank! Captain Struve here is sure enough keeping me outta trouble! All the time! I can't believe how lucky I am to be getting to steer for you two while we go around. I hit the towboat lottery jackpot!"

"Well, you two git down there and belly up to the table. Johnny's got his best Sunday fried chicken and all the fixin's. I can't back away from the table when I'm on a boat that he's on. They're gonna have to pick me off here with a crane when we git to Chicago. I'll be such a tub!"

I laughed and handed the clipboard with the orders to Frank as he took over the controls. "Grab six empties around the corner across from the wharf barge going to the Port Cargill Fleet. There's only about a dozen barges left back there, so it should be easy to git them together. The *Viking* made us a tow of six loads. We will grab and bring them down and set them up as the first six in the next loaded downbound line-haul tow. Looks like we'll be doing the scramble up the Minnesota and back for a day or two and then head south with two loads and six empties. I got 'em all set up and the tow almost completely built in the upper corner of the Packing House Fleet. Had a little time this morning while we were waiting on orders."

"Boy, I can't wait to git pointed southbound. You guys are crazy, you know that, Tommy!? Your brains is froze! I 'bout froze damn to death last night. Had two heaters goin' up here, and Bill had to loan me his heavy jacket. How in the hell do you live up here? And don't you own one of those snow machines? What in the hell? I can't believe anybody'd go outdoors when it gits like this. I am tellin' you, your brains is all froze! That's what it is!" Frank adjusted the rudders as we turned and headed around the corner to get our empties.

"You Southern boys are sooooo soft, Frank! Ha! This isn't anything. Just some nice crisp fall weather. Hopefully, we won't get that snow they're talkin' about tonight. If the ground gits covered with snow, the temp can really go down."

"Well, go on and git yourself some grub. When you come back up to steer, Jimmy, I kin sit back here in back a' ya and sun myself like a turtle on a log. Maybe warm damn up a little bit! You people are crazy, livin' here. Just plain crazy!"

Jimmy and I laughed as we walked down the pilothouse stairway and astern toward the galley. Both of us were born and raised in the Midwest, so we took the ribbing about our winters completely in stride.

"Frank sure is a good egg, isn't he?"

"And like I was telling you, Jimmy, git all the time with him you can on this trip. Don't be afraid to ask questions. Ask him if you can copy his notes from his river charts if he has them along. He is really good, and you can learn a lot from him."

The aroma from the galley was intoxicating.

"Johnny! I heard you got your Sunday best fried chicken! I am hungry. Let's eat, Jimmy!"

Pilothouse view of tow on the Mississippi River.

One of the authors favorite towboat cooks, John Cullen,
serving Captain Larry Moore a sandwich in the pilothouse on the MV Itasca

2. Galley Life

"Lemme give ya s'more a' them green beans. Them's my special ones." John Cullen, our cook, was strutting around like a bandy rooster, having laid out a grand noonday feast for the boys. I never missed a chance to pat him on the back.

"Holy cow, John, everything you make is your special ones!" I exclaimed.

Pilothouse Days

Towboat cooks love folks fussing over their food, and the more you do, the more they up the ante. He was cooking for seven on the *Mallard*. A much more leisurely pace and demand than cooking on a line boat. They carry upwards of twelve or thirteen when you start adding ***engineers, oilers, mates, and second mates***.

John was always in a great mood. His wonderful smile and gentle demeanor made his galley a pleasant and welcoming place. John learned his craft as an army cook and almost made a career in the army but ended up as a school cook in Tennessee. He cooked great food, lots of it, and with the flair of a master chef. He was a skinny 150 pounds, with thinning, silver-gray hair beneath his tall white paper chef's hat, and a long white beard. His pale blue eyes sparkled when he smiled, and you couldn't help but be joyful around him. John was among the top ten of all the towboat cooks I had the pleasure to work with. His hometown was Hardin, Illinois, where he lived with his second wife.

Towboat cuisine is legendary for both quantity and quality. With few exceptions, towboat cooks are seasoned professionals who produce exquisite regional fare (strong emphasis on Southern-style comfort food) and do it effortlessly. Towboat meals are served in two shifts. The first group to be served just got up from a rest and is getting ready for a six-hour shift. Once they are fed and off to work, the crew that just finished their shift gets fed. Breakfast, lunch, and dinner, the same routine. The cook is generally off duty by 7 p.m. until early the following morning, so midnight and nighttime snacks are self-serve.

The heart of breakfast is all the breakfast meat anyone could want. Heaps of freshly prepared bacon, pork sausage, ham, and sometimes side pork. Made-to-order eggs for everyone and a choice of fresh flapjacks or French toast most days. Hash browns or American fries. Fresh-baked cinnamon rolls or coffee cake. Oatmeal and grits. Baking powder biscuits and Southern breakfast gravy every day. Toast, muffins, coffee, fresh orange juice, milk, and cream. Fruit, yogurt, and dry cereal were always available also. Lunch (or dinner, as many call it) is similarly decadent. Most days, a

engineers, oilers, mates, and second mates – referring to additional staff typically on board line-haul boats. Engineers are trained experts possessing the technical know-how to maintain all the engines and sophisticated equipment on board. Oilers assist engineers. Mates and second mates manage the deck crew, one on each watch.

pork roast or beef roast or both, superbly prepared vegetables always southern style, mashed or boiled potatoes with onions and gravy, and all the goodies.

At least one homemade soup or chili each day and again biscuits or hot, fresh-baked bread for the midday meal. Always lots of salads and dressings and all the trimmings. Most mornings, towboat cooks bake pies or cakes or both, and many would make specialty items like hot, deep-fried, raised, glazed donuts a couple times a week.

Dinner (or supper, as it was commonly called) is a combination of left-overs and some main hot dish, lasagna or the like. Same side fixings, fresh-baked bread, potatoes, gravy, and all you could possibly eat. When the tow-boat cook wraps up the chores for the day, the last remaining task is to stock the crew refrigerator(s) with lots of leftovers in portions and arrangements that make it like having all-night access to the best deli anywhere. From dinner till breakfast, there's always plenty to snack on.

***

"D'you git enough?" John asked when I pushed my plate aside.

"I am stuffed, like always, John. I am so amazed at all the food you prepare for us. What really astounds me is that you make it look like magic. You do your work so effectively and without a lot of drama."

"Nice a' you to say that. I like takin' care a' you guys. Working on a boat with you is just about like not workin' at all."

John and I had worked together a lot that year. He was our cook on the *Itasca* most of the summer. I worked ninety-two days straight on board her during July, August, and September. For all but one week of that time, Larry Moore was our pilot and John was our cook. The *Itasca* was tiny compared to the *Mallard*, with much more modest quarters and a very intimate galley. Nevertheless, Larry, John, and I had an amazing cohesiveness, and we had a wonderful time together.

"So, you **built up so many days** this summer," I said to John, "you probably hardly have to work this winter at all. You had dang near ninety days on the *Itasca* with me and Larry, didn't you?"

"Yep. I got a hundred and eleven days built up. I like doin' that. I'm gittin' too old to travel so much, so when I git on a good boat with a good

built up so many days – It is common for towboat workers to get a day off with pay for every day worked. "Building up days" is slang for accruing those days off with pay.

crew, I just stay as long as I can. I like being home with the old woman in the winter so's she ain't got me doin' all them outside chores at the house. She hires them neighbor kids to do all that crap in the summer, and that's fine with me.

"If they don't *lay this boat up* when we git over to Chicago, I'll probably stay on till right after Christmas. That way I can stay home till they put crews on the boats in St. Paul in April. This here *Mallard*, this is a good boat. Better'n most. I like this galley, it's 'bout as good as any I ever seen. And she's quiet with a great room for the cook."

The *Mallard* was a Twin City *live-aboard harbor boat*. Captain, *utility deckhand*, and deckhand on forward watch; pilot, utility deckhand, and deckhand on the after watch. Jimmy was steering, so there were just seven of us on board. Twin City Shipyard, a sister company to Twin City Barge, had a barge – and boat-building facility in South St. Paul, where they'd built the *sister towboats* the *Mallard*, the *Teal*, and the *Lindholm*. One each in 1973, 1974, and 1975. All the same essentially, these boats were wonderfully appointed and spacious compared to the majority of towboats in the Twin City fleet. They were eighty-eight feet long and thirty-three feet wide. All had telescopic pilothouses and two Caterpillar D398 diesel engines producing a total of 1,650 horsepower. The marine architects designed them with very large flanking and steering rudders, and they all handled a tow like a dream.
The quarters were roomy, and the galley extended the entire width of the boat between the engine room and the *rudder room*. The cook had a large industrial kitchen setup with a center island, and meals were served along a diner-style counter that could seat six.

"I sure enjoyed that hitch with you and Larry and the guys on the *Itasca* this summer. Never seen a crew git along so well for so long."

lay this boat up – "Lay up" a towboat means to tie it up and send the crew home.
live-aboard harbor boat – Some towboats that work in harbors have crews living on board. Some harbor towboats are "lunch-bucket," meaning crews change every twelve hours and live at home.
utility deckhand – a deckhand assigned to keep an eye on things in the towboat's engine room, usually at higher pay than a deckhand
sister towboats – towboats that have almost exactly same characteristics, dimensions, power, etc., i.e., built the same or very similarly
rudder room – At the rear of most towboats is a space that houses the above-the-water portion of the steering and backing rudders, including huge hydraulic pumps and cylinders that move the rudders to steer the towboat.

"I loved it, too, John." I sipped my second cup of coffee. "I still laugh when I think about Larry getting that call from Beth Ann." I chuckled to myself.

"What did she say to him? I heard you guys laughing about it but never got the details."

The *MV Itasca*. One of the authors favorites. Twin screw, 1,342 horsepower.

"I'll tell you, John, it was priceless. We were just changing shifts. He was coming on right after lunch. *The marine operator* called and said to go over to channel twenty-six. And, of course, you know everybody in the harbor switched over to eavesdrop. So the marine operator says, 'I have a call for Larry Moore. Go Ahead.' There's a bit of a pause and Larry speaks."

Larry: Itasca here, go ahead.

Larry's wife, Beth Ann: Larry, this is Beth Ann.

Larry: Hello, daaarlin'. How are you doing?

Beth Ann: I'm good, Larry. Just calling to check on how you're doing.

Larry: I am finer than frog's hair. Me'n Captain Groovy Struve just keep rollin' along!

marine operator – This is pre-cell phone time. To make or receive a phone call, a marine operator (a commercial business) facilitated the phone call, making it take place over a marine radio transmission.

Pilothouse Days

Beth Ann: Larry, that's why I am calling. You bin up there ten weeks yesterday.

Larry: I know, honey, I know. I misssss you!

Beth Ann: And I miss you too, but enough is enough. I have asked you repeatedly when you are coming home, and you keep tellin' me you're ***putting in for relief*** but it ain't happenin'.

Larry: I just left a note in the office mail for the ***port captain*** when we were at the wharf barge this morning, honey. I told him I needed to be home by the end of this week.

Beth Ann: Well, Larry, you may have done that, and you may be makin' it up. But, Larry, I want you to know that I have had enough. I know you very well, Mr. Horndog, after all these twenty-six years." I know you well enough to know that you are not going ten weeks without sex. I don't know if you got a girlfriend up there or what, and frankly at this point I don't care.

Here is what I do know, Larry. This coming Friday and Saturday there is going to be a lot of loving occurring in our house in Pekin, Illinois, whether you are here or not. It's your choice!

Larry: Now, Beth Ann—

Beth Ann: Don't "now, Beth Ann" me, Larry. You heard me loud and clear. Git your ass home in the next couple days, or you won't have a home to come home to!

"You should have the seen the look on Larry's face, John. And you should have seen how bright red he blushed, knowing that everybody in the St. Paul Harbor was listening to that conversation on their radios! I felt so sorry for him. I didn't feel comfortable laughing, but then we both burst out laughing together!"

"D'you think he had a girlfriend here?"

"I got no idea, John. He didn't tell me about it if he did. I just think he

putting in for relief – requesting to get replaced and leave the towboat
port captain – towboat company official primarily responsible for arranging crews on boats and crew travel arrangements

---

was enjoying our great working setup, and we had such good crews all those weeks. You were cooking on there and so easy to git along with. You brought our meals upstairs for us in that beautiful, roomy pilothouse, remember? We had the TV from the galley up there and watched till dark each evening while making that gravy train *Pine Bend tank barge run*. I let half the deck crew off to go to town every other Saturday night, and they loved that. Most of them rode for seven or eight weeks." I got up and took my dishes over to the sink.

"I remember you letting the deck crews switch off Saturday nights in town. Didn't you think that was a little risky? Did the office know?"

"I am pretty sure nobody in the office knew, John, but we got so damn much work done, if they had known, I am sure they would have looked the other way. I made all those deck guys assure me that they would come back and come back able to work. They treasured being trusted and having the opportunity to get uptown every other weekend to see a girlfriend and have a couple of beers. Just made the days roll by." I smiled at the memories.

"Everybody on that boat hustled. I swear the dispatchers enjoyed, piling on the work just to see how much more we could get done. And as Sunday afternoon approached, we all jacked it up one more notch so we could get into the wharf barge, get fuel and supplies, and git up to the *Red Rock* before it closed!

"Anyway, I enjoyed all those weeks with Larry more than I can tell. He was fun, a good pilot, and we just seemed to mesh so well. He treated his deck crews with the same respect, and it was all good. Throw in an awesome cook like you, and it's a wonder any of us got off that boat." I got up, ready to head up to the pilothouse.

"It was a good trip, Tom. I enjoyed it too. When they told me I could come over here and cook for you and go around with you, nobody could have been happier." He grabbed a bowl from the counter and moved it toward me. "Now. How about a big bowl of my fresh-baked shortcake with a pile of strawberries and fresh, homemade, real whipped cream?"

Pine Bend tank barge run – This was a time when most oil companies had bulk terminals along the Mississippi, where bulk trucks loaded to move fuel to gas stations. Twin City Barge had a couple of oversized tank barges that were loaded about once a day at the Pine Bend Refinery (now Koch Refinery) about twenty miles south of St. Paul. Towboats would take an offloaded empty down to the refinery, place it for loading, and pick up a loaded tank barge to take back upstream.
Red Rock – This was the nearest saloon to the wharf barge. A good place to get a drink, and the riverman's choice of local bar. Lots of storytelling.

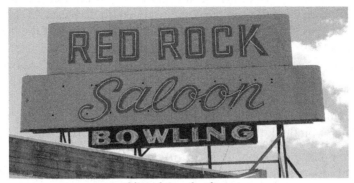

Sign above the door
at the most popular towboat professional hang-out
only about a mile from the wharf barge
in Newport, Minnesota.

Author speaking into marine radio microphone
at the helm of *Itasca*.

Most towboat pilothouses have a couch like this. Good for visitin'

3. More Visitin'

"Come on in here, Tommy. Put yer feet up, and let's visit a bit."

Frank, our pilot, was just *facing up* to our tow of six empties destined for Port Cargill, a few hours upstream on the Minnesota River. Frank was probably forty years old but looked twenty-five. Thick through the waist, broad across the chest but not heavy, he had a handsome, seriously dimpled,

facing up – fastening the towboat to the stern (back end) of the tow with face wires — one on each bow corner. Face wires are approximately one-inch-thick flexible steel cables that are loosened and tightened using winches mounted on the front of the towboat.

almost Clark Gable face, with a warm, contagious smile. Frank dressed like he worked in a bank, not on a towboat. He always had well-tailored pleated slacks and wore high-quality cotton shirts, polo shirts, cardigan sweaters, and always fine shoes. He was a clothes horse without question. He always finished his polished presentation with a touch of excellent cologne. His appearance complemented his gracious demeanor. I never saw him upset or heard him utter a negative word. Frank loved to visit and laugh, and he was always on the verge of a good tease of some sort.

Frank came from the southern tip of Illinois. He had a home in town in Mounds, Illinois, and a summer cabin about twenty miles west on the Cache River near Unity. He and his two brothers all worked on the river, following in their dad's footsteps. Captain Frank senior ran the old Federal Barge Lines steam paddlewheel towboats on the Ohio back in his heyday. Frank quit high school to work on the boats and worked for over two decades for Mobil Oil. In the '50s and '60s, Mobil ran three handsome and prestigious towboats that pushed large unit oil tows throughout Middle America. Over the years, more pipelines were built, and by the '70s, moving petroleum products on rivers became less attractive environmentally. Married for the third time and childless, he and his wife enjoyed camping, mostly nearby in Tennessee and Southern Indiana. He worked for a couple of Illinois River towboat companies before signing on with Twin City Barge.

"D'ya git enough lunch down there? That Johnny is somethin' else! I'm already out a full notch on my belt, and I only been on here a week!" While he talked, he reversed the two hefty diesel engines on the *Mallard* and backed the tow out into the main Mississippi channel. As the tow moved backwards, he poured a fresh cup of coffee and made a quick set of notations in the *logbook*. The wind was blowing strong out of the south, and the damp air and silver-white sky warned of an impending weather change. "I damn sure did, Frank. I love that man's flair for southern cooking. He makes everything so rich and full of flavor. I'm sure my arteries are plugging up as we speak!"

Jimmy, our steersman, came through the door just as Frank moved the engine controls to neutral then to *full ahead*. Frank motioned for Jimmy to

---

logbook – The captain or pilot makes copious notes about all the activities of the towboat. In the case of a harbor boat, dispatcher's helpers use the logbook entries to bill for shifting barges.
full ahead – full speed ahead

have a seat at the controls. Jimmy didn't hesitate. Frank turned and slide in alongside me on the two-seater love seat at the rear of the pilothouse.

Jimmy spoke into the microphone of the marine radio. "The *Mallard* is upbound below Valley Line Fleet checkin' for downbound traffic above the Pig's Eye Bridge, over."

Another towboat responded. "The *Mary Jenny*'s jist leavin' Yard A up here. How about we **switch over to channel twelve?**"

"Ten-four. Channel twelve," Jimmy then keyed the mic again. "The *Mallard* to the *Mary Jenny*, over."

"The *Mary Jenny* back. We just left up here. I got six empties, is all, so I kin git by you jist fine."

Jimmy looked back at Frank and me. Neither of us responded. Making these kinds of decisions is an essential part of being a steersman on a towboat. The *Mary Jenny* was the downbound towboat in this scenario, and because of that, she had the right of way. Because Salami Hanken, the captain of the *Mary Jenny*, had not indicated how he wanted to pass, towboat pilothouse courtesy provided Jimmy with the opportunity to suggest how they might best pass one another.

"How about if I stay over on the right bank and go through the **shore span** and leave the **river span** for you comin' southbound? I am only a few thousand feet or so below the bridge, and once I am in the bridge, I will **cut 'er back** and stay over here out of yer way. That work for you?" Jimmy asked.

That will be fine with me, Captain. You should be looking at us here in about thirty seconds or so. He's got the bridge swung open, so we're good. I will **see ya on the two**. I'll be down through that river span in no time and outta yer way."

switch over to channel 12 – Marine radios have one or two channels designated for boats to call one another. Once contact is made, mariners switch to other channels to converse. This prevents a constant chatter that everyone would need to listen to all the time.
shore span and **river span** of bridge – In the case of a turntable bridge, there are commonly two choices to navigate through. The one closest to the shore is the shore span, etc.
cut 'er back – slang for slowing down
see ya on the two – slang for selecting to meet on the two whistle, side to side, starboard to starboard. Facing forward on a towboat, port is to the left, starboard is to the right.

Pilothouse Days

Pigs Eye Railroad Bridge discussed here.

Frank had asked me about those Shiely Company harbor boats early during that trip.

"Salami Hanken is one of the best captains I have ever seen," I told him. "He is a true gentleman and one of the nicest guys you will ever know. He lives in Prescott, Wisconsin, just down the river from here. Same town I'm from. Shiely's got two boats. The *Mary Jenny* and the *Joe Al Jim*. They have two mines alongside the river about seven miles down from South St. Paul. One produces limestone, and the other is sand and gravel. The *Mary Jenny* brings two tows a day up and delivers to Yard A. The *Joe Al Jim* takes two tows a day up through the locks to their Minneapolis yards. Both towboats got a day shift and an evening shift. Eight hours and maybe a little overtime when the ***water gits up*** and slows 'em down. What a great job that would be. Home every night."

"Salami his real name?" Frank asked.

"Not sure. Think it's a nickname. I'll have to ask him when I see him next. He is a real character. I run into him pretty often downtown at a local hangout, the Pilot House, in Prescott."

"A bunch of you guys workin' out here from Prescott, eh?"

"I guess there are. Don't think about it all that often. When I was

---

water gits up – when river water levels rise and current increases (flooding)

deckin', I worked for a mate named Bobby Lubich over at Material Service on the Illinois River. His brother Johnny is one of the captains on the *Joe Al Jim* for Shiely. They're from Prescott. I think there was a bunch of Beelers that worked out here and several brothers named Schickling. I been relief captain for Denny Schickling the past couple summers down there, running the MV *Sioux* up the St. Croix. Web Severson, Dallas Eggers, Tom Filkins, bunch of others outta Prescott, I guess.

"Probably the most legendary of all of 'em from Prescott is a guy named Popeye Tronnier. Great big guy. That's where he got the nickname Popeye, I think. Arms like big pipes. He's been around on the river forever and works a lot *on the Lower*, they say, as *trip pilot*.

Pilothouse window view of twenty-five-barge tow on the Lower Mississippi.

Captain on just about everything and anything. Worked on the *Delta Queen*. Loves to raise hell and have fun!" I reached for the ashtray and snuffed out my smoke.

"I was in the next bar down the street from the Pilot House one day last winter when Popeye came in from ice fishing on the St. Croix right nearby. He *shook for the pot*. Popeye and the bar owner, Fat Albert, disagreed about

on the Lower – referring to piloting on the Lower Mississippi River (Cairo, Illinois, to the Gulf of Mexico)

trip pilot – a pilot job that is contracted day by day, for an agreed-upon fee typically far above a regular pilot's daily pay. In the 1970s, trip pilot pay was commonly $200 per day (compares to $785 today).

shook for the pot – The player spends a quarter — or whatever the fee is — for the privilege of rolling a set of five dice three times. Most of the time, four of a kind wins a twelve-pack. Five of a kind wins the pot. Sometimes it's weeks before the pot is won, and the quarters in the pot can total hundreds of dollars.

one roll of the dice. Popeye was sure he had won a twelve-pack and would not take no for an answer. When Albert refused to award Popeye the pot, Popeye stormed out to his car and returned with his ice auger. He started her up, stepped from a stool up onto the beautiful historic mahogany bar, and proceeded to drill a hole in it. In the end, Albert backed down, and everybody had a big laugh. Popeye is famous for stunts like that!"

Frank and Jimmy had a great laugh at that story. Visitin' like that is how men aboard towboats spend their leisure time. Some tales taller than others, and most of the time a fair amount of embellishment is included. I got up and started toward the port side pilothouse door.

"I'monna go down and hit the sack for a bit. You two keep her in the channel and try and stay outta trouble!"

Neither Frank nor Jimmy acknowledged my departure. Already deep into the next story, Frank began, "We have a crazy guy like that where I live too. One day I was having lunch at this bar called The Library, and he came in…"

Captain "Popeye" Tronnier at the helm on the steamer *Delta Queen.*

View from pilothouse navigating through Fort Madison Railroad Bridge downbound on the Upper Mississippi River.

4. Goin on Watch

"Rise and shine there, buttercup!"

Charlie, the head deckhand on the after watch, always woke me up with those words. Always with his charming smile and never too loud. My guess is that he was sixty years old. He had thick red hair and a million-dollar smile created by a denture expert. Slow Southern slang just added to his charm. Most everyone on a towboat gets awakened by someone assigned to do that. They may already be awake, but usually someone checks to be sure. Sometimes sticking their head in the door and turning on a light is all it takes. I always requested a 5 a.m. and 5 p.m. wakeup in order to have time to shake off the cobwebs completely before going on watch at six o'clock. Each worker except the cook on a live-aboard towboat works two shifts of six hours offset by a six-hour shift to rest in between.

Pilothouse Days

Most crew rooms, or "quarters" as they are called on a towboat, can be completely darkened because some of your sleep occurs during daylight. The size of the room and the amenities vary based on the size of the towboat. Since live-aboard towboats are pretty much always moving, two characteristics about crew quarters are common. With massive diesel motors working hard, the most serious environmental concern is cooling a room, not heating it. And the second thing that goes with the territory is some level of noise along with constant vibration. That is why when I got off a live-aboard towboat after *my hitch*, before doing anything else, I would typically treat myself to a high-quality, QUIET hotel room for some sleep in a bed that wasn't moving.

The quarters on the *Mallard* were relatively spacious and nicely decorated because she was only three years old. Each room had an upper and lower bunk, and you shared your space (and your personal hygiene habits) with your room partner. In my case, the pilot and I shared a room. Substituting for a closet, each of us had a roomy metal locker and a modest dresser. A floor lamp provided some soft mood lighting near a tiny writing desk and a sturdy, comfortable chair. A fair-sized bath had a nice shower, a stool, and a small sink and counter. I always made my bed and kept my space very tidy in consideration of my roommate. I appreciated the same. The pilot/captain's quarters and pilothouse on most towboats get cleaned, to one degree or another, every day by someone on the deck crew. That improved the chances of your room being that much more pleasant. Each room on the *Mallard* had a healthy-sized air conditioner in the outside wall with an adjustable thermostat. Our room was toward *the bow* on the port side, farthest from the engine room. While underway, the underlying noise was noticeable but tolerable. You get used to it on a towboat. It just is.

I cleaned up and put on a light jacket for my trip to the galley to get my first round of coffee and a bite to eat. As I walked toward the stern on *the guard*, I noted that we were in the Port Cargill Fleet alongside a gray loaded barge that was part of our downbound tow. Almost fully dark at 5:10 p.m., the towboat *flanking lights* shone on the barges adjacent to the muddy slope

my hitch – slang for the time that you spend working on a towboat. Common period for a hitch on towboat is thirty days.
bow – front of any nautical vessel
the guard – Along both sides of most towboats is a walkway (the guard) alongside the part of the towboat above the main deck. This walkway is almost always on top of the fuel tanks.
flanking lights – Towboats are equipped with lots of bright lights that shine to the sides of the boat. Very valuable for navigating in close quarters in the dark.

of the Minnesota River bank lined with huge, leafless cottonwood trees. The sharp sounds of rigging being thrown on the decks of the barges helped wake me up as did the cool, brisk air, a complete contrast to my cozy room.

Photo showing how barges in a tow are fastened together using rigging.

Passing the open doors and windows of the engine room, cupping my hands over my ears, I breathed in the smell of the river. A pungent combination of organic material in various stages of decomposition mixed with silt, general runoff, and the treated, but still odiferous sewage effluent released into the waterway from the wastewater treatment plants on the bank at every town for hundreds of miles upstream. Nothing else in my world had that same odor. It was part and parcel of that phenomenal career I so dearly loved. These were the smells I learned to love as a young boy growing up endlessly fascinated along the St. Croix and Mississippi Rivers in my hometown.

I entered the galley and was treated to one of Johnny's best eye-twinkling smiles. "What can I git ya, Captain Tom?"

"I tell ya what, Johnny. I'm still full from lunchtime! Maybe…though, you got some of that roast beef there, thin sliced on a slice a' bread with a little taters and gravy?" I poured a cup of coffee. It smelled terrific.

"Absolutely!" Johnny said. "Comin' right up!" He followed that with, "Did ya sleep good?"

I laughed. "I don't remember. I was busy sleepin'!"

Johnny grouped the thin slices of roast beef on the cutting board then laid them alongside a pile of hot, fresh homemade mashed potatoes. Covering it all with dark gravy, he set the plate down in front of me and had a seat on his side of the counter.

"Mmm mmm!" I said. "How can everything you cook be so damn good!?" Suddenly I was hungry, almost instinctually responding to the excellent aroma of the food. That was the problem with Johnny's cooking. Everything smelled and tasted so good that you couldn't exercise any self-discipline to limit your portion. Your will power was out the window.

"D'ya think it's gonna snow, Captain Tom?"

"They got snow in the forecast, but it's hard to tell. This time of year, I think the weather news folks all are trying to outdo one another with the early snowstorms to be the first to sound the alarm. I've seen that so much, living in the Midwest all these years. Kinda like the weather forecasts during State Fair week. The fair is a huge economic boon to the area, and the weatherheads hardly ever forecast rain for fear that people will change their plans to go to the fair. One time, I tore the shingles off my house during State Fair week. Left it bare overnight, planning to shingle it the next morning. Big thunderstorm got me outta bed at five thirty next morning. No word of that from them turkey weathermen!"

Johnny smiled and moved some hot, fresh-baked dinner rolls down the counter and opened the cloth that was keeping them warm. "Here. Let me git ya some butter to go with them."

Simply the best food anywhere. Easy to be gluttonous. I turned down Johnny's offer of fresh-baked apple pie and ice cream for dessert. Gotta draw the line somewhere. But I'd probably have some at midnight before going to bed.

"Have a great night, Johnny. Thanks for the excellent food. Wonderful!" I said, exiting the galley and heading for the pilothouse. Walking up the stairs, I could see and hear the deck crew *fastening the rigging* in the *steering coupling*. Stepping through the door,

I watched Frank looking through the binoculars at a group of four whitetail does.

"Man! I ain't never seen so many deer as you got up here! You a hunter, Tommy?" He passed the binoculars to me.

"You bet, Frank. I camped for two whole weeks last month hunting ducks and bow hunting for deer up in Northwest Wisconsin. Lotsa birds, and I let a couple of small bucks go by my stand. Not lookin' for the little guys. How about you. You hunt?"

"Naw, Tommy. Me'n the old woman stick pretty close when I'm home. She likes to go downtown and visit with the locals. We both bowl in leagues, and we got a bunch of camping friends. We got a nice RV. We camp at the state parks in Southern Illinois and Tennessee all summer when I am off. Little fishin'. That's about as sporty as I git!"

He and I swapped positions at the helm. "Another few minutes, they'll have these loads wired up," Frank said. "I heard the *Mike Harris* northbound about two hours ago at the Minnesota River mouth. The guys on the *Viking* went home for the night, so you got the whole place to yerself. Jimmy steered till about four thirty, gittin' them empties up here, so he's likely takin' a nap right now. I'monna git some grub, and I'll be back up in a bit." Frank threw on his jacket and headed for the galley.

The boys turned me loose, and we moved upstream and *topped around* to face up to the tow.

"All gone!" shouted Billy, my utility deckhand, as they let the *shore*

fastening the rigging – Groups of barges are fastened securely together into a tow by rigging so they maneuver as one big vessel. Rigging consists of flexible cables, ratchets, and chain straps that fasten the barges together.
steering coupling – Tows are comprised of barges fastened together end to end. Each connection is called a coupling. The coupling closest to the towboat (one barge length forward) is called the steering coupling. It gets the most stress when the towboat steers, so it must be fastened more securely than any other coupling.
topped around – to turn around 180 degrees
shore wires – Moorings are installed along the riverbank, connecting barges or tows in fleets to flexible steel cables called shore wires. They hold the barges in place along the bank.

wires drop into the river alongside where the tow had been laying against the mudbank. I shifted the throttles to about three-quarters astern and moved the backing rudder sticks so the reversing flow of river water would shoot down between the bank and the tow. The ***stern*** of the tow moved out into the channel, and gradually the entire tow did too. I moved the throttles to neutral for a moment and then to full ahead. The two mighty Caterpillar diesels growled, and crackled, issuing their customary black smoke while coming up to speed. Our ***sternway*** stopped, and gradually we picked up forward momentum. Moving down around the corner, I saw the spotlights of a northbound tow down around Lyndale Bend. I cut her back, and we slowly moved by the fleet where northbound empties were stored on the right bank.

Guessing it was the *Mike Harris*, I got on the radio. "The mighty *Mallard* to the *Mike Harris*."

"Mighty *Mike* right back. What channel, Tom?"

"How 'bout channel six, Bobby?"

"*Mike Harris* on channel six."

"Did you ever know Lucky Buzbee, Bobby?"

"Name doesn't ring a bell. He from around here?"

"Maybe you never ran into him. He made a few trips up here, but mostly he works down in Chicago. Anyway, he stutters, and he has a great sense of humor. Whenever he would git his days in and git close to going home, he would always say the same thing on the radio when you would meet him while passing. He would say, 'D-D-D-D-Don-n-n-n't-t-t-t-t start no l-l-l-l-ong c-c-c-c-c-conversations!' indicating he was just about to get off that boat and head home." I chuckled to myself. "Makes me think of what you must be thinkin' right now. Almost beer thirty for you. You'll crew change up here, right?"

"Yes, sir, Captain Tom. I just saw the ***Capital Barge pickup*** on that gravel road on the riverbank upbound by the salt dock. Soon as we drop these empties, we will crew change right there at the Cargill dock. They're actually

stern – rear end of any nautical vessel
sternway – momentum while moving backwards
Capital Barge pickup – The Capital Barge Company used a recognizable company pickup to move crews at crew change time.

sending a watchman to be on the boat overnight. We'll be *yankin' loads* first thing tomorrow that loaded overnight ta git 'em down for a line boat." He continued, "We got the end of the season party tonight down at the Pool and Yacht Club. Our fearless leader, Mr. Robert Drain, pulls out all the stops every year for this deal. Really well done, top-notch."

"Holy cow! You must be chomping at the bit! How fun for you!" I said. "I am just about to the lower end of the fleet, right above *Dredge Cut*. How many you got?"

"Six. They were gonna hang eight on us, but I was able to talk 'em out of it. We'd a' never got to the party till ten if they'd a' done that! Ol' Mighty *Mike* ain't that mighty!

"I will tuck my lead barges into the right bank north of the salt dock if that's OK with you, Tom. Just don't waste any time gittin' down through there 'cause yer cuttin' into my party time!"

Jimmy came through the door and took a seat behind me. He circled his coffee cup with both hands, shivering after the chilly trip up the stairs.

"You make me laugh, Bobby," I said. "Good thing we got that rain these past weeks or I'd be floatin' through Dredge Cut right here. I got the old girl *hooked up*. We'll be down by you there in just a few minutes."

"Ten-four, Mr. Struve. I am waitin' here on the two whistle. Have a super night. Prob'ly see ya up here sometime tomorrow again."

"All righty, Bobby. Be safe tonight. Hope you all have a great time!" I hung up the microphone and moved my two spotlights to maximize the view of both banks. That stretch of river can be a real challenge during low water.

"See that little shelf of rocks sticking out there, Jimmy?" I asked. I moved my starboard searchlight up and down, highlighting the location I wanted to point out to him. "When I first got into the pilothouse for Twin City in 1973, I had this hot-rod mentality. We did everything quickly, and I think

yankin' loads – slang for removing loads from loading areas
Dredge Cut – Often a new river channel is dredged to bypass sharp horseshoe turns. The new straight channel is called a cut. Dredge Cut is one of several locations where the Minnesota River was dredged to eliminate those severe bends in order to increase the ability to move larger tows up and downstream.
hooked up – full ahead or full astern

our boats and crews probably broke some records for the number of barges we moved around the St. Paul Harbor in a day's time. Not long after I broke in, they put me on the *Viking*. Triple ***screw***. Three engines, three sets of rudders. Twelve hundred seventy-five horsepower. Nice boat. We were running up here in the middle of the dog days of summer. No rain. This nasty old Minnesota River gits more and more shallow during periods of no rain." As we passed through that spot, I moved my light farther down the bank.

MV *Viking*. Triple screw, 1,275 horsepower. Telescopic pilothouse.
Shown pushing a tow of 6 empty barges upbound in St. Paul on the Mississippi.

"Anyway, that little jut out from the bank is the only noticeable reminder at the surface of a small rock ledge that the Army Corps of Engineers ran into in the sixties when they dredged the Minnesota River. They took out several of the severe ***horseshoe turns*** between the grain terminals up here and the mouth of the Minnesota about fourteen miles downstream. Apparently, they found some rock, but it was so close to the required dredged depth that they weren't concerned about it.

"Now, when the river gits realllly low, it's easy to find that damn rock ledge and git hung up on it. I had it in my mind as a new pilot that there should be the correct 'slot' that you had to find to git down through there. Time after time. I would git her hooked up, fully expecting to hit bottom but thinking if I favored that left bank, I could power through there. And time after time, we would hit bottom and git completely and hopelessly hung up. I'd end up with

screw – in nautical speak, screw means propeller. For example, single screw means one engine and propeller, twin screw means two engines, and triple screw means three engines.
horseshoe turns – The Minnesota River had several severe turns that resembled a horseshoe shape prior to dredging.

that same scenario. Twisting and backing and finally ***breaking up the tow*** to get the grounded barge off that ledge." I shook my head at the memory.

"One night, I was headed down on Dredge Cut with six loads, dreading getting hung up again. Right ahead of us was the *Kiowa*, about to enter that same tight, shallow area. The captain was an old boy named Ed Smith. The *Kiowa* is a sister to the *Viking*. Same towboat, almost exactly. Ed was a super nice guy, Jimmy. A veteran on the river, quick with a smile, and generally a very modest character. Thing is, it drove me craaaaazzzy how he and lots of his fellow older captains seemed to take forever to do everything. I was wondering if he and the *Kiowa* were having the same issues gittin' down through that that ***slack water area*** as I was. I watched as the ***wheel wash*** leaving the stern of the *Kiowa* disappeared. I was puzzled. How was he gonna make it over that rock hump without hooking her up? I called him on the radio.

"You havin' trouble gittin' down through there with a loaded tow, Ed?' I asked. 'Not so far, Tommy. I just float 'em through there, and that seems to work out OK. Lemme pay attention here fer a minute, and I will git back to ya,'" I continued to explain. "So, I watched what he was doing carefully. They got right above the upper end of the cut, and he ***knocked the boat out*** and ran around the downstream end and faced her back up! I switched our engines into slow reverse and continued to watch. I didn't see that Captain Ed was making any downstream progress. I eventually stopped the reverse of our engines and floated slowly downstream. It seemed like it was taking forever! Eventually, it looked like he was clear of the shallow, impossible-to-navigate area. A bit more time passed. He brought the *Kiowa* back up alongside her tow, turned a hundred and eighty degrees and faced back up to the six-barge tow. The ***familiar black smoke*** erupted out of the ***stacks*** of the *Kiowa*, and I noted generous wheel wash as Captain Ed brought the three Caterpillar diesel engines up to full ahead.

"I called him again. I couldn't believe what I had just seen. I said, "Ed,

breaking up the tow – After running aground, oftentimes you need to disassemble the tow of barges to get unstuck.
slack water area – any shallow spot
wheel wash – propulsion coming out of the stern of the towboat. Evidence of forward marine propulsion. Towboat propellers are often called "wheels."
knocked the boat out — removed the face wires and separates from the tow
familiar black smoke – Most diesel engines spew black smoke when accelerating. More fuel is sent to the combustion area than can be burned for a period, and that uncombusted fuel exhausts as black smoke until the engine gets up to speed.
stacks – the exhaust pipes of a towboat. Generally located high so exhaust smoke doesn't make a mess.

that was the longest thirty minutes of my life watching you do that. Having said that, I'm embarrassed to say that we have spent no less than two hours each trip downbound for days hitting bottom there and having to tear the tow apart, yank everything through there, then get it back together and downbound again. My hat is off to you, sir. We're doing just what you did, right now. You had your engines dead slow backing down through there, right?'

"He just laughed at me. 'That's the trick, Tom. Instead a' being hooked up and running all the water out from underneath yer tow, you just float 'em through any spot like that.' I told him that I had also just faced up on the downstream end and hadn't even bumped bottom there. I was dumbfounded. That is exactly what happened and how the conversation went, Jimmy. He really taught me a lot. I was so hell-bent on running everywhere full ahead, and that was precisely what was causing us to repeatedly get hung up there. There was so little water in the river that I was pulling what was left out from under the loaded tow!"

"Makes sense, Tom," Jimmy said.

I moved out of the captain's chair and motioned for Jimmy to slide into place and steer. We had moved southbound through Dredge Cut and were coming down on the Upper and Lower Lyndale Bends. Jimmy shined the two searchlights down each side of our six-barge loaded tow and pulled back the throttles to let our *headway* run out a bit.

"I'm gittin' the hang of these Lyndale Bends, I think," Jimmy said. He moved the port searchlight to see the remainder of the bend and continued. "It took me lots of trips down through here to learn to let the lead barges drop way down into the bend before starting that first hard steer to port. Always feel like the boat is gonna hit on the stern as we go around the lower bend, but that's where ya gotta be with six to git through there. Kinda glad they got them *picket fences* on all these Twin City boats. Gives a little comfort as you come skiddin' around there!"

"The Minnesota River is really good shallow water training for you, Jimmy. Nothin' but mudbanks on both sides, and pretty much the worst you

headway – a measure of how fast the tow is moving forward
picket fences – All of Twin City's harbor boats had a series of structural pipes extending down parallel to the outside of the openings in the hull where the propellers and rudders were. Pilots called them "picket fences." They kept the rudders and propellers from contacting the shore or rocks, etc., when the towboat got in where it was shallow or dangerous.

This view shows the "picket fence" that Jimmy is referring to.
Installed on many harbor towboats, they protect the propellers and rudders

can do is get too far up into them old nasty cottonwood trees." I took a sip of coffee and lit a cigarette. "'Nother thing you gotta watch, Jimmy. When you get movin' loads around in these slack water barge-loading areas, you can git yourself all tangled up gittin' **horsey**.

"My first trip on the old *Santee*, as a brand-new pilot. I was trying to yank a load out of the Cargill slip, and, of course, I was in a perpetual hurry! Tryin' to do everything fast, ya know! Back and forth and full ahead, full astern, twisting! I looked out, and we were pinned to the bank opposite the loading dock. The more power I used, the worse shape we were in. I finally gave up, stopped everything and walked out of the pilothouse down to the main deck and took a leak over the side."

Jimmy smiled at me, and I continued, "Got back upstairs and noticed the coffee pot by the couch had tipped over. Not a lot of coffee in it, but a mess, nonetheless. I turned on the pilothouse light, tidied up, and took an additional minute to catch up on my logbook with the last few switches we had made. Everything back in order, I turned off the light and took my position between the sticks. What I saw through the window in the light of the bright flanking lights was a complete surprise. In the few minutes since I'd last tried to use brute force to move the barges, everything had changed. The barges next to the boat had shifted over to dockside of the loading area, and there was now all kinds of room to move the barge I wanted out of the slip. We were soon underway, backin' that load out and on the way to our southbound tow.

"So, here's what I learned, Jimmy." He looked at me, interested in this

horsey – getting in a hurry

impromptu lesson. "In shallow places, less is more. I'd been determined to use all the force the boat could supply to do our work quickly. Instead, I'd moved so much water around that I'd literally sucked the barges on my starboard side over and up against the side of the boat. The barges pinned the ol' *Santee* against the bank, and nothing I'd done had helped. It was simply blind luck, thanks to my call of nature, that I stopped doing anything and let the water settle down. Only then did I understand what was happening."

As we were coming down on the Upper Lyndale Bend, Jimmy pulled both throttles back to ***dead slow***. He'd clearly understood what I was just talking about.

"I watched lots of guys pile tows up on this tight, little muddy Minne sota over the years I bin deckin' here, Tom. Trying to run full ahead and force their way. Even backin' up a little in these tight bends seems to work best for me. Only means a few minutes more at the end of the day, and you ain't stuck and up in the trees all the time!" Jimmy looked at me, hoping for affirmation.

"I like the way yer thinkin', Jimmy. Yer gonna be all right, young man. Best things you kin do is watch and learn from everybody else's mistakes. "I'm gonna head down and make a pit stop. ***You got 'er***, OK?"

"We're guiding and gliding here, Captain Tom. I'm good. Take all the time you want."

I left the pilothouse feeling good about working with Jimmy. He wasn't near the impatient greenhorn pilot that I started out as. That was a good thing. As I moved down the stairs and onto the head deck, I ran into Frank, heading up to the pilothouse.

"You people is crazy, Tommy! You know that? Your brains is froze!" He laughed, hurrying past, rubbing his hands together, on his way to partake in a post-evening-meal-nightcap story or two before heading for ***the box***.

What a great day.

dead slow – as slow as a captain can go and still steer. Engines engaged but very slow.
you got her – slang for "you are taking the helm"
the box – It's fairly common on a towboat for a bed to be enclosed with some modest side rails to keep sleeping folks from falling out if the towboat bumps, thus "box."

Two powerful searchlights at use here helping the captain navigate during darkness.

5. Night work

I could see my breath as I moved forward from our quarters up onto the *head deck*. Jimmy had all the flanking lights on, and you could see the muddy banks of the Minnesota River slowly passing by. I noticed the deck crew had placed a two-way *safety line* between *the bits* and the center of the stern of our six-barge loaded tow. I untied the thick, well-worn *Poly D* head

head deck – Staging area — working area at water level on the bow of the towboat. Equipment and lines are stored there.

safety line – Workers will install a line between the bow of the towboat and the stern of the tow. If anything happens to the face wires, the captain can control the tow while stopping.

bits - mooring kevel-like arrangement on the center of the bow of the head deck of a towboat. This is where a safety line is fastened to barges being towed.

Poly D – Poly D is the name brand of premium line used on towboats. Extremely strong, a little larger in diameter than general use line, it is the premier go-to line for the toughest service on the river. Most lock lines (lines used on the tow while going through a lock) are also Poly D.

deck line and reworked it, making it a *four-way line*. Jimmy had her *backing slow* as he dropped down deep into the Upper Lyndale Bend. Entering the pilothouse, I watched as he and Frank passed the binoculars back and forth.

"Man! Look at the rack on the buck farthest to the right!" Frank said. He passed me his 7 x 50 pilothouse binoculars. We were no more than one hundred feet from the group of five deer, which just stared back up at us. In the bright lights of our towboat, it was as if you could reach out and touch them. There were two bucks and three does, and when they weren't staring into our lights, they kept glancing at each other. My guess was that romance was in the air. I counted twelve points on the bigger buck, and he was indeed regal. What a gorgeous animal!

As we watched, he and the lesser buck squared off and started to wrestle with their antlers. Just a little buddy-like sparring at first, but then the big guy backed up about five feet and coldcocked the little guy! Tossed to the ground, he jumped up then spun around, and all you could see was that long vertical white tail and bottom. He was gone in two bounds. The three does looked longingly at the victorious, massive male. He held his head even higher, giving a show of confidence for the girls. He was clearly in command of his miniharem, and he followed the three ladies closely as they walked calmly back into the thick brown vegetation, now frozen and ready to collapse and decompose under a layer of snow during the coming months.

"I'm thinking that big guy isn't getting much sleep this time of year. Probably full-on rut right about now," I said.

Jimmy had moved the throttles to neutral as the towboat, fastened to the stern of the tow dropped very slowly and deeply into the bottom of the bend. "Very well done, young man," I said. "What you are doing is one of the hardest things to teach a new pilot. Being patient and letting the boat get deep into the bend is all part of *shaping a bend* in every downbound scenario. Typically, a new pilot wants to steer too soon in a shallow little river like this. All you do then is run aground or end up forcing your way through the bend. Or

four-way line – the number of around-and-back times a line is installed accounts for a two-way, four-way, six-way, or more designation. The more ways the line is installed, the more strength it provides.

backing slow – diesel engines in reverse at minimum or slow power

shaping a bend – going around a turn with a tow closer to the outside of the turn ("deep" in the bend).

you actually *stick the tow* and end up fighting to get her off the ground. It really is a matter of patience to get out of this river *at normal pool* with six loads." Jimmy smiled, acknowledging my positive feedback.

"Did you notice that I snugged your safety line on my way upstairs? ALWAYS use a safety line, Jimmy. I can't tell you the number of times I have had a winch let go or even a face wire break. A safety line gives you the chance to keep the tow out of trouble while you kill out your headway. And, here's another thing I will do sometimes. When you get deeeeep down into these bends like you are right now, I might slack that shoreside face wire a bit to give yerself a little extra cushion in case the stern of the boat is draggin' along the mud back there. If you have a safety line on nice and snug, you still have enough flex so the boat just kind of snakes along behind the tow without breakin' a face wire. Make sense?"

Jimmy nodded as he nudged the throttles forward to about one-half ahead to give us a little push into the Lower Lyndale Bend. Looking forward across the three lengths of barges, it seemed like the port bow corner of the tow was about to climb the bank as Jimmy began to steer to starboard. He was doing a wonderful job of steering that tow.

"These two Lyndale Bends gave me fits the first few times I was up here," Frank said. "I spent my first fifteen years in the pilothouse runnin' *unit tows* for Mobil Oil. They ran the *Mobil Leader* that was five thousand horse-power and the *Mobil LaCrosse,* that was thirty-two hundred horsepower on the Upper and Ohio and some on the Lower River. Lots and lots of room in most cases. Nothing like this little pisspot of a river. Between this and that upper end of the Illinois River, I don't know which is worse. It took me a while to git used to these close quarters, that's for sure!"

"You were always goin' like a bat outta hell, too, weren't ya, Frank, with them unit tows?" Jimmy asked.

"Damn straight! Those *long rakes* on the bow and stern of the tow were designed for speed. Makes it even harder fer a guy ta git used to pokin'

stick the tow – run aground and get stuck
at normal pool – when the river level is normal. If dams are present, the level of river that is normal backed up behind the dam.
unit tows – a set of barges or a pair of barges end to end and a rake in each direction. (The rake is the sloping curved bow portion of a barge.)
long rakes – Some barges are built with an exaggeratedly long sloping front portion. Barges with long rakes have less water resistance so they go faster.

around in these tight spots and bein' as patient as you gotta be up here on this river!" Frank said.

"I've had some experience with that high-speed stuff, Frank," I said. "Twin City runs a towboat called the *North Star* with a **hot shot** unit tow mostly between Wood River, Illinois, and locations on the Tennessee River. I made one trip on there about three years ago. The *first watch I stood* down-bound in the dark, south of St. Louis, I thought I might crap my pants. The river was up, and you could make eighteen miles per hour southbound hooked up. That's way fun in the daylight, but at night it was more than I wanted!"

Photo of MV *Victoria*, formerly the MV *North Star*. Twin screw, 3,200 horsepower

Jimmy and Frank had a good laugh, then I continued. "That same trip I had to change drawers again one afternoon after we ran into a fogbank on the Tennessee River. Goin' along upstream hooked up, almost fourteen miles per hour, it was like somebody pulled a shade down on the front pilothouse window. Complete, shut-out fog. Way out in the middle of one of those huge pools on the Tennessee. Couldn't see five feet. *I set her to backin'*, but how was I to know when the headway was killed out goin' fourteen miles per hour? The radar showed me where I was relative to the *sailing line*, but it was not nearly sophisticated enough to tell me anything about headway or sternway!"

Jimmy swung his searchlight from side to side, illuminating the water intake on the right bank just above the power plant. The lights of the power-

hot shot – slang for moving barges quickly between destinations
first watch I stood – first time I took over at the helm of a particular towboat
set her to backin' – engage the engines in reverse then increase to full power astern
sailing line – On river charts, a dashed line shows the ideal location for you to travel or sail.

house in the background made it challenging to see all the features of this last sharp downbound turn before the Minnesota River straightened out all the way to its mouth. Jimmy pulled back the throttles once again and let our headway run out.

"They used to load coal barges out here at the Black Dog Power Plant," I said. "When I first started in the pilothouse, we ran two loads from here down to the mouth and then went north all the way to the head of navigation in Minneapolis to the Riverside power plant. Same power company, but these guys had a rail spur here where they delivered Montana low-sulfur coal. They loaded two barges here almost every day. The old *Santee*. Went through Lock One and the Lower and Upper St. Anthony Locks. It was a gravy train run, man. Two loads up and two empties out. Monkey Rudder Bend just below Lock One was a hoot with two empties downbound, flyin' down through there!"

The old dock where they loaded the coal barges was just coming into view as Jimmy dropped our six barges deep into the final stages of the bend. About the same time, we could see construction lights for the piers and shore structures for the new Cedar Avenue freeway bridge being built about a half mile downstream.

"I had my share of adventures on the mighty *Santee*," I continued. "You'll see the old Cedar Avenue Swing Bridge comin' up here in a minute just upstream from the new bridge. They closed it to traffic, but it's still there in open position till they git traffic on the new bridge. We hit that son of a bitch with the *Santee* when I was deckin' on her in 1972."

Historic Cedar Ave Bridge on Minnesota River. Used between 1920 and 1980

Pilothouse Days

"You hit that bridge?" Frank said.

"I didn't!" I laughed. "The pilot did. It was the dangdest thing. This was when I was deckin', before I got in the pilothouse. Old boy named Carl Bales was the pilot. It was super high water in the spring — water running hot! Carl was just back from all winter off. He would ride the whole summer in St. Paul and then take the whole winter off. I felt really sorry for him. He had the worst hangover I had ever seen. Heavyset, short, raspy, harsh voice that was almost painful to listen to. I would come to the pilothouse to watch and visit sometimes *off watch*. On more than one occasion he asked me to tell him what the signals were coming from the deckhands on the head of the tow. When it was dark, he complained that the reflective patches sewn to the lifejackets blinded him from seeing the men.

"For some reason the dispatchers sent the MV *Sioux* up to Cargill to get a tow. Skeeter Ransom was on there and never been up the Minnesota. He backed the *Sioux* into the point right at the Cargill slip there and bent a steering rudder on her. So we had to take her back down to the shipyard in St. Paul to put her on *dry dock*. They put the *Sioux* on the downstream end of two loads, and away we went," I continued.

"So, that old bridge at that time had a reallllly slow manual operation to turn the turntable and *swing the span*. Carl comes screaming around the corner right here, blows for the bridge, and sets her to backin'. He was almost able to stop, but the old *Santee* had small backing rudders, and he got way *out of shape*. Couldn't git her ass to lift back up against the current. I was off watch, but he started blowing danger whistles, so I got up to help out if I could.

"He managed to stick the bow of the tow through the bridge, backing full, making sure the *Sioux* got through OK. Just never got the *Santee* back over far enough to starboard. The *Santee* hit the end of the bridge dead-on.

off watch – not on duty while on board a towboat
dry dock – a platform that is filled with water allowing a towboat or barge to be placed on it. Then the water is pumped out and the barge or towboat is raised out of the water in order to be repaired.
swing the span – Some bridges are located on a center pier, and when the bridge operator swings the span, the bridge is open and no longer perpendicular to the river channel.
out of shape – slang for "not maneuvering in the correct way," letting the tow get where it should not have been

The pilothouse just folded over backwards right under the very end of the bridge. Right about the same time, they fired up the engines on the *Sioux* and pushed the whole operation into the bank below the bridge. Poor Carl stayed right with it. He never left the pilothouse. I went up the stairs and used a fire axe to cut a hole in the collapsed steel pilothouse wall to git him out!

"Know what the first thing he said was?"

Both Frank and Jimmy were listening intently.

He said, "'Anybody got anything to drink on here?' I think that somebody did get old Carl a half-pint from their locker to help him get settled down. Poor guy!"

Jimmy brought us back up to full ahead, coming out of the lower end of Black Dog Bend. The lights around the airport were more visible, making it seem like we were in the middle of a city instead the middle of nowhere.

Frank said, "Well, I am gonna hit the rack. Eleven thirty comes soon enough. You keep old Cap'n Struve outta trouble, will ya, Jimmy?"

Frank opened the starboard pilothouse door, stepped out, then stepped quickly back in. "Holy shit! The temperature musta dropped fifteen degrees. I don't know what you people see that is desirable, living in this frozen tundra. You are absolutely out of your minds!" Frank continued mumbling about his disdain for the cold and headed down the pilothouse stairs again.

Jimmy laughed and pulled her back a bit as we headed down around the corner above Black Dog Bend. Along the banks there, the trees thinned out and you could see a fair distance away from the towboat. The area is combination state park and river floodplain, so lots and lots of wildlife. During annual spring flood along with occasional summer high water, the ten-foot-high mudbanks lining the channel can go underwater. With our telescopic pilothouse as high as it could go, we were about three stories above the water. Jimmy had all the lights off for the time being because we could see better than if they were on.

"I hope all my pals down near Kenyon git their corn in before this wet cold hits us," Jimmy said. "The moisture in the corn being harvested now is knocking the shit outta the prices this year, but they're really up against it right now. Gotta git it outta the field. I hope this new ethanol thing pans out fer everybody. Talking about six- or seven-dollar corn next couple a' years when they make it mandatory for regular gas to have ethanol."

Pilothouse Days

As we rounded the bend above the Mendota Cut, the **channel lights** on the Mendota Bridge shone brightly, marking the edge of the channel. We were making good time now, and Jimmy **called for upbound traffic**.

"The *Sophie Rose* to the *Mallard*. How about channel seven?" Jimmy unhooked the microphone and stretched the spiral cord a bit, handing it back to me. He switched the radio to channel seven.

"Good evening Mr. McGonahue. How are you this fine night?"

"I am finer than frog's hair there, Captain Groovy. Yer southbound just above the river mouth, huh?"

"Yup. I am sitting in the back watching the world go by while my man Jimmy is making things happen. We are whistling outta here tonight. Nice six-pack with rakes on both ends and makin' time. As Lucky Buzby used to say, 'Don'tttt start no long conversations!' Gittin' ready to head south and go around!"

"Ten-four," McGonahue responded. "I am just about to clear the Omaha Bridge heading to Minneapolis one last time. I think this might be the last two loads they are gittin' up there. They sure got a mountain of salt up there at the Upper Harbor Terminal this year. I hope that is not going to determine how bad our winter will be!"

Gary McGonahue was one of my favorite fellow St. Paul Harbor captains. He was **a regular** for Dakota Barge Services, and he was upbound down in St. Paul with his tow of two salt barges going to Minneapolis Upper Harbor. Gary and I visited about everything and anything whenever we could. He was fun, intelligent, and generally very positive and upbeat. About the same age, we had lots in common. Made the time go by — visitin' with him.

channel lights – All bridges over rivers have colored lights illuminated at night to mark the channel. Red lights are straight up from the edges of the navigable channel, and there is a green light above the center or the channel.

call for upbound traffic – Today, towboats have technology that tells them where other vessels are. Prior to this technology, a captain would announce his position before entering an area where passing would be challenging. If someone was coming the other way, they would call and make arrangements for passing.

regular – The majority of employees working on towboats are "regular". They typically enjoy full benefits, possibly seniority, and are paid an average salary.

"You stay around here all winter, Gary, or do you head south somewhere?"

"No, I am gittin' outta here soon as they lay this boat up. My girlfriend has a girlfriend who has a little apartment on Fort Meyers Beach. She rents us one of the bedrooms. Been goin' there for the past two winters. Love it there. How 'bout you, Tom?"

"I'd like ta take some time this winter, but depends on when we git over to Chicago and if they are busy over there. If I kin stay workin' till Christmas, I'll take a couple of months off after that. I got a place in Northwest Wisconsin. Up by Webster. Some of the best snowmobiling on the planet.

"Hoping ta do some trip piloting this winter too. Had a couple of good hitches last year working for Valley Line over there in January and February. Two hundred dollars a day now. A guy can get healthy quick doin' that!"

Gary chuckled a bit and said, "I heard that too, Tom. I wasn't lookin' to do any extra this winter but, man, they sure make it tempting! Hetrick said he worked all of October and the first three weeks into November, and he put enough in the bank to stay home all winter. Me and him and Couthart are talkin' about a trip down to the Florida Keys this year. That'd be a blast!"

"I see your running lights down there. We are just above the Pool and Yacht Club. How about we just stay over here and slide down this right bank and see you *on the one*? Jimmy's been workin' hard on stayin' deep down into every bend, and he is doing terrific at it."

"Ten-four. One whistle. So, is he gonna git to go around with you guys?"

"You bet. I told him he hit the pilothouse lottery gittin' to do that. Frank Rhymer's on here on the other watch, and he's lettin' him steer all he wants to. Between our two sets of charts and strategizing to see most of the tough stuff, it's a chance of a lifetime."

"All righty, sir! I'monna let ya go, Captain Tom. Fuzzy just come

on the one – slang river-speak for "Let's pass on the one whistle side" (port-to-port meeting or overtaking with the other tow on your left — port — side)

through the door with a fresh cup a' coffee and told me we might be gonna lose an engine. He found a little fuel leak down in the engine room, so I better pay attention to what's goin' on here for a bit. If I don't talk to you before you all head out, have a great winter. Maybe we'll cross paths over there on the Illinois River if we both git some trip pilot work."

"Ten-four. Good talkin' to you, Gary. You take care. See you down the line."

I handed the microphone back to Jimmy as he pulled the throttles back and got up out of the captain's swiveling pilothouse chair. He felt like approaching this bend in the river required his full attention. "Give me your best advice about heading downbound above the Omaha Bridge with six loads, Tom. Do you stay tight to this point like I am doing here, or should I be deeper down into the bend as we come around?" He moved his searchlight across the width of the river in front of us, providing a good examination of our location.

"Yer doin' good, Jimmy. If it's normal pool water like this, it's better to favor the right bank a little. You'll always have a little slide goin' downbound comin' around here, and you want to always leave yourself a little throttle so you can give yourself that needed push to keep your point while the tow runs out of its slide. *Hold in the dark*, just like you are doing for just a little bit more and then hook her up, and you'll be down through there like a dream."

A few moments went by. Black smoke poured from our stacks as Jimmy moved the throttles to full ahead. He steered the tow gently back to port, letting the head of the tow drop safely into the slot along the left pier of this swing span railroad bridge and continued into the next steer, shaping our tow deep down into the bend approaching the High Bridge in the downtown St. Paul Harbor.

"Like that?" Jimmy asked.

"You did everything jist like I woulda, Jimmy. Nice job, kiddo," I said. Moving through the St. Paul Harbor that time of night was enchanting. Once

hold in the dark – When steering a tow around a turn, a captain must sometimes hold the bow of the tow in a location where it appears it will crash (into a pier, for instance) while the tow is sliding (going sideways). After a time, the captain will steer back into the main channel to miss the pier.

we made that final turn below the Omaha Bridge, all the lights of downtown on the left bank high up in the distance came into view. The high, mostly wooded riverbank to the right made you think back to the days when the dozens of caverns located there were used to make and house moonshine during prohibition. Now the openings in the prehistoric limestone bank were bricked over to keep kids out of trouble and cave explorers from needing rescue. The beat-up, trashy wharf housing Minnesota Harbor Service was tucked against the bank. A couple of misfit towboats were moored there along with barges being cleaned and repaired. Along the left bank, the decades-old power plant illuminated the underside of the Smith Avenue High Bridge. The giant smokestack had strobe lights that lit up the mammoth pile of coal just behind the plant. The original High Bridge was constructed in 1889, and she looked it. I wondered how long it would be before somebody decided it was time to build a safer bridge to provide the vital connection between St. Paul and the bedroom communities on the south side of the river.

Toward the river in front of the power plant, Bob Draines' Capital Barge Service wharf-barge-office was located right smack under the High Bridge. Immediately below were piers and shore wires along the concrete-lined bank where his main fleeting area was. No barges there tonight. The mint-green barges moved by his primary customer, the Cargill Companies, were all downbound downstream safely south of the oncoming winter ice. The Paddleford tourist packet boats docked against the park on the right bank were the upstream anchor of a row of docks housing year-round houseboaters. A robust crew, those folks had to deal with frozen river ice all winter long and spring floods almost every year.

I got up to grab a pack of smokes from my carton and said to Jimmy, "Just ahead you can do same as you have been. You can drop yer tow nice and low into this bend above the Robert Street Bridge and slide right down through there. If the water gits up, there is *a pretty good set down onto* that left *sheer fence*, but at this stage of water there is almost none."

Jimmy called for upbound traffic, and nobody responded. Once again, he shaped the tow down nice and deep into the bend and held his point on the right pier of the railroad bridge, waiting as our tow ran out of its slide. The busy collector roadway right at the top of the riverbank — Warner Road — carried cars and trucks just one or two hundred feet or so to our left as we

pretty good set – a push sideways by the current
sheer fence – Many bridge piers have a series of wood or metal pilings upon which a timber "fence" (or timber wall) is constructed. That surface is intended to provide protect the pier in case the tow hits it.

MV *Viking* downbound at Robert Street bridges. Warner Road along left bank.

sliced down through the bridges. Lots of hustle and bustle, vehicle headlights, coming and going. State Street Fleet and State Street Cleaning Station, both belonging to Twin City Barge, were the two main features on the right bank, just ahead between us and the Lafayette Bridge.

"Wish I had a dollar for every barge I have shifted in and outta there," I said to Jimmy.

Twin City Barge had a prominent and premier presence in the St. Paul Harbor. They were there in the very beginning and had made many good decisions, positioning themselves for success. The State Street Cleaning Station was a hub of barge clearing and repair activity every day during the towing season. Run by a group of brothers, the operations were smart, efficient, and profitable. When your barge arrived in St. Paul in a northbound tow, Twin City Barge provided a secure fleet (for a daily fee) for your barge until your barge was shifted (for a fee) to its destination and the cargo was offloaded. Their harbor towboats shifted your barge to the customer, and when it was unloaded, they shifted the barge into State Street to be cleaned. State Street even had a dry dock used for lifting towboats and barges out of the water for repair.

While your barge was there, it was inspected, and the owner was told if repairs were needed. Most times those repairs were made then the barge was either moved back to a Twin City Fleet or shifted somewhere to be loaded for its downbound trip. After loading, most barges returned to one of their fleets and then (again for a fee) a Twin City Barge harbor boat would build a group of barges into a large downbound tow. Each step of the way generated revenue for Twin City Barge in return for excellent service while visiting the port of St. Paul, Minnesota.

We continued our downbound trip, sliding under the channel lights of the main channel of the Lafayette Bridge. Below, on the left bank, a railroad shifting yard was wedged between Warner Road and the multishaded dark limestone bank rising up hundreds of feet above. More fleets. Minnesota Harbor Service Fleets to the left, and Twin City Fleet to the right. Behind the Twin City Fleet, the many colored lights of the runways of the St. Paul Downtown Airport. The airport was built on a floodplain, and with each new upgrade they moved parts of it higher ground to lessen the impact of spring flooding. The 3M Corporation, a major commercial giant in the Minneapolis-St. Paul area owns the giant 3M logos applied to the hangars next to the river housing their fleet of industrial commuter jets. Looking downstream from there, there are fewer lights, and the black of the night on the horizon is set off by the soft golden glow of lights from the Twin City Metro Sewer Plant and another massive railroad switchyard.

"Do you ever run the shore span of the Pig's Eye Railroad Bridge, Tom?" Jimmy asked.

"I never have, Jimmy. The two spans are about a hundred and seventy-nine feet each. I been through them so many times back and forth shifting barges, it just seems natural as breathing. Just like all these bridges up here, you can hold in the dark, making the turn and just drop the head of your tow into the bridge right above. Even if you're still sliding, you got plenty of room in there. Every line boat I have run out of St. Paul left outta the lower fleets, so I never had the occasion to run the shore span. I am sure I would if I was gittin' fifteen down through there."

Just as with the other bridges, Jimmy was *in good shape* coming downbound, and I offered no advice. None was needed. He let the head drop into the span like we'd talked about and hooked her up as we sailed down past the tall timber sheer fence protecting the center span. I got up and walked out of

in good shape – slang for maneuvering precisely the way you should

---

59

the pilothouse, leaving Jimmy to continue moving downstream to our destination, one of Twin City's lower fleets. We could see the flanking lights of the MV *Mary L* a mile or so to the south, lying next to her tow ready to accept the last six barges we were pushing. I hurried down the guard and back to the galley to make a pit stop and get a fresh cup of coffee. All was quiet. Johnny had retired for the night, and the deck crew had headed out to the tow to get ready to **make the drop**. I poked my head into the fridge, thinkin' about a snack but decided against it and headed out into the crisp fall night.

As I came back through the pilothouse door, the captain of the *Mary L* was talking with Jimmy about how to land our tow.

"Back her right up in here in front of where I'm sitting. We are all set for ya. My center **string** can take that **three-piece unit** that's yer port string right in front of the **break coupling**. Once that's done, we got two boxes that we'll use to make the starboard string with your two rakes on the ends, over."

Jimmy made a slow sliding steer to starboard and set her to backin', falling right over to port and alongside their tow. He turned on all our forward deck lights and operated the winches as the deckhands took off our face wires and hung them up. Bill, our utility deckhand, removed the safety line, and Charlie, the deckhand, lifted the remaining **head gear** up and over the **head log** onto the head deck. Jimmy moved the boat over to the side of the six loads and had the guys **catch a line** that slowed the side motion of our barges now settling in alongside theirs.

"Once you git them slid back here, come alongside me, and we'll

make the drop – get ready to deliver the barges or tow — i.e., "drop" the barges at a fleet

string – In the case of a line-haul tow, barges will be assembled longitudinally three across. The center "string" is the center longitudinal row of barges.

three-piece unit – rake pointing backward, a box (square on both ends) barge, and another rake pointing forward, assembled end to end

break coupling – The most common line-haul tow is twelve or fifteen barges assembled together. The majority of locks on river systems have a main lock chamber that is 600 feet long. Tows are assembled so they can be temporarily broken in two and, once the locking occurs, reassembled into a tow. Where that break and reassembly occurs is called a "break coupling."

head gear – slang for all the equipment that is typically used on the head (or bow) of the tow. Lock line, bumper, running lights, transducer, etc.

head log – the front vertical face of the towboat where it contacts the tow. Like the front bumper of a car.

catch a line – fasten a line between two objects — barges or barge and towboat, etc.

swap out the riggin' you got on these," the captain of the *Mary L* said.

Jimmy used our ***pilothouse flashlight*** to find and switch off all our flanking lights. It is pilot-to-pilot courtesy to be respectful of the other's night vision by limiting lights that might be blinding them. He responded affirmatively to the captain of the *Mary L* about the rigging swap. While our deck crews counted and swapped rigging, I turned on the pilothouse overhead light and used the time to catch up on my log work.

Jimmy, yawned, stretched, and grabbed his jacket off the hook on the back wall. "I'monna hit the rack, Mr. Tom. Hope that's OK. Been up and workin' almost all day, and I'm afraid I am runnin' out of steam."

"Absolutely! Git yer butt down there and take a break, Jimmy. You earned it. I gotta tell you, I'm impressed. There isn't a lot I see that you are doing that needs comment, let alone correction. You got some pretty nice natural talent, kid. That's not something me or anybody else kin teach ya. Ya either got it or ya don't. I've had a lot of guys steer for me and broke in several pilots and you are right up at the top for doin' good. Git some rest. We git done here, we are gonna head into the wharf barge and get supplies and top her off with fuel. Dispatchers told us to *lay by* till morning, and if nothing else changes, they might let us head south by midday tomorrow."

"Thanks for sayin' them nice things, Tom. It helps with my confidence. I am really enjoying working with you and Frank. Thanks a lot for everything." He smiled as he opened the door, letting fresh air in and cigarette smoke out.

"Git some sleep, man. Gonna git you a bunch more steerin' time tomorrow, Jimmy."

"The *Mallard* to the *Mary L*, channel six, please."

"*Mary L* on six. Go ahead."

swap out rigging – When barges are delivered to another boat or a fleet, sometimes the rigging holding them together stays in place. In that case, the two towboats will trade for an equal amount of rigging.
pilothouse flashlight – When maneuvering in the dark, a captain needs the pilothouse as dark as possible as his eyes have adjusted to the low light. A very specific flashlight is always nearby (on the console) and is used sparingly.
lay by – when a towboat stops for a period of time.

Pilothouse Days

Towboat MV *Mary L,*. Twin screw, 4,300 horsepower.

"I think we got ya all squared away there, captain. Anything else we can do for ya?" I asked.

"No. Once we git this outside string made up, we'll be ready to face up and head out. Man, it's gittin' cold! I hope we can git down through here without too much ice."

The cold was on everybody's mind. Once river operations become winter river operations, lots of thing change. And none of the changes make life easier. Falling snow makes moving at night intolerable because you can't see anything. If it snows hard enough in daylight, you can't see long distances. Once you are actually pushing a tow through any amount of ice it becomes nearly impossible to turn a tow. Getting in and out of locks gets more complex, and breaking and reassembling the break coupling at a lock in ice can be a huge headache. Lines become stiff as a tree if they get wet and then freeze. In addition, perhaps the most concerning issue related to winter conditions is worker safety. Towboats and barges have steel decks and working conditions become very hazardous with accumulating snow and ice.

"I know what you mean," I responded. "We're gonna take this boat around over to Chicago for the winter, so we'll be right behind you probably later today."

"Well, maybe we'll visit down the line here. Take care and stay warm!"

Good photo of pilothouse console and captain's chair.
Note two engine controllers and the sticks used for steering.

6. A Flood of Memories

The crew removed the line running between our head-deck and the Mary L as they stepped over our face-wires carefully.

"All gone," yelled Bill. He and Charlie had swapped out rigging with the Mary L crew and were busy tidying up their work area right below me on the front deck. I had the front window open about ¼ of the way as we turned and headed *light boat* for the wharf barge around the corner inside the entrance into Pigs Eye Lake. The electric heaters necessary this time of year

light boat – slang for operating towboat without towing any barges

to keep the pilot house warm posed some operating challenges. No matter what you did, the floor of the pilothouse was always freezing cold while the space above the steering console was almost always too hot. A small opening in a window sometimes helped offset that imbalance. Making the turn shoreward and heading back north, the lights around the Peavy Grain Terminal and Twin City Shipyard came into view. Lots of otherwise homeless-for-the-winter marine equipment was scattered around, now dark and secured, waiting to be locked into position until spring by two or three feet of ice. Several construction barges with cranes on board, the last few brand-new hopper barges built right there at the shipyard that didn't make it south, and the balance of Twin City Barges towboats that were selected to winter is St Paul. The towboats surrounded the wharf barge, lit up and plugged into **shore power**. Just enough of an opening for me to bring our towboat alongside close enough to hook up the huge hoses used to take on fuel.

Each of the towboats moored there had been my river home and workplace on at least a handful of occasions. Anchoring the north end of the wharf barge was the MV Sioux. The pride of the Twin City Fleet, she stands four stories tall. Originally a line-boat from the Brent Towing Company Fleet out of Greenville, Mississippi. Twin City Barge bought her in the late 60's to tow barge loads of coal between Prescott, Wisconsin (on the Mississippi River) and the Northern States King Power Plant on the St Croix River just downstream from Stillwater, Minnesota. She was a perfect fit for that work and the pristine St Croix River environment. Spit-shiny clean and always hosting a veteran best-of-the-fleet cook, Twin City Barge considered her their "showcase" towboat and the company frequently arranged for day trips up the river on board for VIP clients and important business associates. Her four stories of visibility made her perfect for down-bound tows of now empty barges frequently carrying high piles of stacked covers. Line-boats that dropped loaded northbound coal barges in Prescott picked up the most recent emptied barges and brought them north to St. Paul to be cleaned and loaded with their southbound grain cargos.

The St Croix deserves its National Wild and Scenic Rivers Designation and is a regional magnet for pleasure boating. Lined with recreational boat docks, summer homes and extravagant year-round abodes, summer recreational boating traffic increases dramatically on weekends making towboat trips too risky.

shore power – Electricity on board is supplied by diesel generators. Where available, a cable providing electricity can be attached to the towboat allowing the generator to be shut off.

Each weekday morning at dawn, John Gray, the Chief Engineer fires up the two 900 horsepower GMC diesel engines and she moves gently across the river to the fleet on the right bank opposite the town of Prescott. The northbound loaded barges are assembled into a tow destined for the King Plant and the upstream journey begins. The deckhands finish laying and *tighten all the rigging* on the tow as she slowly makes her way past downtown Prescott into the pre-1900 era railroad swing bridge and through the decade's old highway lift bridge. Captain Dick Schickling steps out onto the gas-pump-side deck of his small marina called Captain Dicks Boat works, right below the railroad bridge, and gives the hands-raised-above-your-head wave to his brother, Denny Schickling, the primary Captain of the Sioux.

Towboat Sioux pushing a tow of coal upbound passing through the Prescott, Wisconsin highway bridge, entering the St Croix River.

The *Sioux* runs only weekdays between April and November. Home every night, Denny seldom takes any time off during the summer. Over the last three years he did take a couple weeks each season and I was offered the chance *to be his relief.* I leapt at the opportunity! It was a dream come true to

tightening all the rigging – Barges in a tow are fastened together with a series of ratchets and flexible steel cables. Once these "sets" of rigging are installed, they must all be tightened. The ratchet, or "turnbuckle" is turned, pulling the wires tight.
to be his relief – replace him as captain

be piloting this regal towboat, the pride of the fleet, on this gorgeous river where I spent all my summer hours and days as a young boy. I would be lying if I said that I was not beaming with personal pride as a super-young Captain piloting the Sioux daily in front of the town where I grew up.

I was very close to my father. One day as we were moving through the US Highway Ten bridge entering the St Croix, I stepped out onto *the flying bridge* on the downtown side. The sun was just coming up and there was a light misty fog just above the glassy surface of the river. There, on the cordoned-off concrete bridge roadway at the river's edge, was my father snapping a picture of the *Sioux* passing close-by. We gave each other a wave. I still tear up anytime I remember that moment. How proud I was.

Piloting the *Sioux* on the St. Croix river is pure joy. She has a *perfect straight rudder* characteristic. The twenty miles of the St Croix River between Prescott and the King Plant consisted of three wide-open segments divided into thirds by two narrow areas. Traveling upstream, first is the Kinnikinic Narrows where its lovely trout-stream size and quality of water enter the St Croix River. Second is the Hudson Narrows, a mile-long slender stretch between the Highway 94 Freeway and the old railroad bridge crossing the river next to the Minnesota bank opposite Hudson, Wisconsin. You could set her on straight rudder in those wide, stunning expanses between those tight areas and sit down, relax, and pay little attention.

The trip upstream took between four and five hours and the return trip, around three hours. It was a job that almost did not seem like a job. Lots of binocular time. Never a shortage of scantily clad gals on board passing pleasure craft and on beaches at numerous locations. Above the old Hudson Railroad Bridge, a vast pristine sandy beach on the right bank hosted nude sun-bathers on almost every bright sunny day. I found it more than a little challenging to pay adequate attention to maneuvering our tow of empty barges directly above, and moving into the bridge, down bound, while making sure I didn't miss out on the shoreside view through my binoculars! The icing on the cake was being off each night and enjoying being at home like all my friends and family that had shore-side jobs.

flying bridge – a platform alongside and just outside the pilothouse door that provides an unobstructed view of fore, aft, and sides of the towboat

perfect straight rudder – This is an expression that describes when the captain can set the steering rudders on a towboat, and the tow will continue to go along that straight heading for a long time without any moving of steering levers. Very unusual.

Along the stern of the *Sioux* was moored her smaller St Croix River coal run counterpart, the MV *Cheyenne*. At only thirty-three feet long, it took all her three-hundred horsepower from twin diesel motors to shift barges in and out of the automated unloader at the King Power Plant on the St. Croix River. Northern States Power company installed a state-of-the art turning bucket unloader on piers over the water against the bank connected to their coal piles by a high-speed conveyer. It did not perform exactly as designed but by and large it was super-fast. The mammoth machine could unload about ninety percent of the 1400 tons (2.8 million pounds) of coal in a loaded barge in just over 30 minutes.

The *Cheyenne* shifted the next loaded barge to be off-loaded from the last upbound tow under the unloader while pushing the previous barge out of the way. That barge with the remaining ten per cent of coal in it would be shifted to a crane barge set up where workers would quickly clean up the remaining coal. The *Cheyenne* would then place that empty barge in the Sioux's next down bound tow and repeat the process. In the early 1970's, I worked occasionally as a deckhand on the *Cheyenne*. Most days, we played a card game called *"towboat cutthroat euchre"* between shifting the barges. My deck mate Bernie Jensen and I would frequently *"sandbag"* our captain, Bill Lawson while playing. An otherwise wonderfully friendly, mild-mannered man he would fly into fits of rage in response and threw a perfectly good deck of playing cards out the second story pilothouse window of the Cheyenne almost daily!

Alongside the *Sioux*, also secured for the winter, was the MV *Pawnee*. Once a formidable member of Twin Cities live-aboard harbor towboat fleet, she was now mostly the designated "fleet tending towboat". Boxy, only sixty by twenty feet, unsophisticated and bordering on ugly, she makes a perfect fleet towboat. Lots of time spent building tows and occasional a short run to shift a barge a short distance. Short and agile, her twin 400 horsepower diesels give her the needed authority to serve as the boss-boat of Twin Cities fleets. Now *a lunch bucket towboat*, her crews live at home in the local area. *Crew changes* are easy around the St. Paul harbor at six in the evening and six in the morning. Her deck crews are solid men who do back-breaking labor. A

---

towboat cut-throat euchre – a euchre game we played allowing sandbagging and other dirty tricks
sandbag – When playing this game, players could conspire to force the selected victim to lose.
lunch-bucket towboat – slang for a towboat where workers live at home and bring their lunch to work

twelve-hour shift ***building tow*** consists of lugging, laying and tightening sets of rigging without a break.

Photo of rigging and lock lines on head deck of towboat.

The tiny towboat crews' quarters and galley no longer have beds and homey kitchen amenities enjoyed by live-aboard crews in the early-to-middle years of Twin City Barge. The *Pawnee* was considered luxurious in the early years of Twin City's history, especially alongside her similarly tiny and un-sophisticated older sisters in the fleet, the MV *St. Paul* and MV *Pine Bend*. These three narrow and short rock-hard towboats built the Twin City Barge legacy in the St. Paul harbor during the very early years.

In the icy cold winter of 1973, a month prior to getting my Captains license, I served as a steersman on board the *Pawnee* working over in the Chicago harbor. Her telescopic pilothouse earned her a slot as a Chicago harbor live-aboard towboat that year and a wonderful captain and fabulous friend named Larry Hetrick sat patiently behind me in the pilothouse for many days as I learned my new craft.

A significant contrast right alongside the nasty old *Pawnee*, was the MV *Teal*. A sister to our towboat, she was only five years old and huge leaps

building tow – shifting and assembling a group of barges and installing rigging to fasten them together. A fifteen-barge tow will have approximately eighty sets of rigging.

forward in sophistication and amenities. Eighty-eight feet long and a luxurious thirty feet wide, her 1,650 horsepower made her a steadfast workhorse of harbor towboat. Just like our towboat, she was designed and equipped with enormous backing and steering rudders and performed like a dream. Nobody aboard right now. Slated for some upgrades over the winter, she was quiet now, hooked up to shore power and taking a nice siesta.

Tied alongside her was the MV *Paul H Lambert*. She was built in 1965, the first towboat built by the brand-new Twin City Shipyard division of Twin City Barge. She is twenty- and one-half feet wide and 79 feet long. One thousand two hundred horsepower. Narrow so that she was able to tow a two-barge-tow into Minneapolis through the slender locks up there. Boxy, very spartan in every way but a good little towboat.

Towboat MV *Minneapolis*, previously the MV *Paul H Lambert*.
Twin screw, 1,200 horsepower.

She was designed by some well-intended but less-than-sophisticated folks whose idea was for her to have a state-of-the-art control of her fuel system. That idea turned into a labyrinth of piping to and from engines and fuel tanks that was close to impossible to manage. Fuel tanks on a towboat run down the length of the boat on each side under the area that appears on top to be a walkway. They are divided by multiple bulkheads to ensure watertight wellbeing and provide ability to fill or empty as needed for ballast. The designers of this array of tanks down both sides and many, many pipes and lines connecting them from side to side did not consider that it would a full-time-job to manage the volume of fuel in each of the twelve separate compartments at any given time. The result was that the *Paul H Lambert* had an almost permanent *list* to one side or the other. Each time she started to lean the utility deckhand would have to switch valves to shift fuel in the other direction until

list – nautical term meaning the boat is tipping sideways one way or the other.

the list went the other way. Then the same corrective process would need to occur.

I was one of many utility deckhands who rode the *Paul Lambert* in the very early seventies who fought that fuel system valiantly but on no occasion did I come out on top. A never-satisfied-with-the-constant-list captain named Junior Jogurst declared one day over the loudspeaker that I was, inequivalently, the worst example of a towboat professional he had ever known. Only he didn't use those same carefully chosen words. His face was beet red as he screamed out profanities over the loudspeaker that I didn't know existed. I was sure he might stroke-out right there. So that was that.

We continued taking fuel, tied adjacent to the wharf barge about midway between the ends, and hooked up to shore power. Our main diesel engines were shut down as was the operating generator down in the engine room. Nice and quiet and still. I relished the quiet and still after so many days underway. I had some nice calming music on the compact radio on the pilothouse console. The door opened and Bill came in with a damp mop smelling of Pine sol floor cleaner. "Spilled just a trace of diesel fuel when I was hooking up the fuel hose and thought while I was cleaning that up, I would make a pass through here."

Bill was as good hand. Always busy, he was constantly tending to some task or another. Fortyish, slender and light frame, heavy dark beard sticking out from under a permanent dirty stocking hat. He wore ultra-heavy-duty black steel toed logger style work boots and their giant heels gave him an assist with his vertical impairment. Grew up in northern Minnesota and loved being a riverman. Not much for telling stories but always an avid listener. "Do I need to wake anybody up for midnight watch if we are just layin by?" He asked.

"Not if you have your fuel loaded on board and all the other supplies we had in our locker. I am gonna head down to the box myself in a little bit- just finishin this letter to the girlfriend so I can stick it in the ***wharf barge mailbox*** before we head out tomorrow. Did you git to call home? The watchman said there was something wrong with the pay phone.

"Yea. Somebody jammed up the coin thingy, but I called the wife collect and got through fine. She was excited to hear that we were heading out

---

wharf barge mailbox – Mail was stored in a mailbox until the towboat came by to get it.

Wharf barge and examples of towboats discussed here.
Just down the ramp from the offices where the dispatchers worked.
Twin City Barge is now Upper River Services.

and goin' around, so I got a better chance a bein home fer Christmas." He finished up mopping and set the mop outside on the stairs adjacent to the pilothouse. He sprayed some Windex around on the console, moving items as he cleaned. He dumped the half-full ashtray into the plastic garbage can and replaced the liner. "Them tires always been on the Itasca like that? We oughta git some of them around the sides of the guard on here. Bet that softens any bump!" He was referring to the heavy truck-sized tires encircling the water-side edge of the deck on the *Itasca*, the next Twin City harbor boat tied against the wharf barge just to our south.

"She is one of my favorites, Jimmy. When she showed up here there were a lot of pilots who were critical of her. She was built by a shipyard in the deep south where ***watertight doors*** and bits on her stern for towing are more common. They tow barges behind them on a ***hawser*** on lots of the intercoastal where there can be waves so high, they prevent you from being able to face up to your tow. Same thing with the tires. They put tires around the sides 'a boats cause the tow barges ***on the hip*** a lot. She's got a ***model hull***

watertight doors – Doors on the water-level story of a towboat are able to be securely fastened to keep out water caused by high waves.
hawser – If waves are so high that you can't face up to a tow, you commonly tow the barges behind the towboat. The heavy-duty line or cable used to tow is called a hawser.
on the hip – when the tow is secured alongside a towboat instead of in front
model hull – a curved ship-like shape below the waterline

---

under her. Quite a difference from the boxy boats up on this end of the river. I think she's the nicest boat in the harbor for almost all harbor work. She's got steering rudders that go so far *hard down* that it almost shuts the flow of water off. She can steer around anything. And, she also has that perfect straight rudder. Just set her and leave it alone. Beautiful, huge pilot-house and great visibility that high up. On her bow she's got that *second deck* that is excellent for moving lines and rigging on and around empties. And the tires make her a super-soft ride when yer digging around in these fleets. Every other harbor boat we got runs Caterpillars. She's got *screamin Jimmys*. I gotta agree with not likin that! The one other thing is that the cook sleeps in the deckhands' room and some don't like that."

"Me'n Larry Moore and Johnny, the cook on here rode her for weeks and weeks together a while back. I like stayin busy shifting in the harbor and a couple of times a day she makes the *Pine Bend run* and that is gravy. Its fine with me that some folks don't like her. More time that I git to ride her!" Bill finished cleaning on the console and carefully put Franks binoculars back on their folded bath towel bed. "So, the only other Twin City boat still left up here is the *Viking*, right?"

I nodded positively.

"They keep that here for winter towing?"

"Yep. They got her makin the last of season shifts up at Cargill and then they'll put a *skeleton crew* on her for winter towing. You should try to git that gig. You come from this north country. Little cold weather don't bother you!" He shook his head yes. "I told them at the office I wanted on there but I ain't heard nothing back yet. You've worked on winter towin?"

hard down – rudders all the way to the side. Steering as sharply as possible.
second deck – Some harbor towboats have a second deck on the forward end for storing equipment and ease of access around empty barges.
screamin' Jimmies – Slang for GMC diesel engines. These were no-frills industrial diesel motors, and a muffler to quiet them was not a consideration. Known for being very loud while operating at high rpms.
Pine Bend run – About twenty miles downstream from St. Paul, Minnesota, is a massive refinery — the Pine Bend Refinery at that time. Many major oil and gas companies doing business in the Minneapolis and St. Paul area had bulk fuel facilities along the riverbanks in St. Paul. Refined products like gasoline and jet fuel were offloaded into those terminals via tank barges loaded at Pine Bend. Moving those loads upstream or empties downbound was called a Pine Bend run.
skeleton crew – bare minimum number of crew members to operate. No cook.

"I did as a deckhand, but Denny Schickling and Bill Lawson got it sewed up in the pilot house. They're the most senior pilots Twin City's got. They swap out a week or two on and off and it works out great for them. I gotta tell ya man. It's pretty brutal. If it gits realllllllllllllllly cold a two hour Pine Bend run can turn into hours and hours and hours. Can't steer. Just keep hammerin back and forth. Back up and git a run at it and run out of headway and do it again. Just a single crew so ya just sleep when ya kin and you never really get enough. It's just super damn cold, let me tell you! You're surround by ice and the wind blows and it is a bear. Coldest I ever been in my whole life. Only redeeming thing was working with Buddy Bilderback. One of Twin City' old hands. Kind of a character. I call him Builder Buddyback and that gits a chuckle outa him. He cooks when he's on there and he can really cook. Awesome soups and hot dishes and the like. Super good!"

"Yea. It'd be nice to be closer to home, but the office people didn't sound optimistic about it. I probably ain't got enough seniority." Mike slipped up and into the pilothouse chair and lit a cigarette that he had just rolled. I was still sitting in the back with my writing tablet on my lap. "So, which boats they got over in Chicago? I never been over there. If I git a choice what should I go for?"

"You really can't make a bad choice over there now, Bill. They used to have some rats but lotsa good boats over there now. They got the two sisters to the *Viking* over there. The *Kiowa* and the *Northland*. All three are 66 x 26, telescopic pilothouses. Built by same shipyard in Greenville, Mississippi. The *Kiowa* was first. Built in 1966. The *Northland* was built in 71. The *Viking* was built in 70. All 1275 horse triple screws. Pretty nice rooms and galley – nice boats. The other sister to this boat is over there, the *Lindholm*. Pretty much the same as this- roomier and a real horse. Not sure if they're still runnin the old *Manco* but you would love that old sow. Everybody's got their own

The MV *Manco* was a beautiful historic towboat.
Single-screw, 1,150-hp direct-air-reversible Morse-Duesenberg engine.

room. She's a single screw with an old ***direct reversable diesel engine*** that chugs like a steam train engine. I was on her when I was deckin when she burnt. We were breakin ice in a place called Acme Steel Bend overon the ***south side*** and one of the deckhands left an electric heater sitting on a chair and it fell into his bed. Hell of a fire, but the old engineer on her kept her from burning all the way to the water. Huge galley and lots of features from boats from years and years ago."

Bill took one last draw from his homemade cigarette before snuffing the last quarter inch into the ashtray. His fingers were tobacco stained as a result of his smoking them all the way to the end. I continued. "The other two boats over there are the *Donald O'Toole* and the *Windy City*. The *O'toole* is brand new and she is a beaut. Model hull again and 1800 horsepower. She was built by a shipyard in Strugeon Bay on Lake Michigan. They say she could take a full sideways turn in heavy water to the side and will always come right back up centered. Replaced two old tugs Twin City used to run there. The *Red Wing* and the *Gopher State*. She runs across the south end of Lake Michigan to Gary Indiana shuttling oil tank barges. Make some regular runs in and outa the city too."

"The *Windy City*. Now that's a piece of work. She was another home-built job by Twin City Shipyard and somebody came up with the genius idea of electric shitters. So, you got seven guys on there eatin hearty and takin their dumps. Each time you use one of those things it takes about an hour for the crap to completely burn up. All of them vent thru the roof and stink to high heaven. So at any given time you got at least a couple of'em cooking up a storm. That smell is everywhere all over the boat and constant. I've ridden her a few times and I guess ya git used to it. But man! What a crappy deal!"

My attempt at making a pun made Bill laugh. Getting out of the pilothouse chair, he wiped some of his errant cigarette ashes from his belly onto the floor. "I'm gonna head down and hit the box. We got everything outa our locker and full'a fuel. Anything else you kin think of that we need?"

Direct reversible diesel engine – This diesel engine requires no transmission. When it runs forward the propeller hooked to it propels the boat ahead. When stopped or turned off the propeller stops turning. It can run the other direction and that turns the propeller in reverse.
south side – Barge operations in the Chicago Harbor occur in two regions. The Upper Illinois River splits in two just upstream from Lemont, Illinois. You either go northeast up the north side or east and southeast to the south side.

"Did ya check on the lock lines like I asked ya?" I said.

"Yep. There was about *a hundred-footer* down *in the front hold* that's in pretty good shape. And, we got that 300-foot *coil of line* from the wharf barge that you ordered on board. I'll cut a good long length of that in the mornin and *spice an eye in her* so we'll be all set." He got up and headed out the door. "Yer a good man, Billy. I'll be heading down right behind you in a little bit. Have a good sleep, man."

I finished my letter and grabbed my jacket, turning off the pilothouse light as I stepped out into the cold night air. All was quiet as I walked the steps down to the deck and stepped onto the wharf barge. A few industrial type noises coming from the 24-hour operations of the shipyard up on the levee behind the wharf barge. They put out a barge each week. About 100 welders workin there. Pungent river scent mixed with diesel and heavy machinery oil smells were noteworthy here just outside the two-story metal doors along the front of the mechanics shop that occupied about fifty percent of the wharf barge. Her aging galvanized metal roof supported by dirty, weathered metal beams gave this space a lonesome feel and the damp cold here was even more biting than on shore. I walked to the watchman's shack and stepped inside.

Two electric heaters, fans singing away, made it nice and toasty in there. The walls were glossy white paint and a table and assembly of schlocky half-wrecked chairs surrounded the aging metal Formic-surfaced table in the center of the ten by twenty-foot room. I slipped my letter into the mailbox near the permanently stained stainless sink. The always existing smell of burnt coffee com- ing from the Mr. Coffee machine in the corner. Scott Williamson, the watchman, looked up from his book. He had a couple of textbooks spread out and some diagrams of nerves and blood vessels of humans in graphic display.

"I gotta give you credit, Scott. Goin to school in the day and workin all night here. Studying your ass off. Never seen a more determined dude. How long you got left to go man?"

hundred-footer – common length for general purpose lock line
in the front hold – open area below the water line under the head deck used for storage on the bow of a towboat.
coil of line – New line delivered from manufacturers generally arrives in a 300-foot-long coil.
splice an eye in her – Most times, workers splice an eye in one end of a general-purpose line by intertwining the strands of the rope to create a loop.

Pilothouse Days

Scott laughed at my observations and put his book down. His eyes were bloodshot, and it made me tired just to look at how worn out he was. "I git my diploma in March. I'm in the middle of the labs now where we do chiropractic procedures to fellow students and that is really giving me confidence. Beginning to feel like it's real. Pretty likely I will be outa here by the time you git back up here in the spring. I got a spot scoped out on Main Street in Prescott. If everything goes right that's where I am gonna open my own shop."

"Good for you, man. Wow. I can't imagine how challenging it will be to go on your own and start your practice from scratch there. You can count on me to give you a visit and I will tell everybody I know to use you. Good for you. I am proud of your hard work."

"Thanks, Tom. That means a lot to me. I am thinking all this studying will prove to be worth it. I can almost see the end of the line. It will be good to get some patients and get my practice going. Looking forward to it!" He leaned forward over the table stretching. "Good chance we're outa here in the morning Scott," I said. "So, if I don't see you tomorrow night here, we'll catch up with you somewhere down the line." Scott and I shook hands and I headed out the door. "Have a good night- git some shut eye!"

Back on board, I carefully and silently opened and closed the door to our room without turning on any lights. Frank was snoring lightly in the top bunk and I slipped out of my clothes in the dark. The crisp sheets smelled good. Just changed them this morning.

As I dosed off, I smiled at the thought of heading down the big river the next day. Several days of easy running with new views around every bend. Locks, bridges, towns along the banks. Lots to keep occupied and make the time go by. Might even be a story or two.

I am quite sure that I had a smile on my face all night.

Modern towboat pilothouse console and controls including today's technology.

7. On Our Way.

I looked at my watch and yawned again. It felt so good to sleep with no noise and no movement! Quietly, I visited *the head* adjacent to our quarters. I noticed that Frank was not in his bed, so I turned on the light before slipping into my clothes. I pulled the wool blankets tight to the top of the bed and tidied up the pillows, all set for my next visit. I shivered as I stepped out onto the guard and the crisp morning air. Only the lights from the shipyard illuminating the sky. A full hour until daylight. Coming through the door into the galley, I smiled, grabbing a cup, as Frank slid sideways to give me the corner seat opposite Johnny, the cook.

The head – a restroom on a towboat

Pilothouse Days

"Just made this coffee, Tommy. Me'in Frank figuring out all the problems of the world this morning!"

"I told him you people is crazy, Tommy! Yer brains is froze livin' in this crazy cold place. We never git a frost down home till at least December! I ain't never seen anything like this here! I was gonna go fer a walk, but I can't even git up the ramp from the wharf barge without slippin! Let's git our tow and git the helloutahere!" Johhny opened the oven door and removed a metal cooking sheet placing it up on the counter. Something under the foil smelled terrific. "If yer goin up ta the office, take this here on up there with ya. My good cinnamon rolls. Tell em' there from me, if ya don't mind."

"Sure will, John. I'm gonna see what they got in mind for us. Yer a smart man, thinkin to do this for them. They don't fergit things like this. Yer gonna git a reputation!" I topped off my coffee and tucked it onto the corner of the baking sheet. John handed his homemade treasures to me at the the screen door and begged me to be careful not to upset the tray. John handed his homemade treasures to me through the screen door, being sure that I wouldn't bump something and upset the tray. The warmth and sweet yeasty smell were almost too much right in front of me. I started across the wharf barge and Bill, our utility deckhand, intercepted me. "You got as much of a chance a'gitten up the icy ramp with those things as the man in the moon. Here. Let me help you!"

We made it up the ramp and across the parking lot to the office. Opening the double entrance office doors, I led the way. Bill set the pan in on the conference room table in the brightly lit dispatch center.

"Oh goodness!" Bob Jorgens, the head dispatcher said and was up and out of his office chair grabbing a napkin and plate. The first to cut into the warm, sweet treats. John came around the corner from the lunchroom with a plate of butter as Ed was hefting a double serving onto the paper plate found lounging on the corner of his desk he kept on the corner of his desk, ready to go. Big smiles, and unusual quiet for a minute or two, as each man savored the rich, fresh-baked treats. Reaching for napkins, liking fingers, squinting looks of ecstasy and even some modest moans.

"Jeepers!" Bob said. "Do you eat like this all the time? I would be as wide as a house if I had as many of these rolls as I wanted every morning!"

"Johnny is one of the best that ever was. He's always got some kinda fresh-baked something and most times two or three choices. You gotta be careful not to eat dessert before yer meal with him as cook. He sends his best wishes and said to tell ya all good morning!"

"So, I bet you guys are ready to get moving on down the river," Bob said. "Gotta git you outta here before we git ice on Pepin.

"I'm gonna have you go up and *turn the Viking* somewhere around or above the St. Paul Harbor and then you can head out. They picked up a wire in their starboard *wheel* this morning, and they're down to two engines. They are limping out of the Minnesota and heading for the dry dock at State Street. They have a couple more trips in and outta Shakopee, and then it'll just be winter towing." Bob slid another golden glazed roll onto his napkin and placed it carefully on the corner of his wooden desktop. He slid his chair forward and leaned in, getting a bite but avoiding getting his blue-and-gold tie messy. Bob was always dressed very professionally. His golden-blond hair was parted perfectly and swept back on the sides slightly over his ears. He had a warm but not over-the-top smile. Careful and deliberate in all things, Bob almost seemed out a place in this industrial environment. He looked like he would have fit more comfortably behind the desk in the corner office at a bank.

"Which of you three gits the first vacation once everything is done?" I asked. Dispatchers worked long hours including nights and weekends during the busy towboat shipping season, and once things froze up they took turns enjoying generous sabbaticals.

"I'm on a plane for Disney Saturday morning," John said. "This'll be the first time for our two little ones, and I am really excited for them. Five and three. The boy can't stop talking about it. Christmas present to go. I don't think he's slept since we broke the surprise news to them a couple weeks ago."

John Schwab had a modest but athletic frame topped with a full bushy head of brown hair cut in the style of the day: over the ears and mutton chop sideburns. He had a devilish, constant smile. It made him look half his age, and he was the most engaging and social of the three dispatchers. Loved to

turn the Viking – "Turning" is slang for meeting another towboat and taking their tow or swapping tows.
wheel – Marine propellers are often called "wheels." The flexible steel cable fastened to a piling on shore got sucked up into the propeller farthest to the starboard (right, facing forward). When that happens, most times it needs to be cut out with a torch.

chat. The third dispatcher, Ed Williams, was a super friendly fellow with a dark brown mustache and sparkling brown eyes that highlighted his careful smile. Gregarious and very social, he talked loudly and with a sometimes awkward, staccato tempo. He was constantly upbeat and always gracious and pleasant. He dished up his fourth roll, licking the still warm shiny frosting from his fingers, then wiping his hands on his pants. He was skinny and tall. One of those folks who never met a calorie that stayed around for very long.

Bob looked up from his yellow legal pad. "The *Viking* has four loads that will eventually be our last Upper Mississippi Towing tow outta here. U-M 2-2-0-3, U-M 1-7-1-7, U-M 6-6-6, and U-M 3-3-2-1. The MV *Leslie Ann* gits 'em. Whenever you are ready, head upbound light boat and swap out with her. Drop those four at the Valley Line Fleet. You can leave the rigging on them. The *Viking* is heading back up this afternoon and will bring out the last six overnight to complete their downbound tow. They're leaving here with ten loads, picking up two loads at Red Wing and their final three at Winona."

"You said you had your tow ready to go in the **Packinghouse Fleet**, right?"

I nodded, my mouth full of fresh hot sweet cinnamon roll.

"Got the last of your groceries and supplies, full a' water and fuel?" he asked.

"All set and ready to go. I dropped off the logs and the last of the laundry and everything else I can think of in your mailbox down at the wharf barge. I got that order sheet that you put in our mailbox for ordering groceries from Economy Boat Store at Grafton. We'll call that in a day or so ahead and grab that stuff when we swing in there to get fuel. Jim Fleming is sending some radios and parts and this and that around with us. Bill's got several boxes of stuff that Jim wants sent over there down in the engine room. I can't think of anything we're forgetting."

"Maybe give us a shout just before you are ready to face up and head out in case something else comes up." Bob set his most recent roll down and wiped his mouth.

Packinghouse Fleet – Immediately across the river was the iconic South St. Paul Stockyards. Now a more modest footprint, the area warranted naming one of the fleets there the "Packing House Fleet."

"We will do that, Bob," I said.

Bob got up from his chair and extended his hand. I shook it and followed up the same with the other two men.

"Thanks for a good season, Tom. You guys set some records this past year. It was a good year for everybody in the harbor, and we had our biggest revenue year ever. Lotsa smiles next door at the main office. Take care, be safe. We'll see you in the spring."

"Let's head on down, Billy, and get underway."

The eastern horizon was pink and lightening as we stepped back out into the cold. I slipped, and luckily, Billy caught the sleeve of my jacket, keeping me from tumbling to the icy sidewalk. "Careful, there, Tom! Man, they need to get some salt on these icy patches up here. Guy could git killed slippin' around!"

Stepping across the head log onto the *Mallard*, I felt glad this was the day we would be heading south. Bill started the generator and main engines, and I heard him unhook the one-inch-thick shore power cable and drag it along the guard until he could coil it up and hang it on the holder mounted on the dingy galvanized metal wall of the wharf barge. I noticed Charlie standing alongside the face wires ready to unhook them and hang them on the ***tow knee***. He was bundled up like it was winter. Green Bay Packers stocking hat surrounded tightly by a hooded sweatshirt over which was the fur-lined hood of an arctic parka. He clapped his thick leather mittens that encompassed both his hands together and blew his breath in between them. I slid the window open and called out to him.

"How you feelin' about this Minnesota November weather, Charlie!?" I *clutched* both engines slow ahead. He looked up at me and laughed, and I slid the window closed, the pilothouse now fresh with the cooler morning air. I pressed the buttons that loosened the face wires. Charlie took the port one off, and Bill removed the starboard wire. I shifted into neutral, paused, and then engaged both engines in slow reverse.

tow knee- Twin vertical structures about ten feet tall that are part of the front face or headlog of a towboat. If the towboat is faced up to empty barges, workers use the built-in steps installed on the back slope to access the deck of the barge.
clutched – slang for moving the throttles from neutral to just into gear, forward or reverse.

Pilothouse Days

"Three-one-five to the *Mallard*." Bob, from the office, was calling on the marine radio. I responded and we switched over to channel ten.

"If you haven't gotten too far, I need you to grab a couple of empties to take with you up to State Street. Right across from the wharf barge there should be a couple of empty hoppers mixed in with the most recent new barges the shipyard just built. You are looking for two Mid America empties, MAT 2-7 and MAT 3-1. Grab them, and when you get to State Street, spot them two abreast on the wall at the very upstream end. They're saying they are going to build a platform onto them tying them together, and then they're gonna load a giant crane on them to work on the 35E bridge late in the winter."

Off our starboard side, I could see one of the barges we were discussing. "Ten-four. We'll grab 'em, Bob, and get 'em right up there."

We **dug the two barges out** and were soon underway. Rounding the point, turning to starboard, we made a wide, sweeping turn upstream into the brisk early morning breeze. I hooked her up, and we moved swiftly upstream past the giant leafless cottonwoods lining the left bank. Lots of daylight now to see the city awakening around us. Cars and trucks moving along roads on the right bank. Two trains passing each other in the switchyard directly behind the **revetment structure** built to displace repeated flooding.

Bill came in and brought me a fresh cup of coffee brewed downstairs with the drip pot. He sat behind me and got out his tin of tobacco and rolling papers. I watched him slide the lovely brown strands of tobacco out onto his cigarette rolling paper in a row as straight and even as could be. It was like watching someone make art. Slipping the tin in his pocket, he brought the glued edge of the paper up to his mouth and slid it across his moist tongue in a well-rehearsed motion. Tapping the end, he spun the body of the new cigarette and placed it between his lips. Opening his mini box of Ohio Blue Tip Matches, he swiped one against the side of the box, and the bright, fragrant flame leapt up and onto the end of his smoke. He drew a healthy pull into his lungs. Two great smells. A farmer match being struck and that first flush of freshly lit cigarette.

dug the two barges out –slang referring to the process of entering a barge fleeting area where several barges are moored and moving barges around to get to the barges you need to pick up for your tow or to shift.
revetment structure – In locations where riverbanks are prone to erosion, bank protection is installed. Revetment structures are most commonly dikes built to contain floodwaters.

A low ghostly layer of **foggy mist** hung just a few feet above the water in areas out of the wind. Wisps of steam rose from the water, soon to be snuffed out for the winter by a coating of ice. The sun, just breaking the horizon, created *sun dogs* of ice crystals along the sides of the river. Their halos had colors between orange and blue, surrounded by brilliant white. I shook a fresh pack of Winston's out of the carton sitting alongside Frank's carton of Salem's on the console. I slid the front window open a bit and lit up. I pointed at the sun dog on the right horizon, and Billy looked where I was pointing.

"My dad always said that sun dogs are a sign of snow within twenty-four hours."

Billy nodded and took a sip of coffee.

"We gotta get outta, here, Billy. Not one day too soon!"

At State Street, we dropped the two empties on the wall on the upper end as instructed. Jerry Chapman came out of the dirty cream-colored office trailer and strode past Charlie, who was tying a line between the kevel and the fitting on the wall. He checked the two *stern hatches* as he walked over and stood in front of me. I slid the window open.

"I thought you was headin' out, Tommy. You need to git your asses outta here. Snow comin!" He laughed and smiled, giving a high five to Billy, who passed him getting ready to knock out the boat. Jerry looked the part of the Minnesota outdoor construction worker. Oversized insulated Carhartt coveralls opening to a vee at his chest, a Minnesota Wild hockey T-shirt under it. His dirty, sweat-stained, used-to-be-blue fur-lined down vest was adorned with holes, burns from welding sparks. His full high collar was tight up and under his blue hard hat liner.

"We're tryin, believe me! Headin up to turn the *Viking* and get her down here so you can get her on the drydock and do your magic. Soon as we git her tow down to the lower fleets we are gone!" I said.

"Really a pain in the ass to git the dry dock ready for her. We had it all winterized, and now we gotta do that all over again!" Jerry said and laughed again. "Oh, well! That's life in the big city, I guess! Be good, Tommy. See ya

sun dogs – optical atmospheric phenomenon where a bright spot appears on one or both sides of the sun
stern hatches – entryways to the watertight stern area of a barge

---

next year. Don't do anything I wouldn't do!" He waved and started toward the bow of the two barges, checking hatches as he went.

Towboat *Itasca* high and dry on drydock at State Street.

We backed away from the barges and headed upstream light boat. The traffic on Warner Road was picking up as we passed under Robert Street and the raised railroad lift bridge.

"We were going by here one day this past summer on the *Itasca*, Billy. Almost in the exact same place as right here this morning. Less than two hundred feet from the road on our right, here come a guy heading south on Warner Road in a tandem dump truck. Just about this same time a' day. And he is movin'. All the sudden, the dump box on the back of his truck starts goin' up. I could see this all happening, and I couldn't believe it. I snapped on our starboard searchlight and swung it over onto him quick and flashed it around thinkin' he might figure out what was happening. He never slowed down. The box slammed into the railroad trestle above him. You would have thought the box woulda broke off backwards. It didn't. Sixty miles an hour to zero, just like that! It did flip the truck over onto its side. Damnedest thing I ever saw! I always wondered if he made it."

Jimmy came through the door. I got up, moved aside, and he put his coffee on the console and slid into the captain's chair. He was freshly shaved, clean clothes, and looked like a new guy.

"Good morning, young man! Top of the mornin' to ya! You look all refreshed and ready to go."

He arranged things on the console and got settled. "I think I slept for about ten hours," he said. "It was super nice to be tied up overnight, and I just relaxed and stayed in the box. Did a little laundry this morning. All caught up on my sleep!"

I sat down in the back of the pilothouse and updated the logbook. Finished with that, I got up to head downstairs to do some of my own laundry. "Keep heading upstream till we meet the *Viking*. Keep an eye on the head deck to make sure you ain't gittin' any ice on her while running light boat. They left out of Cargill with four loads, but they're down on two engines, limpin' along. No tellin' how far down they are. They're gonna put them on the dry dock at State Street. We'll grab their tow, take it to Valley Line Fleet, and then we are outta here!"

"Sounds good to me! I'll holler if I need anything," Jimmy said.

After I finished hanging my two pairs of pants and some shirts along the walkway in the engine room, I stepped through the door into the galley. Johnny was baking, as he did every morning, and I watched him reach for his always available dishtowel to slide the two fresh pies out of the oven and onto the center counter. I filled my coffee cup and had just set it on the counter, when Jimmy touched the starboard tow knee against the tow the *Viking* was passing off to us. He bumped a little generously, and a bit of my coffee spilled. A moment later we were subjected to a jerky side-to-side motion when the powerful electric face wire winch motors cinched the thick steel cables up tight. I'm sure Jimmy and the captain on the *Viking* agreed that he would grab their tow *on the fly*, so hurrying to get faced up is understandable.

"Seen some sun dogs this morning, Johnny. You know what that means. Ain't gittin' outta here any too soon!"

on the fly – slang meaning swapping out tows without stopping and securing the tow to something. Switching tows midstream.

Pilothouse Days

Johnny smiled and responded, "I'monna make a big pot a' chili this mornin', Tom. I reckon everybody is gonna need some warmin' up over the next couple a' days!"

Jimmy came full ahead, and the rumbling noise of the propellers put an end to our casual gabbing. John cut me a piece of apple pie and set the plate down next to the copy of *The Waterways Journal* I was reading. A real luxury, I had grabbed it in the office earlier. I enjoyed this magazine filled with information about towboats and towboating. I grinned as I touched the fork to the pie, the hot crust flaky and sparkling with a sugar topping. I blew on my forkful, hoping to avoid burning my tongue, and tasted it. "I am gonna weigh six hundred pounds when we git off a' here, Johnny. You are something else!"

John gave me one of his best twinkling smiles, took off his white apron, and lit up a cigarette. The barely discernable picture on the TV mounted near the *port* bow corner of the galley ceiling featured a morning weather guy with a caricature of a huge cloud with eyes and a mouth blowing snow forcefully out of it. While underway, it was impossible to hear what was being said unless you placed your ear directly in front of the speaker. A constant on all towboats, most galleys have a TV going around the clock, snowy picture and all, whenever you were near a town. Reception was always spotty, so getting interested in anything is kind of a crap shoot. You might not get to see the end of a show. Johnny sat down opposite me, his cigarette hanging off his lip as it did most times. He seldom used his hands to smoke. Just let it hang there, and the ash dropped off whenever gravity won out.

"I was a deckhand on the MV *Ida Crown* the year I was eligible for the lottery for the draft."

John looked up from his dog-eared, well-worn copy of the *National Enquirer*.

"The moment they drew my draft lottery number in 1971, the *Ida Crown* went under a bridge, and the TV went snowy. I almost had a heart attack. Everybody on there thought it was hilarious! I was so pissed! It wasn't

The Waterways Journal – a remarkable weekly magazine that provides news related to industrial river transportation and towboats. The only resource of its kind for decades and known for its excellent coverage of issues important to inland mariners.

until the next day, when the lockman at the O'Brien Lock on the south side gave me a day-old copy of the paper, that I found out my lottery number assignment. I ended up only a couple of numbers short of getting a free plane ticket to Vietnam. Damn close!"

John slid his baggy sleeve up his right arm to show me an Army tattoo beginning at his wrist and circling north. "I got drafted, but it turned out OK. I signed up for the Army. I got assigned to a cook job right out of basic training and ended up serving all my time at **Fort Bragg in North Carolina**. The CO liked me, and they kept me there. I cooked my ass off to make sure I didn't get sent to 'Nam. Just like you, I didn't want nothin' to do with that nasty bastard war. They made it so good that I signed up for a second hitch. Was thinking a' bein' a lifer, but a new CO came in and changed everything. I got the hell outta there. Moved east. California was too crowded. I stayed with some family in Tennessee for a while and got a job as a head cook at a school in Chattanooga. Worked there twenty-eight years. Got a little retirement outta them. Cousin that worked on the boats said they was hirin', so I tried that. It was a couple years after I retired, and I was bored stiff. Towboat cooking was just what I needed. I keep payin' them dues to the *NMU*. I should check, sometime, see if I got enough time in to get a retirement check from them."

"You said yer from Hardin, Illinois, right? Know any of those other boys from central Illinois? Jimmy Murphy or Danny Partridge?"

"I know Murphy," John said with a smile. "Crazy son of a gun! We worked together some over there, and I worked on the *Paul H. Lambert* with him early this spring up here. Never seen a man that kin drink like that."

"You got that right, John. Last month he and I were on the *Itasca* for a couple weeks together, and he got completely out of it three times in those two weeks. I'd git woke up and come up to the pilothouse, and he was so drunk he couldn't talk. And laugh?! Jeez, we'd laugh. Me'n a deckhand would help him down into bed and wouldn't hear from him for eighteen to twenty hours. I would just work through that whole time. Dispatchers probably wondered what was up. Then when he did come up and take over, he'd spend two or three hours puking in the wastebasket. Never seen anything like it. I'd take some extra sleep time, then when I came back upstairs, he'd be all apologetic

port – means left in marine terms
NMU – National Maritime Union. I belonged to that union as a deckhand. After a failed merger with a different maritime group in 1988, the union merged with the Seafarers International Union of North America in 2001.

and almost tearfully sorry. A few days later he'd do it again. Such a fun guy and awesome pilot. I didn't want to let anybody know what happened. He wasn't hurting anybody."

John set the dishes he'd just cleared from the counter in the sink and over his shoulder said, "Ya, them boys from Southern Illinois all know how to drink hard. That and fight. You ain't a man down there 'less you git drunk and git into at least one bar fight every weekend!" He laughed, rinsing the last of those dishes and setting them on a towel to air dry. He came back to the counter, shook another Camel out of his pack, and lit up. Exhaling, he said, "I think I might have some in-laws that are related to Murphy. The old gal I'm with now is my second marriage, and she's a native from around where he lives. We never had no kids, but she's got two from her first marriage. Two grandkids. Close by, down in St. Louis. Grandma likes to call 'em. She's always puttin' 'em on the phone. I can't hear good, so not sure what the heck we're talking about most a' the time, but that's OK."

John continued, "I got three kids from my first marriage. My oldest is a boy. He went into the service. Made corporal the beginning of this past year. Damn fine young man. He really made somepin' a' hisself. The two girls never turned out so good. One of 'em's been in rehab so many times I lost count. Been straight for a good while this last time, so maybe she's got a chance. Their mom never was no good. Left me for this truck driver, and that didn't last. She drank up all the money I sent for the kids, and they just sorta made do. Her liver gave out couple years ago, and she tipped over. Her sister buried her. Pretty sure nobody noticed she's gone. Hell of a way to end up."

John busied himself layering fresh noodles in a pan, looked like the beginnings of some lasagna-like dish. I got up, opened the door to the engine room, and grabbed my pants and shirts off the line where they had been drying in the one hundred-plus degree heat above the diesel engines. I folded them and set them on the table near the water fountain. A good temporary storage spot till lunchtime, when I could get in my room.

Stepping out onto the guard, I was again reminded that mother winter was poised to strike in our area before long. The sun struggles to loosen the grip of the far horizon that time of year in the north, and the silver sky behind and around it made it look creamy and liquid around the edges. The air was full of moisture, and the cold wind seemed like it could be carrying snow swiftly sideways at any moment. Jimmy had just backed into the Valley Line

Fleet, and the boys threw the **grapple hook** out into the water a little upstream and shoreward of the **marker can** for the farthest upstream shore wire. Charlie slowly reeled in the line, noting the feel of the hook slinking along the bottom. Then, feeling the resistance from contact with the shore wire, he and Billy worked in tandem to pull the line in. The wire broke the surface of the water, and both men lifted it, simultaneously grabbing a segment long enough to pull it aboard and wrap it around the kevel on the shoreside corner of the stern of the tow. Charlie pulled a section of **cowtail** out of the back pocket of his coveralls and wrapped it around the wire where the last of the turns on the kevel intersected.

I got to the top of the stairs and stepped into the pilothouse, shivering. "Man, it's cold, Jimmy!" I didn't really expect a response, since I was stating the obvious. I went over and filled out the log, entering the latest moves, and called the office on the marine radio.

"How are we looking, Ed? Good to go, or you got other things for us to do?" I asked.

"Grab your tow, Captain Struve, and get outta town!" Ed shouted, laughing.

It was exactly what I wanted to hear. We made a quick stop at the wharf barge, dumping our garbage and logs and grabbing the mail. Back at the fleet, we stopped on each bow corner to place lock lines, bumpers, and running lights. We had built the tow with two strings of three empties, one on each side of our two loads made up as a unit, creating a **duckpond** on the bow in the center of the tow.

"What do we want to *ALWAYS* remember on this trip, boys?" I said into the **loudspeaker microphone** as we were facing up. I slid the front window

grapple hook – looks like a treble hook used in fishing on steroids. One or two feet tall, the hook is made of steel rods, tied to the handy line, and thrown into the water to latch on to the shore wire, which the deckhands secure to the tow.

marker can – a buoyant marker (often a used freon container) tied to the end of the shore wire, marking the shore wire's location on the river bottom

cowtail – Workers create a cowtail by separating strands of unrepairable river lines and cutting them to a handy length. Think twine. Cowtail is used when you want to fasten something temporarily.

duckpond – when a collection of barges is assembled into a tow that is three wide and the front end of two outside strings extend ahead of the front of the center string, that opening in is called a duckpond. Workers need to exercise extreme caution not to fall overboard into that area.

loudspeaker microphone – Most towboats have a loudspeaker arrangement so the crew can hear what the captain is requesting out on the tow or on the head deck of the towboat.

open while Jimmy pressed the buttons to tighten up the face wires.

"NEVER *walk the notch*!" Charlie shouted.

"Atta boy, Charlie! You win the prize!"

Charlie wrapped a four-way safety line around the bits and onto the center kevel of the load we'd faced up to. **Bill and Charlie headed** for the bow to turn our tow loose. The only downside to this tow makeup was that the noise from the engine room would reflect at our towboat because the rearmost empty barges were immediately alongside the boat. On the plus side, the pilothouse was one hundred feet closer to the two bow corners, and our tow assembled this way made a slick *single locking* without having to knock the boat out and *set over*.

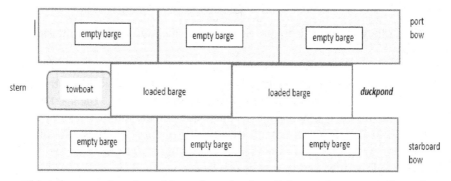

This is how our downbound tow of two loads and six empties was configured.

Charlie threw his hands up in the air, gesturing "all gone" on the head of the tow, and the two deckhands did a little dance and pretended to box and throw each other around a little bit. They were as excited as I was to begin our journey south. They would have one super easy watch after another, only having to get out on the tow while going through locks. It was too cold to do

walk the notch – when a collection of barges is assembled into a tow that is three wide and the front end of two outside strings extend ahead of the front of the center string, that opening in is called a duckpond. Workers should always walk on the side of the barge opposite the duckpond. Walking on the duckpond side is called *walking the notch*.

single locking – Most river lock chambers are 600 feet long and 110 feet wide. When the tow and the towboat can fit in the lock chamber at the same time, that is called a single locking.

set over – In the most common configuration of an eight-barge tow (three barges wide and three barges long) the towboat will be unhooked from the tow and will be moved into the notch — set over — where a ninth barge would otherwise go.

any maintenance on the boat, so reading, visiting, and just enjoying the time going south would be a great treat for them.

Jimmy backed the tow hard for a bit till the bow started to shift to the port, and he slowed the engines and let her *top around.* The wind was whistling out of the north, and it grabbed our 600 feet of empties and gave the tow a serious push along the starboard side. Once past the halfway mark topping the tow, Jimmy shifted to neutral and then came ahead full, starting the steer that would put the tow into a trajectory to get us around the bend and down through the I-494 freeway bridge just downstream. Overall, I was very pleased with Jimmy's journeyman abilities. He was confident, used good judgment, and I hardly ever felt like I would be doing something different. It was a treat to watch him work, and he asked all the right questions when he needed advice.

Frank came through the pilothouse door, fussing as usual about the cold. He smiled that big smile and settled into the seat in the rear of the pilothouse, making a show of clutching his coffee cup close to stay warm.

I laughed and said, "I'monna go get some lunch. You boys got her for a while. Last I heard, there was a couple northbound tows between Locks Two and Three, so we may have a delay at Hastings. Hope we git down outta here before the big snow hits!"

I zipped my jacket and pulled up my collar on the way down to the galley. Pausing for a moment as we slid under the freeway bridge, I said a private prayer asking God for good fortune and safe travels on this trip. Another day where I felt fulfilled and joyous about life and my career on the river. Thank you, Lord.

Top around- river slang for turning a towboat, barge, or tow 180 degrees.

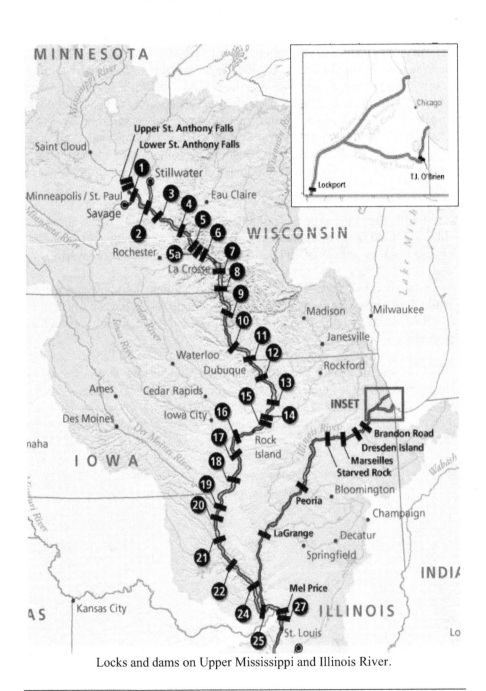

Locks and dams on Upper Mississippi and Illinois River.

Photo showing the confluence
of the St Croix and Mississippi River at Prescott, Wisconsin.

8. Passing by Home

At 5:15, I heard the door to my room open and close, and the light was turned on. It seemed like I had just fallen asleep. I was dreaming I had a big black Lab in the duck blind, and she was licking my face all the time. We were in a boat in a chair that was in another boat, and we were up a ladder about thirty feet higher than water level. I didn't shoot any ducks — I just pointed, and the Lab went and got them when they landed on the water. Isn't it amazing how all the dots don't have to connect in a dream?

Pilothouse Days

I stretched and rolled out of my bunk, sliding my feet into the slippers next to the bed. Teeth brushed and dressed for the cooler pilothouse, I got my coffee and a light snack from John. I was excited to get upstairs and see what was going on. As I climbed the stairs to the pilothouse, I noted that we were moving along dead slow around Buck Island, just above Lock Two. One of the two searchlights was pointed at the long flood control dike that extended from the channel approximately 2,000 feet toward the right bank above the lock. Frank was steering when I entered the pilothouse, and Jimmy was looking over at that dike with my binoculars.

"Man! That's a long dike!" Jimmy said. "It looks like there's a *spillway* built into it on the downstream side along part of its length."

Frank explained a little about how the Army Corps of Engineers constructed the locks and dams on the Upper Mississippi in the late '30s. "They needed to increase the depth of the channel to nine feet. Had to raise the water in places where there was rapids and even rock along the bottom. Between Davenport and Rock Island is a good example. All rock. You git out of the channel along there, you are in trouble! I reckon they had to try to keep from flooding out towns along the riverbank, so that probably has something to do with where they put 'em too."

I grew up just downstream from there, so I had a little local knowledge from reconnoitering in small boats in the area as a youngster. I said, "This dam must be in a critical location. Look to the left as we enter the lock, and you will see a huge set of *roller dam gates*. When the water gits up here, they open them gates up completely, and water still runs over that spillway yer lookin' at. The whole entire lock was underwater during the '65 flood. The paper said there was four feet a' water above the level of the top of the lock walls. They take the electric motors and all the locking machinery out of there every time they get serious spring flooding."

Frank discussed passing with the northbound tow leaving the lock. "We'll be up here on the one if that's OK with you. You better git on up there and git your southbound tow and git outta here. The locals tell me you gotta

spillway – a location along a flood control dike where the design and construction allow for floodwaters to go over the dike during extreme flooding conditions
roller dam gates – Most Upper Mississippi River dams are constructed in segments, including massive movable gates on rollers that can be raised or lowered to allow water through or hold it back behind the dam.

git down at least through Pepin to keep from getting stuck up here, over." Frank knuckled both engines ahead dead slow and turned off his port searchlight.

The captain on the *Herman Pott* said, "I hear ya. Quick as we git to St. Paul, we are gonna head back out."

Frank stepped aside from the console, and I took over. I turned off our port flanking lights, and the captain on the *Pott* did the same as we approached each other. I moved our starboard light to the left and aimed it at the upper end of the Lock Number 2 guide wall.

"Soon as you two git past one another, we're ready for you, Cap," the lockman said on channel 16.

"Heading your way right now," I responded.

Billy and Charlie stepped out onto our tow and headed toward the bow corners of our two strings of empties. "Careful, out there, boys," I called over the microphone. "Had a little freezing drizzle this afternoon. You might find some slick spots out there!" Charlie waved his flashlight up and down, acknowledging me.

Jimmy asked if there was anything special he should know about getting a tow like ours into the lock.

"Not really. Just remember that your ***pivot point*** is farther back than it might seem 'cause of the loads in the center string. Ya almost gotta think of the whole tow as being loads. If there is ***running water*** or if they have the ***out-draft boards*** out at any of the locks, you might be backin' up to git on the wall. If not, just steer slowly like you're gonna land a barge or a tow against any flat spot. Hold a point till you get right down to the end of the wall and then steer slightly. That'll give you just a little slide that should put you flat against the wall. Be careful to go slow around locks all the time. And always

pivot point – a location along the length of a tow where turning is most pronounced.
running water – towboat slang for flood stage. When it becomes difficult to stop.
out-draft boards – If the water passing by the upstream end of a lock guide wall is moving away from the wall toward the dam, lock operators indicate this by displaying a large round red sign commonly called an out-draft board.

Pilothouse Days

Good view of deckhand holding bumper as the tow passes the bullnose

be on your deck crews to make good use of ***bumpers***. You don't want nothin' to do with doin' any damage at a lock.

"The lockman will walk the headline down the entire guide wall. Or they might want the headline *on their rail that runs down the length* of the long wall. Either way, if your stern starts to set out from the wall, you can always stop if needed and git her back. Once yer clear of the ***bullnose,*** git your second deckhand back here for the stern line. I'monna make these two locks tonight, and we'll git you your first lock downbound in the daylight probably tomorrow afternoon if that's OK, Jimmy."

Jimmy nodded his agreement.

Billy was on the starboard bow corner and signaled that we just cleared the end of the guide wall. I steered a little to the port, and the tow began to

on the rail that runs down the length – Some upstream lock guide walls have a railroad rail welded to the outer edge of the wall running its length longitudinally. It rolls along the entire length of the shoreside wall securing the tow against the wall as it goes.
bullnose – the opposite riverside wall of any lock from the shoreside long wall of the lock chamber has an end that is v-shaped and is called the bullnose. Right side, photo above.
bumpers – Segments of line used to secure barges are woven together in a tubular arrangement one to two feet in diameter, and deck crews place this cushioning device between the tow and whatever is being bumped against.

slide over sideways toward the wall, as I had just explained. I had one search-light aim diagonally to our starboard and the other on the port corner of the tow and the bullnose.

"Just as important in this situation as when you're switchin' barges or any other thing. Always, always, always **watch your headway**," I told Jimmy. "See how I have this light pointed out there? Good way to do, 'specially when your boat is out away from the bank like you are here. I got a story about watchin' your headway. Remind me later to tell ya that one."

We moved steadily forward until the boat was just about to come along-side the end of the long wall. I shifted the port engine into neutral and left the starboard engine engaged dead slow. Charlie signaled that our port bow cor-ner had cleared the bullnose, and he headed back to handle our stern line. I backed both engines gently over the last fifty feet and brought the tow to a complete stop about ten feet inside the upstream gate recesses.

Once they closed the gates, I turned on the overhead light and did a little housekeeping. Jimmy came back upstairs from a trip to the head, and I fol-lowed his lead, shivering in my light jacket as I made my way below. The wind was robust, blowing from the north as if to help us get downbound. Back up in the pilothouse I saw, through the now open lower lock gates, the familiar right bank and boat ramp just below the downstream long wall of Lock Two. The lights high along the massive top arch of the highway bridge directly above downtown Hastings were brilliant against the black, starless sky. Billy signaled all gone from the head as the lockman handed him the eye of the lock line from the wall above. A short blast of the lockhouse horn signaled permis-sion for us to depart. I engaged both engines. Our twin Caterpillar diesels sounded throaty and powerful, the noise echoing off the wet concrete walls of the old lock chamber as we headed out into the river channel.

"Right here is where a captain earns all the money they pay him. The Hastings Railroad Bridge has given every river pilot who has passed this way gray hair," I told Jimmy. "Be sure to ask Frank about it tomorrow and git whatever wisdom he kin give ya about it too."

We steered almost straight down under the center channel light of the highway bridge, and I pulled the throttles back to let her headway run out. "Even with this little tow," I continued, "you gotta be super respectful of this

watch your headway – a cardinal rule operating a towboat. One must constantly look out to the side of the towboat and be acutely aware of how fast you are going so you can plan ahead in case you want or need to stop.

thing. This old *turntable bridge* was built before the turn of the century, and my guess is that she's been hit more times than any other on the Upper. There is almost always a construction crew working on the sheer fence. They say the two spans are a hundred and forty feet each, but I have heard several captains say ya can't git through the shore span anymore. They say the shoreside sheer fence keeps movin' toward the river every time they work on it."

Pilothouse view of historic Hastings Railroad Bridge downbound.

I let our tow drop down deep into the bend and started a play-by-play description for Jimmy. "This is how I make this bridge with any tow more than a couple a' barges, Jimmy. Drop yer tow into the bend. Keep your ass where I got ours right now, 'bout halfway between the center and the left channel light on the highway bridge. Back straight up and let the current on your right side git the tow moving to the port. Once she's settin' over nice, come ahead on a straight rudder nice 'n easy and let her drop down toward the bridge. If it feels right and you got her comin' nice, you can punch her with a tow this size and slide right on down through. If I have a full tow of loads, I am careful to git her right down almost into the span before I come full ahead.

"The key thing here is patience. I've seen some guys try to drive this bridge. When they do, they all end up chickenin' out and either piled up into the sheer fence or against that concrete structure right there." I focused our starboard searchlight on the bump-out on the right bank about 200 feet upstream from the bridge.

turntable bridge – a bridge that sits on a pier under its center and turns sideways to let river traffic pass

"City a' Hastings built that little concrete pad there so they can back dump trucks up there in the winter and dump snow they git off Main Street right into the river. That thing is also constantly being re-built. They no sooner git it redone, and somebody comes along and hits it. Opens that lead starboard barge in yer tow like a can opener. Don't see how the Coast Guard or somebody don't make 'em git it outta there."

Jimmy was standing alongside me acutely interested in seeing how this was done. "'Nother thing I do that some others might not is I just come about half ahead when I git 'er where I want and leave that remaining throttle on reserve just in case I really need it."

The head of our tow cleared the upstream end of the sheer fence, and we moved down into the bridge. As we moved along you could see a gap in the sheer fence on our starboard side where somebody had hit it recently, timbers sticking this way and that. I opened the pilothouse door and waved at Squeak, the **bridge tender**. He had stepped out of his tumble-down old bridge shack and waved his flashlight at us.

"Not sure where Squeak got that nickname," I said to Jimmy. "He lives right there in the second house down from the bridge. Been the bridge tender there as long as I kin remember. He'll be kickin' back with nothin' to do for a few months here in a week or so."

"You grew up right down here, didn't ya?" Jimmy asked.

"Yep," I responded. "Pretty fun to go by here on a towboat. Brings back so many memories from when I was a kid. You'll see how far it is from Prescott to Hastings once we git around the corner here. We used to walk the railroad track along the river and come over to Hastings sometimes in the summertime. I'm guessing it's six or seven miles. The railroad that goes through Prescott is the Burlington Northern. They go to St. Paul. The bridge we just went through is the Milwaukee Road. They go down the Minnesota side of the Mississippi, and the Burlington is on the Wisconsin side.

"As kids, we'd catch the Milwaukee Road passenger train on the Hastings side of that railroad bridge and ride it to downtown Minneapolis. Sometimes we got on in Prescott and went to downtown St. Paul. Just kids riding the train fer somethin' to do. Ninety cents to Minneapolis, and a dollar and a nickel to St. Paul and back. When we got to St. Paul, we would visit

---

bridge tender – person employed by bridge owner who raises and lowers (in the case of a lift bridge) or swings (turns the turntable) the bridge to let river traffic pass.

pawn shops. They had a bakery surplus store there too. We'd git all the donuts and those little pies we could eat for thirty or forty cents. We thought we died and went to heaven!"

Jimmy laughed. "I grew up right on the edge a' town, out in the country. Raised hell down by the crick, about all we did all summer. Zumbro River. More than a crick during spring runoff but nothin' in the middle of summer. Got to go to the Goodhue County fair at Zumbrota sometimes, and couple a' times my aunt let us stay in a tent next to her camper with them at the state fair. Kenyon, Minnesota, where I grew up. Lotta pig farms. Worked for my uncle on his farm. Driving tractor and working at the co-op when I was ten. All that kinda crap. 'Bout eighteen hundred people. My dad runs the co-op and Mom works part time at the municipal liquor store. Never got ta the cities back then 'cept for those times at the fair."

I chuckled at his reflections on his rural upbringing. "That's why you got such good sense and ain't afraid a' work. Murphy told me that you just about worked them regular guys on the *Pawnee* under the table building tow this past summer. Said you could outwork any of 'em!"

My comments made Jimmy smile. His work ethic and good sense were evident, and so I was that much more willing to help him with his training to become a pilot.

"Like you, Jimmy, I was raised on a farm about five miles outside of town as a little guy. We moved to town when I was six or seven. I remember the sound of the pig feeder doors slamming, and the smell of pig shit is like nothing else on earth." I smiled, thinking about how I'd had dozens of imaginary horses wherever I laid one of my feed bag "saddles" across a fallen tree in the small woodlot behind our modest two-story farmhouse. I'd wrap a piece of twine around the log and hold the "reins" tightly as I chased bank robbers and rescued maidens throughout the Wild West.

"Lots of memories from those early years. Man, I can still smell that school bus. Guy named Oscar Reiken drove it. Never saw him smile once. He was my hero. My dad bred cows for Minnesota Valley Breeders in those years, and when we moved to town, he got a job at one of the marinas."

Jimmy was looking through the binoculars at the structures along the train tracks on our port side.

"I love going by that farm a few times a year. My uncle and his family still have a small farm nearby."

The lights on the bluff at Prescott started to become more recognizable as we moved swiftly along just upstream from where the St. Croix enters the Mississippi at Mile 811.5. I pulled the throttles back to slow, more to spend time watching my hometown go by than anything else. Frank came up the stairs and joined Jimmy on the couch at the rear of the pilothouse. Toothpick stickin' out like always, he was likely looking for some post dinner conversation.

"Ran over a pleasure boat right there last summer." I waved our port searchlight at the center of the channel just downstream from the railroad swing bridge.

"You did what!?" Frank almost choked laughing.

The memory of how serious that incident could have been was still strong in my mind. "Comin' down outta the St. Croix on the *Sioux*. Couple of clowns there didn't git their motor started, and I ended up goin' right over the top of them."

Jimmy looked at me incredulously. "Wait, wait. Back up to the beginning. You gotta tell us this whole story!"

"Lotsa pleasure craft on the St. Croix every summer day. 'Specially Fridays. Not many days when we didn't have some sorta close call. They got absolutely no idea how close they are to danger, most of 'em! Somebody drops a skier in front of our tow at least every couple a' days. Anyhow, we got nine empties, and they were all stacked covers except one. Bill Lawson put that on the bow of the center string. I was good with that. I called Lyle Kidd, the railroad bridge tender. He said he had a train. I slowed way down and waited and waited. Little wind outta the west and still no train, so stopped, shoving the head of the tow up onto the sandy bank in the trees right above the highway bridge.

I had the engines pulled way back as we moved slowly past the Prescott waterfront. I shined a searchlight around the waterfront, across the dozens of boat slips, now empty, waiting to get frozen in for the winter.

"Two trains went through, one in each direction, and Lyle sounded his siren, warning that he was about to turn the turntable railroad bridge. I backed her up and got a little swing going to the port and came full ahead just as Frankie Huppert, the highway bridge tender, blew his horn, indicating the highway lift bridge was all the way to the top.

I lit a smoke and continued. "Web Severson and Larry Simpson were on the two bow corners, riding down through the bridges. They got a *speaker box setup* on the *Sioux*. Speaker box on the head to communicate with the guys on the head of the tow. Like most days, somebody over on the bank hollered, or maybe a boater yelled. It wasn't unusual for the deck guys to holler back. I heard some racket like that and didn't really think anything of it. The lead barges were just getting down inside the highway bridge, and there was a pleasure boat in the channel below the railroad bridge. I could see a guy on the bow pulling up an anchor rope just before they went out of sight behind the stack covers on the starboard bow empty of our tow. I had a little slide goin' 'cause of the wind from the starboard, so I still had her hooked up as the boat went under the bridge. The yelling in the speaker box got louder and louder, and all the sudden Web jumped over onto the head deck of that center empty hopper barge, and he was jumping up and down and waving me to back her up."

Both Frank and Jimmy continued looking at me wide-eyed. "I brought both engines back to neutral and *began blowing a danger signal*. I threw the steering rudders hard down to the port and the backing rudders hard to starboard and backed her hard just as the stern of the tow cleared the railroad bridge. Our headway was gone in about four hundred feet, but the unintelligible yelling continued from the speaker box. When Web showed up along the outside guard of the starboard lead barge just behind the stack covers, he was leaned way out over the water, hanging on and looking for something down below. That gave me a pretty sick feeling in my stomach."

"So, you run 'em over?" asked Frank.

"I wasn't sure," I said. "I pressed the call button on the box in the pilothouse asking for somebody to talk to me."

speaker box setup – A speaker box that included a microphone was stationed on the head of the tow and connected to a control box in the pilothouse. The captain could hear the deck crew talk and could talk to them via the wire that connected them.
danger whistle – four or more blasts of the whistle (towboat horn) repeated over and over, indicating some sort of danger, emergency

"They got 'em out!" Larry yelled into the speaker box. "They got 'em out. A boat that was close by come by. They got 'em out. Damn close, but they're safe. Boater come by and picked up both guys!" Cleary, Larry was shook up. His words were clipped and anxious.

"Boy, was that a relief to hear!" I continued. "Turns out they couldn't git their motor started. They tried and tried, and at the very last second, both guys jumped in and swam away from where the tow was. Webby said five more feet to the port and we'd a' missed 'em. The blessed part of the whole thing was that boater nearby who heard the danger whistle and knew what it meant. He rushed over and grabbed the two guys outta the water and got them away from the tow."

"Holy shit, Tommy," Frank said. "I bet you had ta change yer drawers!"

"Damn near, I'll tell ya. Talked a little bit more to the boys on the head, and once I was sure those boaters were safe and over on shore, I clutched her into forward and headed down into the Mississippi. Heard some clunking and felt it before I saw it. I stepped out onto the flying bridge, and out popped their boat. Chunk of aluminum 'bout the size of a big cooler was all that was left after rolling six hundred feet under that tow.

"I called the office and let 'em know what happened. A couple minutes later, Dick Lambert, one of the higher-ups, called back. That's when the gravity of the whole thing began to set in. He was just one of many company officials and Coast Guard big wheels that showed up on shore once we dropped our empties and tied up for the night."

"I'm thinkin' them boaters was the ones that needed new clean drawers," Jimmy said with a chuckle.

"They came down to our boat and were interviewed by the Coast Guard guys. Both drunk. Kept sayin' they were OK. Just wet and scared. No injuries. Man, I was sure glad about that. Changed my perspective forever though, I kin tell ya that. Never again took it for granted that a pleasure boat would git outta the way. It was a jolt to think that I could have been responsible for somebody drowning. I use a lot more caution in those spots now after that whole thing."

"I seen that happen a couple a' times in my years," Frank said. "Both times, nobody got hurt, but like you said, scares the bejeesus outta ya!"

Pilothouse Days

To our left, a Burlington Northern railroad train made the tight turn coming west behind the stone foundations and basement rear entries of business that lined Main Street. Her horn sounded the familiar grade crossing signal I had heard so many times growing up there.

"Something like twenty-four trains a day through there," I said.

Loud bangin' noises as the engines of the train passed over the *blocks* where the shore track stopped and the railroad bridge track started. "See them boat docks right there?" I waved our port searchlight around the covered marina docks and slips of the farthest downstream marina in town. "That is Prescott Marine. Where my dad worked when we moved to town.

"In 1965 we had the biggest flood ever. The Mississippi was record high, completely over these banks that you see. My dad was the boss there. They were in danger of all the boat slips getting away down the river and being destroyed. I remember my thirteenth birthday was spent setting off sticks of dynamite in holes we'd drilled in the ice that was holding all those boat slips in one big piece. We had pike poles and tried to get that ice away from the docks a little chunk at a time. That massive sheet of ice was creating too much strain on the cables holding the docks to the shore. When I look back at it, it was crazy to be doing that."

I brought the ship ups back to full ahead as we passed the last of the lights along the shore at Prescott.

"I better git in the rack for a bit, boys. See ya in a few hours," Frank said as he got up and headed out. He hurried down the walkway, shivering and fussing, giving Jimmy and me a good laugh.

The night sky was jet-black, with clouds blocking the moon and stars. We could see the faint glow of the lights at Prairie Island Power Plant about ten miles ahead off our starboard bow. I leaned back in my chair and felt again an overwhelming sense of peace and satisfaction as we moved along the stretch of river where I spent so much time as a boy.

blocks – slang for the mechanical equipment that connects the railroad track at the end of the bridge to the shore track

View from pilothouse of tow moving into a lock downbound on the Mississippi.

9. Jimmy's First Locks

"Johnny, yer sausage gravy and biscuits are the best!" I placed my plate in the sink, rinsing off the small bit of gravy left on it. Just the perfect seasoning. Not as salty as some, and the biscuits were delightfully tender and rich. Lots of pork sausage crumbles. Dipped in a nice egg yolk, they are heaven. I topped off my coffee getting ready to head up to the pilothouse.

"We're making good time, dontcha think?" Johnny asked.

"You bet!" I responded. "This pair of loads is scootin' right along. It's like the empties are not even there. Sorry about your view here from the galley." The way our tow was configured there was an empty hopper barge alongside the boat on both sides, blocking the view from the deck. "Yer always welcome upstairs, Johnny. This is really pretty country. Come on up anytime. Tons of eagles in the trees, and with the leaves gone, you kin see their nests and the whole deal."

Pilothouse Days

I stepped out onto the guard cautiously, watching carefully for any patches of ice. As I approached the head deck, I could see the vast expanse of water looking past our loaded barges in that wide spot in the Mississippi. Just getting to be fully daylight. Stepping onto the pilothouse steps, I returned a wave from two fishermen in snowmobile suits in a Lund boat out in front of downtown Lake City. Entering the pilothouse, I shivered and decided to leave my coat on for a bit while I woke up.

"We had a couple hours' delay at Lock Three last night," Frank said. "The lockman said a hydraulic line damn near caught on fire when someone left a heater too close. They decided to drain the lines and replace the section of hose that got burnt. Said they didn't want no oil running into the river! We waited for that northbound tow you saw at *watch time*, then they let us go down and tie off on the upper guide wall.

"Holy shit, Tommy. I went down the wall to visit with those guys and got to see their shop. Damnedest thing I ever saw. They got every tool known to man. Best money can buy. And on top of that, two or three of everything. I couldn't believe it!"

Frank moved to the side, and I sat down in the captain's chair and took over. "I've done that too, Frank. We got delayed down at Rock Island north-bound one time, and they invited us up to tour everything. Exactly my reaction, too. Best of everything money can buy. Pretty amazin'! I will give 'em credit though. They kept everything neat as a pin. Least they did there."

There was a stiff wind blowing out of the west as we made the slight turn that had us steering almost straight east for the last seven miles across to the foot of Lake Pepin, right ahead of us. Off to our left, the little town of Pepin, Wisconsin, was waking up for the day. The marina that dominates the waterfront there had one or two holdout sailboats still in the water. Otherwise, crickets.

"Pretty good *rollers* out there," I said. "Good thing we're running with the wind, or we would have a coating of ice a hundred feet back from the head from the splash spray!"

Frank looked out at the head deck with the binoculars. Setting them

watch time – slang for when the two crews change at the end/beginning of their shifts
rollers – long running waves that follow a strong wind on the water

down, he said, "I made them boys wrap that lock line up good out there with a tarp once we left Lock Three. Figured we might have some big waves out here on Pepin."

Jimmy came up the pilothouse stairs and almost dropped his coffee when the pilothouse door lurched forward, caught by our strong following wind. Once he won the fight with the door, he found a spot in the back.

Frank got up to head downstairs for breakfast and a break. "See you birds at noontime. Keep 'er in the rut!" We all chuckled when he struggled with the door on his way out. The breeze blew some papers around, and Jimmy slipped right into the captain's chair when I got up to catch them. I moved to the back, tidied up around the logbook, and began writing a note to my girlfriend.

I pointed to a feature on the river chart and said, "You'll find yer first red buoy about a mile above Reads Landing, pretty close to the right bank. The Chippewa River comes in right there, and then it's a little turn before you come down into Wabasha. Yer gonna make at
make at least a couple of locks here this morning if there ain't no northbound tows."

"Sounds good," Jimmy said. He looked like a kid on Christmas morning sitting among a heap of presents.

I left our steersman to his work and took a break down in the galley. I freshened up my coffee and had a bite of the hot apple pie Johnny had made for lunch. The deck crew went out to get everything ready for making Lock 4. We were going under the highway bridge that crosses the river at Wabasha as I walked up the pilothouse steps. Lots of wonderful old brick buildings for several blocks along the river on the right bank. A couple had remnants of old painted advertisements, so common on sides of business buildings of these once robust river towns.

"Bring her right down onto the wall, Captain. We're ready for ya," the lockman said over the marine radio.

Jimmy responded, "Ten-four" as he hung the radio microphone up and got up out of the chair.

"No out-draft board here." I felt the need to give Jimmy a little direction to make sure we started the lock thing off on the right foot. "That's a good

Pilothouse Days

Note large round sign (outdraft board) on the end of the long wall (far right)

thing. Stay out in the main channel where you have room above these locks. Once you get close, come at the wall at a slight angle with a tow like this, Jimmy. Take her nice and slow. A gentle turn just as you clear the end of the wall, and you'll put yer tow into a soft slide that will cause the tow to set right in flat against the wall. Easy to do with just a couple lengths, like this. If you had a *full tow*, you would do it quite a bit different. I am going to ask you to be reallllly careful about watching your headway. Hard as it is to be patient, you gotta go slow and easy around locks. It's the right thing to do, and if you don't, the lock people go out of their minds!"

Jimmy had pulled back the throttles earlier, and we were approaching the beginning of the signs installed along the bank calling out the distance till the end of the lock's *long wall*. Huge chunks of recycled, broken-up concrete bridge abutments and massive limestone boulders at the water's edge protected the riverbank there where tows backed in during high water causing erosion with their wheel wash. Lots of nasty old used-up railroad ties line both sides of the Burlington Northern Railroad double track that that runs through there. For another 250 miles, their route clings, sometimes precariously, to the left riverbank before reaching Rock Island, Illinois, where it goes both east and west. The tiny, well-worn town of Alma, Wisconsin, was waking up just ahead beyond the pilothouse port windows. An occasional lonesome car, wisp of exhaust in the crisp air, moved past on the Great River Road, the main Wisconsin state highway there. I watched Jimmy, pleased to see him looking out to his left repeatedly, watching the bank and checking his forward speed.

full tow – slang for a full double-locking tow – either twelve or fifteen barges
long wall – Most river locks have one wall extending about 600 feet before entry to the actual lock chamber. Getting flat against this wall before entering the lock is critical.

Bill was stationed on the port bow corner of the tow holding the eye of his lock line, and he caught the ***heaving line and monkey's fist*** the lockman tossed to him. At the same time, he waved the ***all clear signal*** letting Jimmy know that the corner of the tow was passing the end of the long wall. He passed the heaving line through the eye of the lock line and the lockman pulled the eye across the small gap between them. The lockman set aside his heaving line and began carrying the eye of the line slowly along, knowing that at any time he could place the eye of the line on a timberhead if needed. Jimmy made that slight turn we'd discussed after clearing the end of the wall, and the tow ***set*** very gently over and against the lock wall.

Mississippi River lock chambers are 110 feet wide. Our tow was three regulation barges (each thirty-five feet across) wide, so that meant that we had five feet to split between the sides of the tow inside the chamber. As soon as Charlie gave Jimmy the all clear on the starboard corner of the tow, we were in the chamber. All that is needed then is to watch the stern corner against the long wall, keeping it no more than one foot or so away. Jimmy moved the chair over and heaved a sigh of relief.

"Well done, young man," I said. "How's that feel?"

"I am glad I got to steer a lot before arriving here, so I could get the feel of the tow. You were right that it needs to be handled like we are just towing the two loaded barges. The six empties don't make a lot of difference 'cept fer taking up the space. I feel good, man! I feel good!" He smiled, and I patted him on the back.

Charlie worked his way back to the port stern corner, Jimmy slowed and stopped the tow perfectly just inside the gate recess, and Charlie fastened his lock line securely.

"Gonna head down to the can, if that's OK, Tom." I nodded, and Jimmy stepped out into the cold morning. I turned and entered our movements into the logbook. I smiled as I thought back to when I did some piloting for the first time.

heaving line and monkey's fist – Lock workers use a length of lightweight line with a weighted ball (monkey's fist) on the end of it to toss to the deck worker on the head of the tow. The tow worker ties the lock line to it, and the lock worker pulls the line over to the wall.
all clear signal – This is a signal where the deck worker waves an arm up and down meaning that we have passed the corner of an obstruction or other barge.
set – slang for sliding or moving sideways

Pilothouse Days

Jimmy joined me back in the pilothouse as we were passing the little town of Minneiska along the Minnesota side of the river. "You remember that overhead walking bridge over the train tracks between downtown and the lock wall back there at Alma?" I asked.

Jimmy nodded as I got up, and he slid into the chair.

Stately and historic Valley Line towboat, the *L. Wade Childress*

"My very first trip up here as a deckhand on the *L. Wade Childress*, first mate's name was Tubby Smith. He asked me if I would go to town for him at Alma. I was just off watch. On the downtown side of that bridge was a place called the Dam View Bar. Still there. I got all the pints of vodka I could stuff in my pants for him for the twenty he gave me!" I chuckled, thinking back to that hot summer evening. "The captain musta really liked him because there was no way he didn't see me coming back across that bridge with my pants pockets all bulging out!

"Loved that boat and its sister, the *W.S. Rhea*. They were both giant old horses that had been repowered to five thousand horsepower. They were so old that they had all the regal lines and massive quarters from the early years on the river. Ridin' those boats as a deckhand is where I learned everything important about making locks on the Upper River southbound with a full tow. They *loaded those boats up* even in high water! Never *used any tugs to get on the wall*.

loaded those boats up – describing the large-sized tows (overloaded) assigned even in high water
used tugs to get on the wall – At the time (late '70s) it had become very common for down-bound tows to hire a local tug to help get their tow onto the wall above the dam during periods of high water where dangerous out-drafts occurred.

Checked our way in with long lock lines made out of *sisal*. Nothing like today!"

"I'da liked ta seen that," Jimmy said. "Never rode a boat where we had a full *double-locking tow*. Just always towboats in the harbor. Built a lot of twelve and fifteen barge tows but always for other towboats."

Photo of tug helping by pushing the tow towards the long wall of the lock.

I lit up a cigarette, took a good drag, then told him, "Yer gittin' a little taste of it with this tow filling the entire lock chamber. It's kind of all relative. Most of the time, you'll be lucky enough to find yerself with a tow that is sized for the boat yer runnin'. Let me tell you, it can be hairy when it's not. When I was first a trip pilot over on the Illinois River, I got me a couple of doozies where we were waaaaay overloaded. I had to clean my pants more than once, but I didn't have no choice. I had to take whatever came my way at first so I could get the experience I needed to be able to get all the tripping work I wanted."

"So what is the secret to making a lock downbound with a full fifteen-barge loaded tow? How's it different from what we're doing?" Jimmy asked.

checked our way in – The deck crew worked a line on the bow corner of the tow hooked to the lock wall that helped pull the tow over against the long wall. The line was snugged to the point of stress just short of breaking to pull the tow in (*checking* the line).
sisal – The lock lines used to check were premier African sisal (fiber) ropes three to four inches thick that were remarkably strong but would not snap if overstressed. They simply separated. It made this checking process less dangerous.
double locking tow – Most lock chambers are 600 feet long and 110 feet wide. A typical fifteen barge tow is locked in two sections, a double locking. The first nine barges (three wide and three long) are lock through and that is followed by the remaining six (three wide and two long) and the towboat.

Pilothouse Days

"Unless it's *flat pool water*, the best thing to do is get over as close as possible to the shore directly above the long wall. Ya drop yer tow down nice and easy and stay more concerned about keeping your stern over than the bow of your tow. Let the head creep by the end of the long wall, and the lockman'll toss the heaving line to yer deck crew. Once he or she pulls the eye of the lock line over and puts it on a timberhead, you kill out your headway. Have your deck crew check and fasten the lock line till the head of the tow stops moving away from the wall and toward the dam. Then gently come ahead, and as you move forward that lock line will pull the tow toward the wall. That make sense? Can you see this happening?" I asked.

This photo shows a lock line between the port bow corner of the tow
and the lock wall pulling the tow toward the wall as the tow moves forward.

Jimmy nodded while I grabbed the binoculars and checked out a fisherman we were passing who was netting a nice fish.

"Keep your ass over all the time yer doin' this. You never wanna get out far enough for the current to get on your side, forcing the whole tow over toward the dam. If you keep your ass over tight to the shore, the current will be on the river side of your tow, and it'll keep you on the shore. Once you git the tow setting over to the wall, keep yer tow nice and square with the wall.

flat pool water – slang referring to low water. The river is at its lowest stage with much less current, etc.

Be sure not to get in a hurry. You can always back up and do it all over again. Once the head gets on the wall, lots of these locks have a mooring bit that rides down a rail, and you just have your guys on the head tie the head off on that moving timberhead and slide on down into the chamber. Anytime the tow wants to move off the wall, stop at a timberhead, have 'em tie 'er off, and bring the tow back on the wall.

"Like I was sayin', as a deckhand and a mate, I handled that checking of the lock line dozens of times before I ever put fifteen in a lock from the pilothouse. Jist be sure that you don't git horsey. And be super damn careful with these *Poly D lock lines* we have now. They are super strong. But if one ever breaks, it can be crazy dangerous for the deck guys!"

Photo of Poly D lock lines. Super strong.

Jimmy pulled the throttles back and started to *get into shape* to make the approach to Lock 5. We were at the bottom of the second *crossing* in this

Poly D lock lines – Poly D is a brand name that refers to new polyester nylon combination rope that is rugged and super strong. Very dangerous if it breaks/snaps.
get into shape – begin to approach. Put the tow in position for a steer or some sort of upcoming maneuvering.
crossing – The Mississippi River channel shifts frequently along its natural course from one side of the river valley to the other. These long channel directional changes are called "crossings" in river slang.

half-mile-wide pool above Lock 5. The Milwaukee Road Railroad tracks abutted the river immediately in front of State Highway 61 on our starboard side there. Just up a slight rise and off in the distance, a large green combine was moving swiftly, eating up rows of yellow-tan cornstalks, the dust and debris jettisoning out the back quickly blowing downwind. The elevation changed at least 300 feet from the base of the steep bank at the end of the cornfield to the tops of the trees crowning the slope. Thick clusters of gray, leafless trees clinging to that incline. All huddling, full of nuts and seeds stashed in the fortified homes of so many resident critters, all set for the long winter ahead.

Billy waved the all clear once again as the tow cleared the end of the long wall, and Jimmy steered slightly to port and the tow settled tightly onto the long wall. The corner of the tow was close enough to the wall that Billy just handed the eye of the lock line to the lockman, who then walked it forward. Once again, Jimmy was constantly looking out to his right side at the shore moving past, judging his speed and making decisions accordingly. The wind had shifted to the northeast and was blowing easy, straight onto the lock wall. Jimmy brought both engines back to neutral and let the momentum of the tow move us along for the remaining thousand feet until he reversed the engines to stop the stern of our tow just inside the upper lock gates. I was pleased with Jimmy's proficiency, especially given his novice status. With each new accomplishment I grew to respect this young man's natural ability to pilot a towboat.

"Nice job, Jimmy," I said.

He smiled at me and said, "I just want to pinch myself. I have wanted to become a pilot since the first day I stepped foot on a towboat. It all seems to be coming together. I feel confident and comfortable."

"It's a pleasure to work with you, Jimmy. You appear to be a natural."

The lower gates were open, and the lockman honked the horn, signaling we were free to go. Both deckhands raised their hands high in the air signaling *all gone*. "We're gonna be down to Lock Five before lunch." I gave Jimmy a friendly poke in the back. "Yer gittin' three locks in one watch, young man. That's a good thing!"

all gone – when all lines are turned loose, and the tow is ready to be underway

Pilothouse view of beautiful forested river bluffs lining the Upper Mississippi River.

10. Favorite Boats & River Folks

"Git up, Jimmy. Take a break! Yer done for the day." I grinned at him and gave him a friendly pat on the back. He got out of the captain's chair and moved to a spot alongside Frank at the rear of the pilothouse. I hung up my jacket and slid into the chair. We were just starting into the last crossing, taking us back over the Wisconsin side right above Lock 8 at Genoa. The lights of La Crosse and Brownsville, Minnesota, illuminated the edge of the blue-black horizon behind us. It was cold enough to snow and sure seemed like it wanted to. Snow and night navigating with searchlights is not a good combination. Any amount of snow would slow or stop us now that it was dark. No radar on that fine vessel but most likely wouldn't run in a snowstorm anyway.

Pilothouse Days

"How'd our young student do, Frank?" I asked.

"You know what, Tommy," Frank said while Jimmy looked at him hopefully, "this kid is a natural. Good as anybody I ever seen fer just startin' out. Made Locks Six and Seven without a hitch. Kep' 'er in nice shape comin' down on that La Crosse railroad bridge. Did jist fine. I had a hell of a time stayin' awake! This is like a vacation with him on here!"

"That's good to hear, Frank. Yer gonna be all right, Jimmy." I smiled back at him, moving our port searchlight left and set it on the Genoa Upper *Day Beacon* about a mile upstream from the end of the long wall at Lock 8. "Johnny's got yer *Saturday night steaks* all set down there. Damn nice T-bones. Makovech's Boat Store really puts out the best steaks. He said to tell ya that he won't start 'em till you come down to the galley and tell him how you want 'em done. He's got that incredible mushroom gravy that he makes with 'em. Amazing! I'm stuffed. We sure hit the jackpot with him as a cook on here."

"Lock Eight to the *Mallard*. Channel fourteen, please."

I grabbed the marine radio microphone and switched the channel to 14. "Good ahead, over."

"Jist opening the upper gates and letting the *Prairie Dawn* outta here so we'll be ready for ya."

"Ten-four. We'll be right on down there. Thanks." I switched the radio back to channel 16. "The *Mallard* to the *Prairie Dawn*. How about channel nine?"

The *Prairie Dawn* answered, "Channel nine. Go ahead, Captain Groovy!"

"Hey, Peewee! Didn't know you were still up this way!" I recognized the pilot I was talking to aboard the *Prairie Dawn* as Mike McReynolds. He'd worked for Twin City Barge until about a year before then became a regular

day beacon – slang for a permanent marker along the shore. Because it is a day beacon it has no lights.
Saturday night steaks – very traditional to provide crew great quality steaks for Saturday evening meal on live-aboard towboats

MV *Prairie Dawn*. Twin screw, 5,400 horsepower.

pilot working on line boats for ADM. His vertically challenged stature provided the basis for his nickname, but he was always good-natured about it. He was one of several local rivermen who called International Falls, Minnesota, home. Hell of a good pilot and a great guy. He and I had worked together the last three weeks of September aboard that boat.

"Yes, sir! We turned the *Beauty* down below Muscatine, and they sent us back up light boat to grab the last loads of the season outta Winona and La Crosse. We're light boat. I'll head out into the channel and let you run down the bank. See you on the two, OK?"

"Ten-four. Two whistle. So'd you git off there between when you and I were on there in September and now, or'd you jist stay on her?"

"I made it up home in October for three weeks. Fall fishin' and duck huntin'! The walleyes on *the Rainy up there at the Falls* git the feedbag on in late October! Caught a couple a' ten pounders. Best fishing in years."

"Good for you, man! I got some huntin' time in in October too! You can't beat fall hunting. We had some good northern duck flights last week in October. Had a great time. Black-and-blue shoulder. Got to where I couldn't shoot anymore!"

"Trying to git outta here 'fore it gits too damn cold. Frank Rhymer's on here with me. He says we're all nuts, livin' up here in the frozen land! I keep tellin' him it's heaven, but he's not buyin it!"

the Rainy up there at the Falls – slang for up on the Rainy River near International Falls, Minnesota. Home to a number of towboat workers in the '70s.

Pilothouse Days

I flipped on our pilothouse light just for a second and waved as the *Prairie Dawn* passed by. Peewee **waved his flashlight at me** from inside his pilothouse. I adjusted our searchlights and decided it was time to focus on making this lock. The boys were headed out to their respective corners on the bow.

"We'll be right behind you sometime tomorrow, Struve. Prob'ly talk with ya down the line."

"Well, you have a great winter, Peewee, if I don't catch up with you again. Maybe git some a' them Rainy River walleyes fishing through the ice. Be good, man." I hung up the microphone and concentrated on the river.

Frank stood up and grabbed his smokes, ready to head downstairs. "Crazy. That's what you people are. Livin' in this godforsaken frozen hell-hole. Ice fishin', my butt! You don't drive out on the ice, do ya? What the hell are you all thinkin'?" He made me laugh with his constant chiding about choosing to live in the great white north.

"Oh, it's a big deal up here in the winter, Frank. People have well-rigged ice fishin' shacks. Top-notch. Color TV — the whole deal. Little drinkin', some card playing. If you catch fish, that makes it even more fun!"

Frank was shaking his head, smiling, and mumbling as he headed downstairs. The corner of our tow cleared the end of the long wall, and Billy handed the lockman the lock line. I shut down the port searchlight and looked to the side repeatedly, monitoring our forward speed.

Jimmy watched from behind and asked, "So, the *Prairie Dawn* a nice boat?"

"Oh, man, Jimmy! 'Nice' doesn't do it justice," I responded. "Gorgeous. Super nice boat. Agri-Trans bought her from Wisconsin Barge Line. Fifty-four hundred horse. Handles beautifully. Her and the *American Beauty*. My two favorites ever. Both St. Louis Ship towboats. Built solid, late sixties.

waved his flashlight at me – All pilothouse professionals limit the time any lights are on in a pilothouse after dark. A human's eyes dilate fully in the dark. When a light is turned on, the pupil contracts. It takes time to get night vision back after the light is turned off. Repeated, this causes a headache. Many times, instead of turning on a light, another pilot may just wave his flashlight at you to say hi.

Buddy named Kenny Martin referred me over there. I made a couple trips for them as a trip pilot. I'd be damn tempted to take a regular job with them if I didn't have so much seniority here. Their boats are spotless, and that company is reallllly top-notch."

MV *American Beauty*. Twin screw, 5,400 horsepower.

Charlie signaled all clear as we passed the short bullnose, and we continued floating down into the lock chamber.

"You ain't half bad at this yerself!" Jimmy said. He was standing next to me while I put our tow into the lock.

I smiled and turned to give him a friendly thumbs up. "You better git down there and git yer steak, Jimmy. You've had a big day. Take a break, my man. You've earned it!"

A cold chill and the always present smell of our diesel exhaust came in through the door as Jimmy headed downstairs. There was a fair breeze coming right out of the north down onto our stern. Lights of the massive power plant with its tall smokestack against the black horizon just ahead, right below the lock. No stars again. Snow couldn't be too far behind us. Gotta keep moving to stay ahead of it.

Pilothouse Days

A few isolated flakes drifted down from time to time while Frank and Jimmy visited with me after dinner. I occasionally switched on one of the searchlights to confirm what I was seeing close by and on the horizon. Some nights piloting, you can almost see better without any lights. The Upper Mississippi makes a slight turn and then below Genoa runs parallel with the railroad tracks and Highway 35 in Wisconsin all the way until the final crossing that brings us over to the right bank at Lansing, Iowa. We crossed the Minnesota-Iowa border about six miles below Lock 8. Yard and farm lights and the markers along there made running in the dark along here a breeze.

I looked at Frank sporting his perpetual toothpick. "What did ya think a' them steaks?"

Frank grinned at me in dark and said, "Some of the best I ever had, Tommy.

"So, what's the deal with Makovech's Boat Store?" he continued. "He doesn't have any towboats, does he? I hear him talkin' to boats on the radio up there all the time, arranging to meet them and deliver their groceries and supplies. We got groceries from him one of the trips I was on the *Colonel George Lambert* up here." I turned and shrugged. "I don't know Stan Makovech personally, but he's been the grocery & towboat supply go-to guy in St. Paul for years. You know Jimmy Dye?"

Frank shook his head.

MV *Pamela Dewey*. Formerly MV *Colonel George Lambert.*
Twin screw, 4,200 horsepower.

"He's related to him somehow. Not sure how. I think he's got a bunch a' money in Dye's outfit. Dakota Barge Services. You've seen the MV *Sophie Rose*? She's named after Makovech's mother." I switched on a searchlight for a moment to check the location of a line of buoys. "The *Sadie Mae* and the *Dominique Q.* are two other Dakota Barge boats.

"So, you was on the *Colonel George Lambert*?" I asked. "Twin City's only been runnin' her for about a year. Whatdya think of her?"

"She's OK, Tommy. Forty-two hundred. She's one of those new Viking class Dravo-built boats. They're nice boats, but they'll rattle yer back teeth. You go to backin' full on them boats, you better not have nothin' on a counter or it'll be on the floor. They git the job done, I guess. I was spoiled, all them years working those **Mobil boats**. I was on the *Mobil Leader* regular for three years. She was built in sixty-seven. Boats was built more solid back then. Quiet, comfy. Good living boats.

MV *Leland Speakes*. Formerly the MV *Mobile Leader*.
Telescopic pilothouse. Twin screw, 5,000 horsepower.

"Musta got enough pipelines in the ground so they laid them boats up. Not that many oil tows running around up here anymore. Still plenty down on the **Intracoastal**, but that ain't for me. Happy to be over here now. Twin City's a good company. Workin' so close to home over there in Illinois is a plus. Most of the time I just drive up to Lemont to catch my boat. So much easier gittin' back and forth."

"You got a favorite boat over there, Frank?"

"Not really, I don't guess. They've put me on just about all of 'em

Mobil boats – Mobil Oil Company ran a fleet of towboats and tank barges around the inland rivers for years, transporting oil from refineries to customers.
Intracoastal – The Intracoastal Waterway (a marked channel along the Gulf Coast of the U.S.), is a major corridor for oil barge movements to and from Texas and Gulf oil fields.

now. I like workin' in *the canal*. Lots of variety and keeps a guy sharp, I think. Bunch a great guys over there too. Jack Moore has been super to me, I gotta say. He's some good people, that guy, right there."

"I couldn't agree more," I said. "Twin City's got some good people and some real characters." Once again, I turned on a searchlight briefly and checked to make sure the marker I was steering on was the right one. I continued, "A guy could write a book about all these guys we work with! I gotta smile when I think back to all the captains I've worked with over the years at Twin City in St. Paul." I laughed thinking about what story to tell.

"Take Ernie Clay. Came from Columbia, Missouri. Owned an actual Checker cab that he ran on his days off at home. He had at least a sixty-inch waistline and wore a size thirty-inch belt. You coulda held a flashlight in that gap! Asa Briggs. Came from Pepin, Wisconsin. Good-natured old cuss but a real slob. Same size as Ernie and slooooow. Drove me crazy. I *followed him* on the Itasca one time. He was too lazy to git outta bed. Hawked up his loogies and just spit 'em all over the wall alongside the bed. It was the damnedest thing! Bunch a' guys from down near Pepin. Claire Marks. Bill Lawson. Bobby Sinstad. Phil McFate. All good guys. Phil McFate was Twin City's fleet mate. Built tow all day every day and never wore gloves. Skin on his hands was perpetually black. Tough old guy. Lit one cigarette off the other all the time."

"I worked with Phil my whole first summer in St. Paul," Jimmy said. "Toughest son of a gun I ever saw. He would get a *steel sliver* in his hand and just pull it out with his teeth like it was nothin'! He lived on the old *Minneapolis* that was moored to the wharf barge. Had it made there. I think his cigarette smokin' got to him. Had the asthma. I didn't see him around at all this past summer."

I continued through my list of characters. "Preacher. Morri Stanford was his real name. He would laugh and smile and quote Scripture all during a watch and sing praises to the Lord. Then something would go wrong, and

the canal – The Chicago and Michigan Canal. At Joliet, Illinois, the Illinois River turns into a canal that was built to move river traffic up into Chicago and connect the river with Lake Michigan.
followed him – He got off and I got on, replacing him as captain.
steel sliver – The flexible steel cables used to fasten tows together would fray at times, and you could get a steel sliver (similar to a wood sliver) from them.

he would cuss like a sailor! After he'd settled down, he would beat himself up for losing it. Begged forgiveness for letting you down!" I chuckled and continued. "Skeeter Ransom. Ronnie Nolman. Larry Moore. Jay Sampson. Bunch of great Illinois boys! Your neighbors, Frank!" I reminded him.

"I am gonna write a book someday," I continued. "Stories about all the fun and crazy things that happened. All the good towboat people and their ups and downs. It'd be fun to be old and still be able to remember it all!"

Frank got up, shrugged on his jacket and yawned. "Yes, we sure git to meet a lotta guys workin' out here. I made some damn good friends over the years." He grinned at both of us and continued, "Eleven thirty will be here quick. Better head down to the box. Good work today, Jimmy. Yer gonna be all right, kid!" Frank winked at me, gave Jimmy's knee a squeeze, and closed the door on his way out.

MV American Beauty downbound just upstream from Lansing, Iowa.

Jimmy stretched and yawned and said, "I'm gonna turn in too, Tom. Thanks for a great day. It is sooooo good to git all this experience. Let me know if you need anything. Otherwise, I'll see you in the morning."

"It's great workin' with ya, Jimmy," I replied. "See you in the morning."

Pilothouse Days

Lights in the front rooms of a handful of homes clinging to the side of the bluff at Desoto, Wisconsin, off to our port side. An occasional car traveling along cautiously, exhaust visible, testified to the freezing temperatures. Off in the distance to our starboard, the crest of the Iowa riverbank appeared shadowed by the lights of Lansing and the historic highway bridge that crosses the river there. I leaned back in the captain's chair after tuning the transistor radio on our console to an easy listening station with a strong signal. A quiet night, no river traffic, dark, leafless trees moving past on both sides. Ducks, geese, and summer birds all got smart and left for warm Southern winter spa locations. The smells of fall. Smell of snow wanting to fall. The soft glow of the console RPM, gauge, and rudder indicator lights accompanying me. Another good day on the river.

Another *great* day.

Pilothouse view of loaded tow downbound on the Upper Mississippi River.

Pilothouse view of a fifteen barge loaded coal tow.

11. That's God's Country!

"Morning, Jimmy! Did you git a good sleep?" I had just pulled the ship ups back to half ahead as we made our final approach down into Lock 11 at Dubuque, Iowa, when Jimmy walked in. He came and stood beside me, hoping I would hand over the controls to start a new southbound towboatin' day. "You ready to go ta work?" I asked as a I slid over and let him stand at the controls.

"Had a good night's sleep, did a small load of laundry, played a little cribbage with John, got some coffee," he explained. "I'm ready."

Bill and Charlie stepped carefully onto the stern of the load we were faced up to. Charlie, always a comedian, pretended to slide a bit on the few tiny snowflakes that had collected on the lee side of each of the barge fittings. I smiled at them, grabbed the microphone, and reminded them, "Boys, you gotta be extra, extra careful out there not to slip. Promise me you are taking your time and watching every step you take. 'Specially because you are on opposite corners with no way to git to one another quickly. You gotta be super careful, please!"

Both men waved without turning back. Far over to our starboard side, tall plumes of steam sliced through the cold air out of dozens of tiny stacks above the massive John Deere plant.

I cautioned Jimmy just a bit. "You got just a bit of a west wind blowing you off the wall, so once you git down on the wall don't hesitate to stop and get your tow flat on the wall. He nodded and pulled the throttles back to dead slow, watching his headway closely, glancing frequently out the starboard pilothouse windows. He *held a nice little point* as before and just prior to the end of the long wall, he steered to port when Bill waved, indicating he was clear of the end of the wall.

"*Captain Newt* to the *Mallard.* I'm down below here northbound with a construction crane barge. I'll stay out away from the wall till you go by. See you on the one whistle, if that's OK."

I reached past Jimmy and keyed the mic without picking it up. "Ten-four, Captain. One whistle."

A few moments later, Charlie waved his arm indicating the port bow of the tow had cleared the short bullnose. About twenty minutes later, the lockman sounded the horn indicating we could be on our way. Both deckhands waved the all gone signal, and Jimmy moved the throttles to one-half ahead, starting us moving out of the lock chamber.

"You git down around the corner, you'll see the railroad bridge," I explained. "This one is almost a copy of the Hastings Railroad Bridge. 'Bout a hundred forty-five feet each span, but it's out in the middle of the river. *Shape it*, back up, do whatever you feel good about."

Jimmy backed and killed out our headway then leaned the starboard bow of our tow against the long wall once he cleared the short wall bullnose.

He twisted the stern out into the channel.

held a nice little point – This is when a captain steers past the position needed and holds the tow in that position before letting the tow come back to a straight line. .
shape it – slang for steering a tow deep in the turn, "shaping" a turn

Once he ***shipped the engines forward***, I grabbed the radio microphone. "The *Mallard* is downbound departing Lock Eleven."

Jimmy came full ahead and headed out into the channel.

"I got the railroad bridge open for ya, Captain. Bring her on down," came the reply from the railroad bridge tender.

Jimmy steered down through the challenging railroad bridge without any problems. I watched carefully, ready to step in, but he steered like there was nothing to it. I respected his skill but knew also being twenty-something and having a great attitude were giving him a distinct advantage. Ten years prior as a new pilot, I wasn't scared of anything either, and every new challenge was just that, a fun new challenge. Let me at it! It made me smile to remember back to those wonderful first days and months in the pilothouse.

"Nice job, Jimmy. You just made one of the most daunting bridges on the Upper without a hint of a problem. Of the others, prob'ly the two worst are the Burlington and the Hannibal railroad bridges. 'Bout the same as this one. Hannibal, when the water's up, you kin have a helluva time stoppin' sometimes. You just get tight to the bank, back her full, slow down best you kin, and drop yer tow in the hole when you git right down on top of it. I personally don't like the Fort Madison Bridge either 'cause it's out in the middle of nowhere. I prefer being close to the bank. But it's got a nice wide span."

"I felt good back there," he said. "Just kep' a nice straight rudder and kep' it about half ahead like you said." He sat back in his chair, a nice open stretch of river ahead. Fat clutches of sticks assembled into bald eagle nests at the tops of the grandfather cottonwoods along both banks.

"That's yer best strategy, Jimmy. Lots of guys ***git all out of shape*** second-guessing themselves. If you are coming at it square with the world, there's seldom any set that will impact you if you are moving faster than the current. Be sure and ask Frank if you can copy his notes from his charts. He

shipped the engines forward – move the ship up controls forward, engaging the transmissions and beginning forward propulsion
get all out of shape – slang for making steering or operation decisions that get the tow into a bad or dangerous position

prob'ly has notes about ***lights to line up on*** and where to keep your stern if you back up for any of these in high water."

The rest of the day and the next two days passed mostly uneventfully. Jimmy steered each day, and I let him work a few hours after dark each day to help him get confidence with running at night. We got a twenty-minute snow later that afternoon right in the middle of the big stump field above Clinton, Iowa. ***Shut us completely out***. Frank pulled her back, stopped for a bit, and the snow stopped as quick as it started. Wind blew the light snow all off the tow without an issue.

View from pilothouse fifteen loads, downbound on Upper Mississippi River.
Arsenal Island Railroad Bridge, Lock #15 - Rock Island, Illinois.

After dark later that night, Jimmy made the bridges and locks amid all the lights around Rock Island, Illinois. Great experience to work down through a tight channel (rocky areas – must not get out of the channel!) with shore lights everywhere making it a challenge to identify your navigational markers. Next morning, we were treated to a crisp clear sky and sunrise. Mid-morning, the sun dogs were glorious! Jimmy made the Burlington Railroad Bridge, again without any problems.

lights to line up on – Captains watch carefully when successfully navigating a bridge or tight location and note where the stern or bow of the tow was in relation to a light or marker on a structure or on shore. They will note that (in their charts) and use those same lights again and again to line up their tow successfully.
shut us completely out – fog or snow condition when you can see nothing

That stretch of the Upper Mississippi is a lovely step back in time. Sleepy, tiny towns line the riverbanks. Old, scrappy rock and brick facades of the mostly long-shuttered businesses were camouflaged by layers of vinyl or aluminum siding, most of it faded away from its original guaranteed-to-last-forever color. Lots of river bottom agriculture there. Long, low floodplain fields along the river, crops freshly wet from melted overnight frost, were abuzz with giant red and green combines rushing to collect the golden seeds that get dried and stored in metal silos that stand on each farmstead. From the very edge of the river till the banks go almost vertical along each side of the river, these fertile lands that flood once every four years are a gamble well worth it for local farmers.

Above each Upper Mississippi lock, there is a terminus where lowland farmland gives way to the shallow and then deeper backwaters, now critical natural habitat and magnificent, well-populated wildlife refuges that cleanse this great river and help rid her of all the flotsam and jetsam that finds its way into her upstream. Passing through that morning, the river was coated with a thin, crisp layer of clear ice and spotted by snow that had collected upwind from cattails, revealing why all the migrating birds had departed.

Numerous majestic bald eagles nesting along banks of Upper Mississippi River.

Lots and lots and lots of eagles stay the winter there. There'd been a formidable push over the previous ten years or so to save the eagles, and it was working. Nests dotted all the mammoth senior cottonwoods lining the banks. Glorious fishermen, those guys. Everywhere you looked you saw one of those majestic birds. Easily three feet tall, with their white-capped heads, golden beaks spread, too proud of the flopping fish they were holding to begin to feast.

Pilothouse Days

We had no delays from other towboat traffic at the Upper Mississippi locks as we progressed downstream. The last of the upbound towboats, now turned and headed southbound like us, were far upstream, scrambling to get out of the Upper River before freeze-up. Wisconsin became Illinois at Dubuque along the left bank. Iowa became Missouri at Keokuk on the right bank. We were averaging eight miles per hour, including the time making locks. Five days after leaving St. Paul, daylight brought yet another silver sky with a following light north wind. Midmorning, Jimmy put our tow into Lock 25, the last of the locks on the Upper Mississippi. Once the lines were thrown off and the guys signaled the all gone, I grabbed the marine radio microphone, ready to phone in our order to the Economy Boat Store in Grafton, Illinois. They were the go-to folks for marine supplies in the St. Louis area, and we needed to top off our fuel and water.

"The *Mallard* to the St. Louis Marine Operator, over."

"The St. Louis Marine Operator to the *Mallard*. Switch and answer channel twenty-six, please." I changed the channel to 26. A moment later came the response, "St. Louis Marine Operator to the *Mallard*. Go ahead, Captain."

"Good morning, sir. Can you please put me through to the Economy Boat Store in Grafton? I have their number if you need it."

"No need, Captain, we have their number. Stand by."

When the gal came on the phone, we discussed our need to take on some fuel and fresh water. She and I traded some business and billing information that had been forwarded from the office a few days prior. She was extremely courteous and friendly. She OK'd us to land near the lower end of their wharf barge just below Lock 26 for an hour or two. Normally, they would come alongside your towboat as you passed by with a tank barge and transfer fuel directly into your boat without your having to stop. Because we had an empty barge along both sides of our boat that would not work for us on this trip. We made an appointment for midafternoon, assuming we didn't get any delay at Lock 26.

The high bluffs of Jersey County, Illinois, up the hill from Grafton, were immediately in front of us when Frank came through the door at 11:50. "See that?!" he asked and pointed in front of us. "That's God's country right there!"

We all laughed at his outburst, fully aware that this kind of fun ribbing would be coming as we grew closer to his home port. The Mississippi makes one final turn and flows almost due north just upstream from where the Illinois River connects with it. Out the front window, the lovely sleepy tourist town of Grafton lay sliced in two by the highway, snug against the steep bank, a handful of the last faded greens here and there. Many trees hiding from the fall wind still had some washed-out yellows and even an occasional hint of orange. Numerous cabin cruisers, sailboats, and houseboats remained in the water, moored at the marina. Safe behind a low dike, the docks unified that hamlet of boat owners who were hoping for one or two more nice late fall days when they could flee their banking and business jobs in downtown St. Louis and get out on their boat for one more afternoon on the river before freeze-up.

"You boys git down there and git some lunch," Frank said, taking over the controls. He sat back in the chair, toothpick in his broad smile, while he looked out at his home turf. Turning and waving forward he shouted, "I'm so close to home, I kin taste it!"

Being away from home for extended periods only sharpens the joy of familiar surroundings when not at work on a towboat. When a river worker gets close to home or close to getting off a towboat to go home, the feelings of anticipation and joy can be overwhelming. As they say, hard to wipe the smile off your face. Perhaps it's analogous to lovers in absence of their respective betrothed. Towboat worker enjoy the rewarding work and comradery enjoyed working on a towboat but never forget the lover who is waiting patiently at home for your return.

Jimmy and I scurried down the guard of the towboat and ducked into the warmth of the engine room on the way to the galley. John turned just as we came through the door connecting the galley with the engine room. Backing away from the stove, he held a pan of homemade dinner rolls, golden-topped and glistening with real butter basting, which he placed in the center of the counter. That mouth-watering goodness was the centerpiece of a serving area crowded with piping hot sliced ham topped with brown sugar, a heaping pile of fresh home-fried chicken, three choices of vegetables, a huge bowl of real mashed potatoes, chicken gravy, cold cuts, salad, dressings, and tall jugs of tea, sweet and not. He just grinned at us like he always did and stood there waiting to get anything else we might need.

"Dig in boys," he said as we hung up our jackets and took seats at the counter. The smile under his unkempt whiskers couldn't have been broader.

Pilothouse Days

"We are just going by Grafton, Johnny. How many miles from here to yer hometown of Hardin, Johnny?" I asked.

"Johnny turned toward us and said, "'Bout twenty-five or so. I could damn near throw a rock from here to there!"

I laughed and said, "You and I can both thank the same guy from Hardin for gittin' us towboat jobs. Captain Lowell Bailey! What a good guy! And a barrel of fun! The most infectious laugh in the world! How did you meet him, Johnny?"

"He come in the café I run there for a while, and you couldn't help but be pals with him. When he'd come in, it was like he was holdin' court! Everybody in the place was involved in a conversation and laughin'! He knew everybody and everybody's business in the whole town. When he wasn't ridin' a towboat, he was everywhere helping this person and that! One of the kindest guys you ever met! I met his wife a couple times. Mary Ann. What a lovely gal! She musta been a saint putting up with him bein' gone all the time.

"Everybody said he was the Illinois state champion duck caller! Won a bunch of contests. Lotsa duck hunters around Hardin! I still see him once in a while. He's workin' for Illinois Marine. Regular captain on the *Aggie C* last I heard."

I cleaned up the last of my gravy and potatoes with my third hot fresh bun and pushed my plate a bit forward to stop myself from eating more. "You are just the best damn cook in the land, Johnny! My self-control goes totally into the shitter when I got your food in front of me!"

We all laughed, then Johnny moved from the worktable to our counter with a bowl of fresh hot shortcake under a cloth cover. Next came a giant bowl of sliced strawberries, shiny in their clear sugary glaze. After he set those in front of us, he ran the mixer briefly to fluff the homemade whipped cream and placed that alongside the other bowls. He said, with coy smile, "You guys gotta have some a' this. Strawberries were getting ready to go bad, so I made an extra big batch!"

I groaned as he split open a fresh-baked shortcake biscuit, plated it, and dipped into the bowl of strawberries, ladling a huge portion over the top, followed by a monstrous dollop of whipped cream. How could I say no? Like everything he made, it looked too good to be true. He served up a similar giant portion for Jimmy and took our plates over to the sink.

"It'll be nice to call the old woman today and git caught up," Johnny called over his shoulder. "Bill and Charlie said we was stopping at Economy Boat Store to git fuel maybe this afternoon?"

"If we don't git any delay at Lock Twenty-six, we should be in there before supper," I told him. "You need any odds and ends, or we good till we git to Lemont?"

"Naw. We're good," Johnny said. "I made sure we had extra everything 'fore leavin' St. Paul. 'Less we git a big delay northbound on the Illinois, we'll be fine."

Jimmy and I cleared the rest of our lunch dishes from the counter before heading back upstairs. "Awesome lunch, Johnny!" I shouted as we opened the door to the engine room. "Thanks so much!"

I followed Jimmy onto the head deck. He headed up to the pilothouse, and I stepped over the head log onto the stern of the loaded barge we were faced up to. I paused, grabbed a life jacket from a nearby hook, put it on, and pulled up my collar, zipping my jacket up tight. A short walk after that delightful meal seemed like just the ticket. I stepped carefully, walking quickly to try to provide a little cardio to the exercise. Once I got to the coupling, the noise of our towboat was reduced, and when I reached the ladder I climbed up on the decks of the empties on the *starboard string*. I stood there for a bit, enjoying the partly sunny afternoon. The light following breeze moved the scents of fall along the thick, always moving, muddy water. The view beyond the levees lining the Missouri shore was a stark contrast to the cliffs lining the Illinois shore there at Grafton. The Missouri side was characterized by fence lines marked by shelter rows of mostly leafless trees, with multiple shapeless masses that appeared to be collections of sticks and debris, nests for local flying residents.

More massive red and green combines, again racing to gather the fall harvest prior to the real foul winter weather dead ahead. Rich river bottom farmland and only about one mile between us and the last few miles of the Missouri River. The second longest river in North America, the Missouri this river just down ahead of us at the entrance to Lock 27 and the Chain of Rocks Canal. A couple of small barge lines operate between Sioux City, Iowa, and St. Louis on the Missouri River, but the largely uncontrolled channel with no

---

starboard string – Barges strung together end to end are called a string.

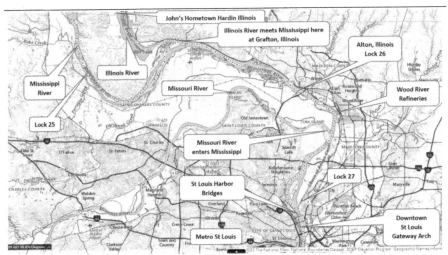

Confluence of Mississippi, Illinois and Missouri Rivers at St. Louis.

locks and dams is constantly alternating between flooding and ultra-low water. Towboating there is a real challenge.

I got back to the boat and climbed the stairs, entering the pilothouse refreshed but very chilled. "Brrrrr!" I exclaimed, shivering top to bottom like a wet hunting dog fresh out of the water.

Frank and Jimmy both laughed, and Frank grabbed the microphone to call Lock 26.

"We got one just putting their tow back together and heading southbound right now, Captain, then we'll fill the chamber back up for ya soon as he clears the lower walls."

"Ten-four. We'll be right on down there. Thanks a lot," Frank responded. "There's a couple a' tows northbound out of Lock Twenty-seven, so we're lucky not to git a delay!" he said to Jimmy and me.

Feet up on the console, front pilothouse windows open, Frank was leaning back in the chair, steering with his right hand and holding a smoke in his left. "Sure is nice to be back down out of that frozen north." Grinning, he continued. "I'm lookin' forward to callin' the old lady when we take on fuel and let her know that I didn't freeze to death! You people is crazy, Tommy! You know that, right?" Frank never tired of teasing about the brutal conditions on the upper end of that river. I decided it was time to remind him the weather in Illinois can be tough too.

"I won't deny that it gits cold up there, Frank, but let me tell you, I've seen my share of brutal weather working the Illinois River over the years too."

Lock and Damn #26. Now replaced by facility with 1,200-foot-long lock.

Frank sat up and pulled the ship ups back to half ahead. Smoke from his cigarette wafted out the window. Straight ahead in a wide spot in the river was Lock 26, anchored to the left bank.

Tall grain elevators perched on the city front of Alton off to our port side. A rusting highway bridge and a busy well-weathered railroad bridge both cross above the lock. Their piers are part of the lock walls above the lower lock gates of Lock 26.

"Let me tell you about Illinois cold. Last winter I was a trip captain on the *Nicolas Duncan*. Below zero for about five nights in a row. We dropped five loads in the fleets just above the Peoria Lock. Beat the shit out of everything getting across Peoria Lake. A good foot of ice all the way across. Bunch of other boats there with, us or we'd still be out there. The rest of our tow, four empty tank barges, to deliver to the Shell Oil refinery at Wood River."

Frank steered very slightly to starboard as Terry, his lead deckhand, signaled that the head of the tow had cleared the end of the long wall on our port corner.

I continued, "We had easy going till we got down to the LaGrange Lock and Dam down at Beardstown. We rolled in there just as it was getting dark, and we were seventh in line waiting to go southbound. The ice was thick, slush ice, thousands of little pieces, nothing solid, and *gorging*. I had ta keep her shipped in reverse to keep from moving down on top of the MV *City of New Orleans*, who was right in front of us. We were talkin' with the guys at the dam, and they had given up on locking boats 'cause there was so much slush ice they couldn't operate the gates and the water was rising. They were busy *throwing the dam*."

"Wait, wait, wait!" Jimmy said. "Back up there, Tom. What are you talkin' about, 'throw the dam'?"

Photo shows wicket dam & ice conditions at La Grange Lock on Illinois River.

Frank backed our engines, bringing our tow to a stop just inside the upper gates and turned, smiling as I continued my story. "The lower end of the Illinois is miles-wide floodplain, and the river floods, most years, several times, Jimmy. They built the last two locks and dams — the Peoria Lock and Dam and the LaGrange Lock and Dam — using wicket gates. These wicket gates can be lifted to hold back the river easily when it is low water. When the river floods, they take all the equipment out of the locks and lower the wickets, dropping the dam. The river traffic runs where the dam was, bypassing the flooded lock. Make sense?"

Jimmy nodded, Frank smiled, fiddled with his toothpick, and I continued.

gorging – when conditions are right, the constant breaking and pushing aside of the river ice causes it to build layers below the frozen surface. If this process continues long enough, the entire depth of the river channel can fill with slushy ice and it becomes a gorge of ice.

throwing the dam – The wicket dams in the story can be uninstalled, letting the river flow over the top of them. Taking them down is referred to as "throwing the dam."

"All through that evening watch I had to increase our reverse engine power a little to keep from moving down. I got up and went on watch in the morning, and we were running about one-third astern. There was only about two hundred feet between the head of our tow and the *City of New Orleans*. There were three tows upstream from us waiting to go southbound, and we were all doin' the same thing. The lock guys kept saying they'd git the dam down anytime now.

"I went on watch at six p.m., and we were backing full and closing in on the *City*. Pretty disconcerting, let me tell ya! The ice just kept building in. Next to the small opening in the water alongside the boat you could see the current smoking along. The river was rising. About seven o'clock, they got the dam down. The tows closest to the dam were froze in place and couldn't move. One of the boats held her tow, and the *Sugarland* came light boat to get on the side of each of the tows to shake me loose. Thirty-three hundred horse, and it's all she could do to get everybody going!"

Frank and Jimmy were thoroughly engaged in this tale, waiting to hear how it all ended up. "So, she got the *City* going in front of us, and I brought our engines to neutral from full astern. Just as the *Sugarland* bumped the head of our four empties, we broke free. I hadn't engaged the engines yet, but we were goin'! At that same moment came a shut-out snowstorm. I turned off all our lights, even the guard lights, but I couldn't see the barge I was faced up on. The radar on there wasn't much, but at the time it was all I had. Away we went. I watched as the tow was coming down alongside the lock, and I was adjusting the throttles trying to determine what it would take to steer. After a bit I realized the steering I was doing had very little effect on where our tow was going!

"All I could see on the radar were the images of all the tows pushed into the bank below the dam on both sides of the river, angled out to hold their positions. Each seemed to be precisely where we would crash. I bet there were a dozen northbound tows waiting, all a target for our out-of-control tow. And then, when things couldn't get worse, it was like we went over a waterfall, right at the dam. You could feel it in your seat. And we picked up even more headway. I knew I couldn't back up. The next tows in line were screaming down right behind us on the radar!

"Longest fifteen minutes of my life! Got down below all those upbound tows, backed into the bank, snow still coming down hard! I had the mate *hold*

hold us there – Our mate stood at the controls when I stepped away, making sure we didn't move until I returned.

us there while I went down and changed my drawers!"

Frank and Jimmy chuckled and looked at me, shaking their heads. At that point I was especially animated, reliving an event that most likely took a year or two off my life.

"Here is the most amazing part of this story, boys. The next day we got down here to Lock Twenty-six. That tow didn't steer worth a shit from the LaGrange Lock south, and I couldn't figure out why. We locked the *little chamber* 'cause we only had those four empty tank barges, and there was lots of other marine traffic. Now, remember we had a tow of empties."

Both men continued listening intently. "They opened the lower lock gates, and the boys turned us loose. I came ahead on her, and nothin' happened. I couldn't believe it. That gorged ice was still frozen and stuck to the bottom of those barges! It was so far below the river surface that it was catching on the *sill* of the lower gates in the lock. I ended up having the guys tie the tow off, and I backed full for a long while to flush some of the ice out of there. We eventually made it to Wood River. That was a trip I will never forget!

"It gits cold down here, too, Frank! I am here to tell ya!"

Frank's shoulders shook with laughter as his deck crew turned us loose when the lock people sounded the horn. He shipped the engines forward about half ahead and said, "Yah, I been there too once or twice, cold winters on the Illinois. That's why I live as far south as I can in Illinois. Mound. You kin throw a rock over ta Kintucky. Ohio River there don't never freeze up! We got green grass most a' the winter!"

He continued to watch the stern of our tow as we moved out of the lock chamber. "I still say you people is crazy to live up there, Tommy. Yer brains is froze!"

Jimmy and I laughed, then kept on grinning, enjoying that lovely towboating early afternoon.

---

little chamber – some lock and dams on American rivers have more than one lock chamber. In this case Lock 26 had a small auxiliary lock chamber that is use continuously because the lock is so busy.
sill – The doors (gates) that open and close on a lock chamber rest against a sill, like a threshold on a door in your house.

Major refineries along the left bank of the Mississippi at Wood River, Illinois.
Missouri River enters Upper Mississippi and top left of this photo.

12. St Louis, Then Up the Illinois

I came on watch as Frank was entering the upstream end of the *Chain of Rocks Canal*, making our final downbound approach to Lock 27. "We are sure having some luck making these locks without a lot of delay," Frank said. "Got one southbound, but they said he'd be clear by the time we git down there."

He moved sideways, I stepped in behind the controls, and with some considerable effort, hoisted myself up and into the captain's chair. I looked at Frank and declared, "Gittin' harder and harder to climb the stairs up here, I swear! Had to let a notch outta my belt tonight after supper. I'm thinkin' I will have gained about ten pounds 'fore we git to Lemont!"

We both giggled then Frank headed down to eat.

Refineries as far as you could see on the port side, steam streaming up from dozens and dozens of stacks. Some of the tallest metallic towers topped

Chain of Rocks Canal – Just above downtown St. Louis there is a rocky section of the Mississippi difficult to navigate during times of low water. A canal was constructed that carries river traffic around this hazard. The most downstream lock (No. 27) on the Mississippi is at the lower end of this canal.

with cones were burping tall flames and black smoke, and some were belching multiple clouds of waste from the refining process. Each flaming stack lit up the night sky, illuminating the similar stack next to it. Made me wonder two things. One, who in the world would live around there. Two, do they wait to burn off all the most severe and smokiest waste until after dark? You can smell the refineries around Wood River, Illinois, for ten miles in every direction. All the big oil companies had river docks, tank barges moored and offloading or loading. Lots of marine commerce along there.

Jimmy came up and took the seat behind me. "Take the rest of the night off, there, young man," I said. "Too much traffic and too many competing shore and bridge lights and crossings between the bridges southbound through the St. Louis Harbor. Even with a tow our size, we gotta be on top of it heading down through here." I moved our searchlights, one on each shore traveling down the canal. Both banks were lined with huge limestone *riprap*.

"Not a problem, Tom. Happy to watch you do it. Never been down here before, so looking forward to relaxing and learning from you." He added, "Must not have been able to find us a northbound tow, huh?"

"I called Bob Jorgens, the head dispatcher, when we were loading fuel. He thinks they will get us some barges going north once we git up on the Illinois. Said he thought for sure we'd have something northbound at Peoria. Last year when we went around, we went light boat the whole trip from St. Louis to Lemont. Made it up there from here in thirty-nine hours."

My deck crew gave a mock salute from the stern deck of our tow as they headed out to make Lock 27. We passed several loaded barges moored in front of the grain terminal on our port side. A bit farther inland you could see the lights of the coal-black towers of the once-active steel foundry that anchored the all but shuttered Illinois town of Granite City. We got in the lock and dropped down uneventfully. The lockman sounded the horn, and the men turned us loose just as Frank came through the pilothouse door. A grin and a toothpick. Just finished supper. Most likely a story on the way.

"Johnny just took all my money playing cribbage!" Frank said. "So far, he's got me for a dollar twenty-five on this trip. I won't be able to put gas in my truck to head home from Lemont!"

riprap – fractured rock and/or debris that is placed along riverbanks to slow or limit erosion. Huge riprap is made up of stones weighing several tons each (three to seven feet across).

I pushed the ship ups to full ahead as we shoved out of the canal into the main river. Lights of downtown St. Louis dead ahead, illuminating the starless night. Industrial, marine commerce with piers, lights and landings on both sides of the river.

Frank grinned at Jimmy. "You ever been down here before, Jimmy?"

Jimmy shook his head, mumbled a "Nope," and yawned.

"Southbound in this harbor after dark will put some hair on yer chest, let me tell ya." Frank laughed and continued, toothpick moving up and down vigorously. "You make the Merchants Railroad Bridge, come right outta there into the McKinley Bridge, make a crossing under the I-70 bridge, then make Martin Luther King and Eads Bridges, then while yer passin' the St. Louis Arch you gotta be ***gittin' in shape*** to make the Poplar Street and the McArthur railroad bridge. All in about three miles. Never less than a strong current, lots and lots of other traffic, and lights along the shore both sides. Mercy me!"

View out the pilothouse window making St Louis harbor bridges downbound.
Note the arches of the historic Eads Bridge.

I laughed at Frank's apt description and added my two cents, "And…if the water is up at all, you gotta hit Eads dead-ass center with yer boat, 'cause ***it's got arches***. And the higher the water is, the tighter the slot between the

gittin' in shape – steering and placing your tow into position ahead of a tight location
it's got arches – The Eads Bridge over the Mississippi at St. Louis has structural steel semicircular arches. Vertical clearance decreases as you move away from the center of the arch.

arches!" Frank and I high-fived, a small gesture of kinship between two captains who have earned the seasoning that comes with those occasional crucial, grab-you-by-the-seat-of-your-pants times at the helm of a towboat where you really do earn your keep.

Frank entertained Jimmy and me with stories of a few of his personal close calls in the St. Louis Harbor and some mischievousness that often accompanied one captain or another "arranging" for something to happen — a slowdown or unnecessary stop —to ensure the trip down through the harbor occurred on the other watch. Jimmy found the Arch fascinating as we passed and studied it carefully through the binoculars. I made the last-minute arrangements on the marine radio to drop our tow at the Riverport Fleet. The captain of the fleet harbor boat came alongside and dropped his deck crew on our tow as I was backing out of the main channel over toward the fleet. Billy met them out at the first coupling, and together they counted the rigging we would swap.

It was a good feeling to be at the southernmost end of our journey. No issues, no near misses, and everyone on board expecting to get to go home in a few days. Lots of good energy as we headed northbound about an hour later. Relaxing, running along light boat at a good clip against the rapid current there. Northbound through the St. Louis Harbor, enjoying a crisp fall night in one of the most vibrant towboat environments on any river. Lots of traffic, lots of chatter on the marine radio. Frank came up at 11:45, and we traded greetings and necessary information. I felt very satisfied, shucking my clothes and getting in between the warm sheets in my bunk. It had been a good day.

***

As I climbed the stairs in the morning, I could smell a snowy day coming. Frank was running along *with no lights*. We had no delays making Lock 27 and then Lock 26 northbound. The river channel between Lock 26 and the mouth of the Illinois River is very wide and easy to navigate. The earliest morning commuters between Grafton, Alton, and St. Louis were cautiously feeling their way along out our starboard windows, watching for slick spots on the roads, the icy Mississippi river only thirty or forty feet below them. A kind of thickness in the air, just shy of light snowflakes, our fine towboat leisurely idling along. No tow in front of her. Engines at a little less than one-quarter throttle, going as fast as we could go without getting water splashing

with no lights – Sometimes conditions are such that leaving lights off provides better visibility than operating with lights at night. (For instance, light fog, snow, drizzle, etc.)

and turning to ice on our head deck. Traveling light boat is a singular pleasure. Most towboats require little steering when not towing, you just move from one main channel marker to the next and stay awake.

We had been fortunate that the Twin City Barge team in St. Paul had found eight barges that needed to go from St. Paul to St. Louis. For a massive grain shipper, that is not an issue. For a harbor company just moving their towboat to vital and robust winter quarters over a thousand nautical miles away, it is a terrific boon to find some *casual* but revenue-producing *barges* that need to be moved along that same route. Twin City's primary goal was to get the towboat to Lemont, where she would most likely begin, the day of arrival, to make profitable trips in and out of the city, moving barges and getting goods and liquids from the upper end of the Illinois River deep into the maze of minute canals adjacent to river docks and businesses in Chicago. If a towboat company can make revenue by towing along the way to offset costs, everyone smiles.

Frank, still in a great mood, yawned, smiled, and said goodnight. Zipping his jacket tight, whistling, and pulling up his collar, he stepped out into the brisk early morning darkness on the way to our shared quarters. I *checked my chart*, making sure that I was where I thought I was, and I smiled, thinking about how lucky I was to be riding a towboat once again with Frank. He was such a good guy and an excellent pilot. He and I trusted each other implicitly, and that is an important component to happiness in the pilothouse. When you know your partner is competent and has personal and professional integrity, it brings you a peace that allows you to completely relax during your off time. Frank was so good and such a great guy. If only every trip could be just like that one.

An hour or so later as dawn was struggling into being, it started to snow. Very lightly but enough to reduce visibility to about a half mile. If we'd had a tow, we would have had to stop. The snow stayed with us up past Grafton, and as we continued upstream entering the much narrower Illinois River it let up just a little. If we had been able to see, the lower stretch of the Illinois River finds flat, crop-covered floodplains in both directions. Some occasional oak-covered hills, more modest than along the Upper Mississippi, here and there. The local highways alongside are constructed close to the river then a

casual barges – Many barges are moved by the owner's towboats. A barge not part of a dedicated fleet or company is sometimes called a "casual" barge when moved.
check my chart – In those years, captains and pilots would check on the river charts if they were unfamiliar with their location.

little inland and then back close to the river again. Age-weary farm trucks with fresh-picked corn or soybeans spilling over their sideboards, heading for the elevator. Occasionally, cabbed modern tractors briskly pulling one or a pair of bulk carrier grain trailers mounted on giant can't-get-stuck-in-the-field balloon tires moving determinedly to the same elevators.

Just before lunch we passed Hardin, Illinois (cook John's hometown), out our port side, and I gave a short blast of the whistle to a couple of adventurous boys skidding on their bikes in the snow down near the boat landing,

River crossing on Illinois River at Hardin, Illinois. The lead barge
of an upbound tow is visible under the raised span of this highway bridge.

stopping just short of the icy river. They hoisted their arms up and down, yanking on the imaginary whistle cord, and I give them a good one. Not one leaf was left on any of the trees lining the river there. Gray, naked, and calm, content in their hibernation-like tranquility. They stood guard, watching as the winter snows and clouds came and went, occasionally warmed with a bright sun on a brisk day. When that happened, all the squirrels and chipmunks would come out and rejoice for a few hours. Touching, playing, teasing. Frisky whenever it appeared to be fruitful and safe. Who can beat that?

Jimmy spent the morning playing cribbage with John. I was happy for him to get a break. He'd had several fourteen- or fifteen-hour days steering while we were southbound on the Upper. He got a thrashing from John, though. John might have been the best cribbage player on the river. I had played with him, and at first I thought he was just super blessed with good card-playing luck. Not the case. He had a sharp mind and most likely could have been a terrific scientist of some sort. He kicked my butt enough times for me to learn that unless I was in the mood to be abused, to just leave the cribbage board on the galley counter when he was around.

Jimmy and I had just come upstairs after lunch, and he was swapping spots in the captain's chair with Frank.

"Man! That sliced turkey open face sandwich! It's a like a great home-cooking café with Johnny serving it up!" I exclaimed.

Frank joined me in the back of the pilothouse on the lounge.

"You guys like playing cards?" Jimmy asked. He was shaking his head, wondering how he got beaten so bad by our illustrious cook.

"I like cards a lot," I said. Then I added, "Pretty good at gin and cribbage. Euchre is really popular up north. Everybody gits taught how to play cards as a youngster where I come from in Wisconsin."

Jimmy picked up the binoculars from the console and checked out a pair of white-tailed deer at the edge of the water on the port side.

"Do they play euchre where you come from in Southern Minnesota, Jimmy?" I asked.

"Oh, yah!" Jimmy responded. "I grew up playing euchre too." He laughed and continued, "I thought I was pretty good at cribbage till this morning. Johnny took me to the cleaners. I still can't believe it! Took four bucks off a' me!"

Frank and I both chuckled.

"Poker's my game," Frank said. "I got some old boys down home that I play with. Nothin' serious. No burned pots or nothin'. Nickel, dime, quarters. We play Saturdays and Wednesdays when I'm home. Got a nice poker table, and the wife makes her tasty kinck nack snacks. She loves when the guys come over. Keeps me outta the bar. Little fire in the fireplace, some ice-cold Buds. We do OK."

"I kinda gave up playin' poker on boats," I said. "Discovered the nitty-gritties about gambling when I came out onto the river. When I was first deckin', played a lot of poker with crew members who didn't have enough money to be in the game. They could never win. Their kids at home didn't have shoes. I was single, plenty a' dough, and could never lose. Taught me if you can't afford to be in the game, you got no business there. I go to Vegas once or twice a year. Play nothing but dollar blackjack. I find a table where there ain't no camera close, and I set myself a limit to what I play before I git up and leave. I always tip good. If you git the right dealer they'll leave your card as good and go right by you as long as you take care of 'em."

The sparse marine radio chatter was interrupted by a call from the St. Louis Marine Operator. Frank picked up the microphone and said, "The *Mallard* back to the St. Louis Marine Operator. What channel would you like?"

The operator responded, "Channel twenty-six, *Mallard*."

Frank switched over to channel 26. We were close to being out of range, so there was a lot of background noise. Sounded like the caller was on the end of a very long string talking into a tin can.

"The *Mallard*, here. Go ahead, Marine Operator," Frank said.

"Good afternoon, Frank. It's Bob Jorgens up in St. Paul. How are you all getting along?"

"Hello, Bob. We are all gittin' along jist fine. Motorin' along here light boat at Mile Marker Forty-one. Kin see the Pearl Railroad Bridge right up ahead a' us."

"Very good," he replied. "Glad I caught you all before you got outta radio range." Frank grabbed a tablet and, reaching over the console, he closed the center pilothouse window to make it a bit quieter. "So," Bob continued, "I found you some barges for your upbound trip. I'll give them to you whenever you're ready."

"Got my tablet right here. Ready when you are," Frank said.

"OK. We have two Union Mechling empties at the Naples Fleet. Should be around Mile Marker Sixty-four. They are in the Osage Marine Fleets there. U-M 1-6-4-3 and U-M 9-9-3. The dispatcher for Osage Marine told me they have someone at the radio there around the clock. They monitor both channel sixteen and channel seven, and they will get you set up and meet you at the fleet to pick up your barges.

"We also have a loaded, *oversized tank barge* for you to pick up at the Meredosia Power Company Nitrogen Dock. The barge number is M-P-D-C 1-4-4-4." Frank wrote the number on the yellow legal pad. "The dock is at Mile Marker Seventy, and the barge is supposed to be ready, or will be ready to go, when you get there. This barge is fifty-two by three hundred, and I think it has some large tanks mounted on it. Hope it fits into the tow for ya!"

Frank smiled and keyed the microphone. "We'll git her for ya, Bob. Don't sound like anything a bunch a' professionals like us can't handle!"

"All right, then," Bob responded. "If you would, why don't you call me once you get into radio range with the marine operator in Peoria? You can call anytime at my home number. I may have some additional barges at either Peoria or Hennepin but still trying to work out the details. It might not be ready when you get there."

"Will do, Robert. We'll keep paddlin' along here, and we'll be sure to call ya before we git to Pekin. You gittin' any snow there yet?" Frank smiled, always sure to be charming with the dispatchers. They all liked Frank and his always-pleasant temperament.

"No, no. Not yet. Just cold. They're already talking about whether the little ones will git a white Christmas up here, but that's still weeks away. The river is frozen over hard, though. I can tell you that. We got the *Viking* doing winter towing, and so far it hasn't been too bad. They are constantly breaking though the ice."

"All righty, Robert! You take care and keep your feet close to the fire or whatever it is that you all do to stay warm up there!" Frank chuckled at himself, *cleared us* on the radio, and hung up the microphone, shaking his head, questioning the reasoning of people who find the cold Minnesota winters tolerable.

I smiled as Frank slid back into the lounge seat at the rear of the pilot-

---

oversized tank barge – tank barges larger than the standard size of typical barges that are 195 feet long

cleared us – When a captain finishes talking on the radio, it is common to say that they are "clear" (transmission completed).

house. He had reopened the front window a couple of inches to help clear out the cigarette smoke. Our cartons of fresh cigarettes, recently purchased at the Economy Boat Store at Wood River, lay together on the far left side of the console. Smokes and the most recent copies of *Playboy* and *Penthouse*. Critical requirements, always at the top of the list of boat store supplies. Followed up by fuel, fresh water, food, and assorted provisions.

Jimmy commented on the width of the river. "Damn. This ain't much more than a crick, is it?" The Illinois River was at low water stage, and from one low, sloping, red-brown mudbank to the other it was no more than eight or nine hundred feet. "You couldn't ***top a barge around***, right here, between this red and green buoy. Not sure how you even pass somebody here if you both got full tows."

View from pilothouse upbound on Illinois River with loaded tow.

"You gotta pick yer spots ta pass somebody! That's for damn sure," Frank said. "Nice thing, ya can't git in too much trouble on this lower end. Worst that's gonna happen is ya git run out onto a mudbank someplace!"

"It's all like this, Jimmy, except for the narrow, rocky places up about Starved Rock and big old, lazy assed Peoria Lake. Plenty wide but shallow there during low water. You kin watch as you go by with a tow, and the water all slips back into the channel once you pass by."

top a barge around – turn a barge end for end

"It's a different river, Jimmy. That's for sure. Lotsa old boys — they start up in here and start squealin' like little girls! 'Specially if they git all the way up above Brandon Road. Whinin' and snivelin' like you never heard!" Frank laughed, and his toothpick jerked up and down.

"I started working as a trip pilot over here in 1975, Jimmy." I put out my cigarette then continued. "I wanted to git my name out there. That's how it works. The first thing they ask ya is where you been workin' and for who. You gotta take whatever you kin get at first. Then once they know you are OK, they put you on their list, and they'll put you to work when you call 'em. The first two years I started trip piloting I took any job I could git. That's kinda the downside. They don't always tell ya everything that's goin' on. Just to catch their boat at such-and-such a location as soon as you kin git there."

"I had just about the same experience, Jimmy," Frank piped up. "My first two years as a pilot, before I hired on full time with Mobil Oil, I was on this boat and that boat and had to take whatever I could git. Kin be some scary-ass shit, I kin tell ya. ***Overloaded towboats***, junk towboats, half-assed, inex-perienced crews, no cooks, you name it!"

"My worst overloaded towboat was the *Herb Schreiner*," I said. "A while ago when Bob Jorgens said we might have a pickup at Pekin, it brought

MV *Aggie C*, formerly the MV *Herb Schreiner*. Twin screw, 2,400 horsepower.

overloaded towboats – The size of tow (number of barges) should complement the size and horsepower of the towboat. A small, underpowered towboat should not try to handle a large tow.

me right back to some of the most terrifying hours of my piloting life. One of my very first trip pilot jobs. The *Herb Schreiner*. Twenty-four hundred horse. Telescopic pilothouse. Steered OK but had single backin' rudders and ***wouldn't hold her ass up*** for shit.

"Comin' down above that damn old Pekin Railroad Bridge. One-thirty in the morning. Just enough drizzle that you couldn't see shit!" I felt my palms begin to sweat, even then, all those years later. I lit up and continued. "We had eleven loads and three empties. Captain dropped a loaded tank barge right above the Peoria Lock before midnight. The lazy dick left the tow with a notch at the stern on the starboard string. The square end upstream. He didn't think it was important to rearrange the tow because we were picking up a load to replace the one we dropped when we arrived in the fleet just below the Pekin Railroad Bridge."

Marine Carbon Arc Searchlight from the 1970's.

Even though this was several years in the past, telling that story had my heart racing. Frank and Jimmy were caught up in the story, nodding and smiling. "Like I said, it was drizzling. One of the searchlights was not working, and the Mickey Mouse utility deckhand on there had no idea how to adjust or ***line up the carbons*** on the other one so we could get the light to focus down

wouldn't hold her ass up – describes a towboat that does not steer well when backing up or going astern

line up the carbons – Carbon arc searchlights were the best available at that time. Two carbon rods mounted on a ratcheting slide lined up together and energized in front of a convex mirror provided an intense light that could reach out thousands of feet ahead of the tow. The lights had to be adjusted (line up the carbons) for the beam to be strong, tight, and far-reaching.

to a tight, long-distance beam. The bridge was cockeyed. Sitting in the river in a turn to the right to begin with. I backed her sorry butt over tight to the right bank but because of that damn starboard stern square-end notch, the tow wants to lay in the river cockeyed in just the opposite direction the bridge lays.

"Empties are on the head. Couldn't see a damn thing, even if I'd had another good searchlight. Pitch-black, and no lights along the shore — thick woods there. The snowy mist skewing what I could see with the one working searchlight. The water was up, damn near flood stage at the Peoria Lock. All I could do to hold her against the current." I couldn't believe how shaky my hand was as I lit another cigarette.

"I'd crawl backwards upstream, git right in tight to the right bank. I'd back her ass out a little bit, and as I started to turn the tow and drop down toward the bridge, we'd start setting down onto the left pier. Didn't look good, so I'd back her up again. Kept doing that again and again. Finally, had enough. We flew down through there. I steered her for everything we had, and our port stern load still landed on the bridge pier. Hard! I thought for sure we tore the side outta that barge. Piled into the mudbank below the bridge. Ended up bustin' some riggin', but the damn tow stayed together somehow. No damage to the barge or bridge! Only because it was a miracle!"

Frank howled and got up and pulled on his jacket. "I'monna piss my pants, but I didn't want to miss a word of that!" Frank said. Out the door and down the pilothouse stairs, quickly but carefully.

"Wasn't there some way to refuse taking that many barges with that small of a boat?" Jimmy asked.

"Not really. I had to take any job that came my way at first. Getting my foot in the door. I was only the pilot on there. Had nothin' to say about the tow. Turned out that was the only badly overloaded trip job I had."

Frank came back upstairs, holding a warm cup of coffee between his hands and shivering as he sat back down alongside me, behind Jimmy. While the door was open for a minute, some of the cigarette smoke escaped.

I continued, "Lots of work back then though. A ton of work and a shortage of trip pilots. Lots of money to be made. I made $29,000 in 1975. Two hundred bucks a day for trip pilots. I worked a lot that year. Ended up with lots of good contacts in my phone book and a ton of great experience!"

Pilothouse Days

I stood up, getting ready to head downstairs for my afternoon nap. As I reached for the door, I stopped and looked back at Frank and Jimmy. "Now that I think of it, that wasn't the only close call riding the *Herb Schreiner*. After we dropped that tow, we went back north and turned another company boat just below Brandon Road. Twelve loads again! Going along OK until we were comin' down just outta Peoria Lake. Right above the Interstate 74 freeway bridge in front of downtown. Setting up to make the railroad bridge directly downstream. Dropping down, nice and easy, over along the right bank. All the sudden both engines start to sputter. I am watching the RPM gauges and they both just go to zero, just like that. The utility deckhand raced downstairs.

I-74 Freeway bridge immediately upstream from Peoria railroad bridge.
Maneuvering downbound just upstream of this bridge when we lost both engines.

"I called the upbound tow coming through the railroad bridge just downstream, right in front of me. I tell him I'm dead in the water. He responds with a serious lack of interest. We agreed on the one whistle, and there he was. I assumed he was going to take it easy. He had a unit loaded tank barge tow, and I watched in disbelief as he hooked her up. I heard our starboard engine start back up. The utility man came out on the head deck and yelled, '*Water in the fuel! Changing fuel filters!*' He raced back to the engine room. I felt a slight sense of relief having one engine, at least for a moment.

water in the fuel! changing fuel filters – Condensation can be a problem in diesel fuel stored in tanks on towboats. A place to catch that water prior to it getting into diesel motors is a fuel filter.

"The minute the bow of that unit tow went by the bow of our tow, his momentum and the water he was moving sucked us right over on top of them. I came full ahead with my one puny engine and steered away for all she was worth. Thought we were gonna crash for sure. Then suddenly, he started to clear our stern, and our tow went wildly out of control in the opposite direction. This asshole was watchin' all this and never let up! Full ahead and never looked back. My tow was almost completely crossways in the river right above the railroad bridge. Luckily, it was flat pool water, so I was able to hold up and get back in shape to make the railroad bridge. The utility guy got the other engine going, finally.

"Another day where I had to change drawers after doing my watch!"

Oh man!" Jimmy exclaimed. "Not sure I spend a lot of time wonderin' if my engines are gonna quit! Is that something that happens a lot?" As a soon-to-be new pilot, it was a reasonable question.

Frank put out his cigarette and volunteered, "Only happened to me once in sixteen years. Always a possibility, I suppose. Damn infrequent that you would ever lose both engines at the same time!" He coughed briefly, grinned at me with the toothpick bouncing, and said, "Better git down there and git some rest, Captain Struve. Might be a little hard sleepin' now that you got yerself all wound up!"

Peoria Lock & Dam. Tow navigating upbound over top of wicket dam. High water.

Pilothouse Days

He and Jimmy were smiling and laughing as I headed downstairs, probably already on to their next story. I couldn't help giggling as I stepped carefully to avoid ice and occasionally looked up the river on that crisp late fall day. The water surface was a flat mud brown with just a hint of ripples from a following wind. Smells of fall. Leaves, damp mustiness. It's a tradition on towboats, these stories. We experience again and again the satisfaction, joy, or terror through the retelling. All these stories equal the sum, eventually equivalent to a towboat career, done well.

In my room, as I lay sliding toward slumber, I reached for and held the pocket-sized, dog-eared copy of the New Testament given to me by my high school friend, Doug Eichman, on a camping trip many years earlier. Always at my bedside. A permanent fixture. During those very dangerous early trip piloting experiences, when worry about the next shift elbowed to the side any possibility of off watch sleep, I read passages from that little faux leather-covered abbreviated Bible. I discovered repeatedly a very real peace provided in His Word that allowed me to rest and give my fears away. I carry that awareness and gift, continuing to be grateful, even more so today. A clear understanding that I will never be given more than I am equipped to handle.

Pilot house view of downbound tow passing another tow in a narrow place.
The upbound towboat here is stopped and standing by out of the channel
allowing the downbound towboat to pass safely.

Pilothouse view of tow upbound on the Illinois River.

13. Narrow River, Ain't it?

The door opened, and my overhead light turned on. I was soooooo close. I was reaching for a plate that had lovely, juicy, fresh bright-orange lobster tails on it. We were at the all-you-can-eat lobster buffet. I was there with this incredible, buxom young lass, and she was enjoying the ambience and meal as much as me. I had just handed the server a five-dollar-bill, and his eyes lit up. He smiled broadly and loaded my plate. Stacked steaming lobster tails three high. My mouth was watering, and then the light turned on.

Dreams can be so real. Even on a towboat. Wouldn't it be fun if somehow we could catalogue dreams with places and times and see if any dots ever connect? I lay for a moment, smiling with joy at this leisurely year-end trip. Noting that the engines were at idle, I figured we must be at the fleet picking up our barges or finishing building our tow. I eased out of my warm bed and shuffled in my slippers toward *the head*. Teeth brushed, into pants, shirt, and light polar vest, I slipped into my jacket and stepped out onto the guard. Fully dark, light snow falling, flakes glistening in the glow of the flanking lights.

the head – The bathroom on a boat is called a head.

Pilothouse Days

We were moored against several lengths of empty barges in one of the fleets near Naples, Illinois. The deck guys were dragging a couple of sets of rigging onto the head of the loaded tank barge, and they worked together to cover the three-foot-high coiled pile of Poly D lock line with a large tarp. As I carefully made my way back toward the galley, the guys turned us loose, and Frank moved our boat out to the bow of the two empties that made up our port string of barges. Puttin' out *running gear*, and then we'd be underway.

Running gear on the head of this tow includes two lock lines, the jack staff, pea light, and two depth finders.

"Johnny, my man, how's it going?" I said as I stepped into the galley.

"Just fine, Captain Tom, just fine." I didn't mention that I had been dining in a seafood restaurant in my dream just minutes before.

I spotted a cast iron pan on the stove, where golden cornbread-coated catfish strips were frying. How about that for a coincidence? John smiled, noting my interest in the fish, and reached into the oven. Pulling out a metal

running gear – slang referring to lock line, bumper, running lights, pea light, and whatever other items might be needed at the bow of the tow

pan full of fried fish covered with a cotton cloth, he began placing the delectable pieces onto a plate as I slid in and up to the counter.

"You are soooooo good, Johnny. My favorite fish recipe!" I exclaimed. I squirted out a big pile of tartar sauce next to the fish and dug in.

I love fish. No other way to say it. And I really love fried fish and seafood. Love anything fried. I always say that you could French fry car keys, and I'd eat 'em. Noise and vibration under us in the galley indicated we were getting underway. Frank was backing away from the fleet. The galley on the *Mallard* was above and immediately forward of the propellers, so anytime the engines were reversed, this spot where meals were taken and lots of visiting occurred would be temporarily overcome with strong vibration and the accompanying clamor of reverse propulsion. Once Frank brought the engines to forward, the noise was reduced considerably. I cleaned up my second helping of fish, and Johnny grinned at me. Every towboat cook is in paradise when anyone fusses over their cooking. Johnny couldn't do enough to please me for precisely that reason.

"You are the best!" I exclaimed, getting up and giving him a generous fist pump. "I am crazy about your fried fish!" I filled my coffee cup, got into my jacket, and headed upstairs. As I walked through the door, we were just coming under the Highway 104 bridge, which crosses high above the cozy Illinois corn-country town of Meredosia. The Cargill dock and barge-loading facility adjacent to the bridge there was lit up like daylight. The covers on the barge being loaded were open on the stern, and the workers were just adding the last beans needed to *trim the barge* perfectly. Behind the elevator, the orange marker lights outlined dozens of semis lined up waiting to unload. They were end to end backed up on both sides of a main road as far as we could see. Farmers racing against wet weather and freezing conditions to get the last of their crops out of the fields and into town to the elevator.

Frank had elected to string out our empties, and he placed them adjacent to our loaded barge on the port side. The huge loaded tank barge had at least *two stories of tanks and superstructure* above the deck. It was a good thing we had a telescopic pilothouse with a thirty-foot-plus height allowing good visibility past all the equipment on the barge.

trim the barge – all four corners drawing the same depth of water (almost always nine feet). To make the loaded barge level.
two stories of tanks and superstructure – Tanks and pumps and miscellaneous equipment rose from the deck to a level of approximately twenty feet.

Jimmy came through the door not long after I did, and he and Frank swapped places behind the controls. "I had the guys move the *jack staff* and *pea light* just a little to the port," Frank said. "The tow is tracking just a little that way, and I been watchin' fer a bit to get her at dead center. We're goin' right along with that *long rake* on this load."

Jimmy commented on where Frank had the boat faced up. Is facing the boat up offset always worthwhile?" he asked.

"Much as ya kin, yah. I always do," Frank said. "Long as you got the opportunity, for sure. Good to try to get yer boat *faced up offset* if needed. 'Specially when yer gonna have the same tow for a while. Make life easy on yourself!"

Jimmy and Frank continued discussing how moving the towboat one direction or another from center when it is attached to the tow can be useful in helping the tow travel straight. Sharing the tricks of the trade with Jimmy was both fun and satisfying.

"D'you see all them trucks waitin' to unload at Meredosia?" Frank asked. "The wife's sister and husband been putting in close to two thousand acres in corn and beans the last couple years. He's got a big farm and leases some other land. They are killing it. Three- and four-dollar corn and seven- and eight-dollar beans. Farmers is gotta haul money to the bank by the wag-onload right now!"

Jimmy asked, "Don't these guys down here git three hundred bushels of corn to the acre too?"

Frank nodded. "Brothers-in-law's farms are almost straight east a' here. Between Tallula and Lewisburg on Highway 123. Flattest, blackest ground you ever seen. Right in the center of that three-hundred-acre corn!"

jack staff and *pea light* – A pole with a flag on —jack staff — is used to indicate wind direction and is typically placed at the center of the bow of a tow. The captain uses this to watch the movement of the bow from side to side. The pea light is a battery-operated light bulb mounted at the top of the jack staff operated after dark and is also used to see side-to-side movement.
long rake – A rake is the front curved end of a barge and a long rake is extended. This makes the barge go faster because of less resistance.
faced up offset – whenever the towboat is attached to the tow anywhere except at the center of the stern. The towboat can be faced up to one side or another from center if it makes steering straight easier.

Frank kept chatting as he got ready to head down for supper. "I was tinkering with the math. Let's just say fifteen hundred of the acres he farms is corn. And let's say two hundred and eighty bushels per acre. That'd be four hundred twenty thousand bushels a' corn. Four dollars a bushel at the elevator?"

Pilothouse view passing by an elevator- barge loading facility
along the Illinois River.

He was grinning and looking like we should be doing the math. He solved the math problem for us. "A cool one million six hundred eighty thousand dollars! We are in the wrong business, boys!" We all laughed, and he stepped out into the cool, dark night.

"I got relatives up in Minnesota that put in lotsa corn and beans," Jimmy said. "It's good black ground up there too, but they need rain pretty regular to git up over two hundred bushels an acre fer corn. Seems like Central Illinois never gets short a' rain. Frank's right, though. Been a little up and down, but the last four or five years when the Russkies been buyin' so much, three and four dollars per bushel is gettin' lots of farmers into the positive numbers." Jimmy adjusted his spotlights and checked the locations of barges in the fleets just upstream from us.

"I coulda farmed," he said. "My uncle and brother both wanted me to go in with 'em, but I just couldn't see it. If we inherited the land maybe. But renting and payin' a big tab to the bank is just too risky fer me. Happy to try this whole 'workin' on the river' thing. Never been happier. Keep pinchin' myself, thinkin' this pilothouse gig might actually be my future. Things are sure looking that way."

Jimmy and I talked a bit more about our common backgrounds, growing up in rural farming settings in the Midwest. We both agreed that growing up among folks who didn't shy away from hard work was a blessing. We'd both experienced backbreaking physical labor as youngsters, and when we had to step up as deckhands we had what it took to succeed.

Frank came back up after eating just I was talking to the lockman at LaGrange Lock and Dam.

"Bring her on up, Cappy. We just let a Valley Line towboat out northbound. Nobody else around. We'll dump the chamber and be ready for ya," the lockman said.

"Ten-four. See you in just a bit," I responded, and hung up the microphone. I asked Frank, "Whadya think a' that fish Johnny had?"

Frank grinned and his always-at-the-ready toothpick slid in and out while he whistled. "Crazy good, all's I kin say. He is one of the best cooks I ever seen." Frank settled in alongside me at the rear of the pilothouse.

The low farmland surrounding us gave nothing away on that dark night. Between Meredosia and LaGrange Lock there was a massive wildlife refuge off our starboard side. The lights of the lock chamber on the right bank ahead about a mile were the only lights around.

"Didn't you work a bunch on those Valley Line *coal towboats*," Frank asked.

"Yep, worked on all of those Valley Line Illinois River coal boats," I said. "*Brandon* and *Dresden* were my favorites. I really enjoyed that coal run between Joliet and Havana. Twelve, sometimes fifteen empties downstream. Hoppers, such great visibility! Lotsa slidin' and glidin'!"

coal towboats – Coal was mined across Southern and Central Illinois and then shipped by rail to Havana on the Illinois River. These are barges and towboats that moved that coal to power plants supplying electricity to the Chicago area.

"Jeepers!" Jimmy said as he lit up a cigarette and adjusted the front window to let a little fresh air in. "I s'pose there was no loads to put into a tow if they were in a dedicated coal run from Southern Illinois up into Chicago for the power plants. Loads upbound and empties downbound. *What'dya do when the wind blew?*"

"You just made do," I said. "If ya got a storm and got blew outta the channel, you jist backed till you got to where you could land the tow to steady it and git back in the channel. Some of the tight places, they couldn't keep buoys with paint on 'em. Even without wind, ya hadda run 'em down to make yer steers in the bends.

"Those were good boats," I continued. "The *Brandon* was thirty-two hundred, and the *Dresden* was thirty-six hundred horsepower. Both of 'em were old Ohio River Company boats. I decked on 'em before I got to run 'em,

MV *Dresden*. Valley Line Illinois River coal line-haul towboat. 3,200 horsepower.

"What'dya do when the wind blew?" – Jimmy was asking about how a captain handled a tow of twelve or fifteen empties when it was windy. A twelve-barge tow is 800 feet long, and a fifteen-barge tow is 1,000 feet long. Either acts as an enormous sail.

and that made it that much more special. They had great engineers on 'em, and there was never anything broke. Top-notch running. Good mates, and no scrimpin' on groceries or cooks."

I got up, put my Winston Super King out, and refilled my coffee cup. I unplugged the coffee maker — last of that pot. "Only downside was their raggedy old barges. The pilots up in the canal would just *put those tows on the wall* and skid all the way up into the city. Ate them barges alive. They had four or five round-the-clock crews welding at their barge repair fleet at Joliet. Went on nonstop. Always had a bad leaker or two in every northbound loaded tow. Every time we took on groceries or water at Will County, they would load a *pallet of shingles* on the boat with a forklift.

"You asked about a load in the tow to help if there was a wind, Jimmy." He nodded, curious to hear the answer. "A handful of times they tried to stick one or two loads into a downbound tow. It was a nightmare. The pivot point moves back so far to the stern that it is impossible to do anything. Only had one tow like that, and I hated that. I think they gave up on that finally. Better to just have a tow of empties and be done with it."

"So you just ran from Havana to Joliet with the upbound loaded tows?" Jimmy asked." He moved the ship ups back to about one-quarter ahead as he pointed our tow a little in the dark at the end of the lower guide wall of the lock. "I forgit that you never been up there, Jimmy. When you come out of the Brandon Road Lock in Joliet northbound, there is a large fleeting area. Think sixty or seventy acres as a farmer. Fleets on both sides, and most of it is Valley Line northbound loaded hopper barges of coal, and on the other side of the river is southbound empties."

The deckhand on the bow corner of the empties on the port string of our tow waved all clear as we went by the corner of the downstream long wall of the lock. Jimmy steered a little to starboard to bring our tow flat against the wall. He turned his head continuously looking out our port windows, keeping his eye on our headway. That continued to please me.

put those tows on the wall – Between the two limestone walls of the channel between Lockport Lock and Lemont, Illinois, a captain could steer the tow carefully and sail smoothly in the center of the channel. Often, they just let the tow lay against the wall and scrape along. This could damage the barges.
pallet of shingles – When barges get old, they often develop cracks, especially near corners and ends where collisions can happen. When the crack, they leak. One way to slow the leak is to drive cedar shingles into the crack. The shingles expand when wet and slow the leak until the crack can be repaired by welders at the shipyard.

View from pilothouse of fifteen loaded coal barges upbound on the Illinois River.

When it would no longer distract him, I picked up my explanation. "From Brandon Road Lock all the way up until you git into the city, it's sheer limestone and concrete walls on both sides. The channel gets tighter up from downtown Joliet, and it's all bridges and docks and fleets and barges moored along the way. Nobody runs any more than two widths north of there. Valley Line has its own smaller towboats that run upbound from there."

The deckhand on the starboard corner on our loaded barge signaled all clear as we continued into the lock.

"They run eight loads from Joliet right on up into the power plants in the city. Back and forth, back and forth. Them boats just keep making those short trips."

Jimmy reversed the engines as the deckhand on the stern of the rear empty in our tow came adjacent to a pin on the wall that allowed our entire tow and towboat into the lock chamber.

"The *Heekin* and the *Des Plaines*," I continued. "*Heekin* was the first towboat I ever worked on. Naaaaasssty, and I mean nasty!" Frank and Jimmy both laughed. "Had just a tiny ***one-story superstructure*** and a telescopic pilot-

one-story superstructure – same as a building on land: one floor house. The deck crew's quarters was below the waterline. Didn't care much for that!" I exclaimed. "I never piloted the *Heekin*, but I did work a hitch on their other short-haul towboat, the *Des Plaines*. **Single screw**. Boy, was that an eye-opener!"

MV *Des Plaines*. Valley Line Chicago area coal towboat. Single screw, 1,080 hp.

Jimmy stood and stretched, turning on the pilothouse light and dumping the ashtray into the wastebasket. Frank and I squinted and covered our eyes, surprised by the abrupt change in lighting.

Frank grinned at me and said, "Young kids," pointing at Jimmy. ***"Doesn't bother them to have that light change quick like that!"*** Jimmy looked at us nonplussed and sat down again in the captain's chair while turning off the bright fluorescent overhead light.

Frank asked me, "D'you ever work on the *Manco*? She's a single screw. Man, oh man! Like ta killed me the first trip I had on her." Frank was referring to the one single-screw towboat that Twin City Barge had in their fleet operating in the Chicago area. Frank smiled, slipped the toothpick in and out a bit and continued. "Twin City musta got a hell of a deal on a lease for her or something. She really doesn't fit with the other boats they are running up here, but I gotta say I grew to love her before it was over. I'll git on her anytime now. I'm one of the only guys who really likes her."

single screw – one engine. No redundancy.
Doesn't bother them to have that light change quick like that – A captain is typically very careful to avoid bright lights in the pilothouse after dark. Once your pupils are dilated to help you see best in the dark, you can get a bruiser headache if someone shines a light at you or turns on the overhead light. Younger persons seem to have fewer problems with this.

"I decked on her, Frank, but haven't piloted on her. I heard they really fixed her up nice after *she burnt*."

I felt compelled to explain to Jimmy the difference in piloting with just one engine. "Tell you what, Jimmy," I said, "if they give you a chance to git on the *Manco*, you don't miss it. The difference between running a single-screw and a twin-screw towboat is extraordinary. You can learn so much on a single-screw towboat that you will never learn any other way. A twin-screw boat, you can *twist* and do this and do that. Single screw, you gotta think. You gotta be two — no scratch that! — four moves ahead a' yerself all the time."

The horn sounded, and the deck crew turned us loose. Jimmy moved the ship ups to half ahead, and we started upstream once again. He did a nice job around close places, and I felt almost no need to give him advice. Jimmy must have watched lots of pilots carefully coming up. He was skilled and used good judgment much like a more experienced and mature pilot. That was something I'd done that gave me a decided edge when I became a pilot. I carefully watched everything I could. Studied every move every captain made and considered how it was done. I spent every moment I could in every pilothouse, observing and learning, from the good and the not so good.

"And there ain't no cutting corners running a single-screw boat," Frank continued. "You learn to use only steering and backing, and you are much more careful setting up and putting your tow into a slide forward or backward. And ya git jist one crack at it.

"I will say this. I've run two single-screw towboats. And both of 'em had wonderfully responsive steering and backing rudders. Far superior to any twin-screw towboat I was ever on."

I jumped in. "I couldn't agree more, Frank. When I first got on the *Des Plaines*, I was terrified. Once I had a couple of days with her, I couldn't git enough. I was learning sooooo much!"

"I think running a single-screw towboat is very similar to sailing. You must *be* the boat. You gotta think like yer the boat!" Frank and I laughed some more, then he got up and slipped into his jacket. "Headin' for the box, boys. Keep her in the rut here!"

she burnt – I was serving on the *Manco* as a deckhand in the winter of 1972 when she caught fire and all the crew's quarters were destroyed. I lost all my belongings.
twist – when a captain uses the two engines — one in forward, the other in reverse — and adjusts the rudders to help turn the tow or towboat more effectively

Pilothouse Days

He stepped out into the cold night, and a welcome burst of fresh, to-bacco-smoke-free air rushed through the door. The pilothouse swayed just a bit as it always did when someone was climbing or descending the stairs. Jimmy was *running one light to the next* and using his searchlights only occasionally. He checked his chart frequently and carefully using the pilothouse flashlight. We didn't talk much for a while. Very peaceful. He *called for traffic* as we approached the Beardstown Bridges. Crickets. Nobody else around. Once he made the railroad bridge, I took over.

"You are doing so dang well, Jim," I said. "Don't know what advice I'd give ya right now. I'm watchin' you day after day, and you just keep impressing me."

A little embarrassed, he said, "This is fun, Tom. You two are so good to give me all this time and your patience. There is no better way to learn than to git behind the sticks here and jist do it." His gratitude was evident. "And the company letting me be on here as a steersman. Don't know how I got so fortunate." He yawned and picked up his jacket.

"Have a good rest, kid," I said. "There'll be more steering for ya tomorrow."

***

We kept running along hooked up, and all was good. Makin' about seven miles per hour. Woulda been faster, but that oversized tank barge had a *square end* that we were faced up to.

For the first time in days, the sky was clear. No wind. A crisp, almost full moon just ahead over the bare cottonwood trees on our port side. Must have been some snow along there earlier. Very light layer covering the frozen mudbanks and topping the crushed mounds of dead overgrowth. Heaps of stars. The brilliant moonlight cast a silver shimmer on the water ahead, and each buoy was easily identifiable without a searchlight. It was a Beautiful towboat evening. I decided to wait till morning to call Bob. Without any traf-

---

running one light to the next – Shore markers are arranged so that a captain can steer after dark by traveling from one light to the next.

called for traffic – A captain would call on the radio when approaching a location where it would not be desirable to meet another towboat without warning. Today, towboats all have technology telling them where any nearby vessels are.

square end – A tow with rakes on both ends goes much faster than a tow that has a square end on the stern. That square end offers resistance going through the water.

---

fic delays we would be in the Peoria area around 9 a.m., and I would call then.

Bill came up to check on me.

"Thanks anyway, Mr. Bill," I said. "No more coffee for me tonight."

MV *A. H. Crane*. Formerly MV *Brandon*, 3,200 horsepower, twin screw. Valley Line Illinois River line-haul coal towboat. One of authors favorites.

He sat down for a bit and rolled one of his custom smokes. Lit it with his aged but polished beat-up Zippo. Clicked it shut firmly, and I caught the characteristic whiff of lighter fluid. He sighed as he exhaled his initial smoke. One peculiarity of Bill's was that he would never look you in the face. Gazing out to our port side, he asked, "We'll be up there day after tomorrow, ya think?"

I was enjoying the smell of the Prince Albert tobacco he used in his homemade cigarettes. "Depends on whether they have more barges for us to bring north, but, yep, if no delays and no more tow, we'll be there sometime Friday."

"Have they said anything about *laying this boat up*, or d'ya think they'll keep runnin' us?"

"You know, I should ask the dispatcher when I talk to him tomorrow. He might know, and if he doesn't, maybe he kin see what he kin find out."

laying this boat up – removing the crew and stopping operations temporarily

Pilothouse Days

Bill was quiet for a bit and then told me, "***Got my days in***, so I'd be happy to go home if they lay us up. Hopin' I kin be off over Christmas this year. The daughter got the new grandbaby, and her little boy, Tommy, is six this year. I got him his first BB gun and wantin' to be there to take him out in the woods the first time with it."

I turned on a searchlight briefly to check the mileage on a ***day board*** we were passing. "Tell ya what, Bill, we should get to the Peoria Lock tomorrow in the morning. If they got a pay phone that's workin', I'll call the office in Lemont and see if I kin talk to Jack Moore and find out what's gonna happen. I've talked to everybody on here, and the only ones that are OK with staying on when we git there is me and Charlie. Everybody else wants to go home. So I will check and see."

Satisfied with my answer, Bill got up to go downstairs. "How about I take this nasty old coffee pot down and wash it up?" he asked, looking back over our stern.

"That'd be a good plan, Bill. Thanks a bunch!"

He stepped through the door into the cold fresh air, flicking the remainder of his smoke over the side into the water. I was so enjoying the beautiful late fall evening. I tuned our transistor radio to a local country station, put my feet up on the console, and leaning back in the chair, said a modest prayer of thanks.

A good night on the river, indeed.

got my days in – When a crew member came to the end of their standard thirty-day hitch, they "had their days in."
day board – a daytime marker and aid to navigation in one of several standard shapes. Color indicates side of channel. Red downstream left, green downstream right.

Pilothouse view upbound at Pekin Railroad Bridge with fifteen barge tow.

14. Almost There

"Sounds good, Bob. We'll just keep heading northbound with this tow." I was just finishing up talking to Bob Jorgens, the head dispatcher in the St. Paul office. They hadn't found any additional barges for us to add to our tow going north on the Illinois River. "Did anybody from the Lemont office mention what they are gonna do with this boat and crew when we git over there?"

Bob replied, "Haven't heard anything, Tom. Sorry. I have no information for you."

We finished up our marine operator phone call, and I took over for Jimmy so he could head downstairs for a break. I steered our tow gently to port as we approached the bend directly below and up into the Pekin Railroad Bridge. I had a lot of memories of that area. It was common to add or drop barges there when I worked on towboats as a trip pilot. Just a few miles downstream from Peoria, Pekin had a fresher generation of industrial manufacturing, a major power plant, and at least four significant grain terminals. What Caterpillar is to Peoria, grain and chemicals are to Pekin. I slowed a little as we passed fleet after fleet, and I blew our horn for a youngster waving vigorously, perched on the corner of a baby blue blanket on the grass at the waterfront park just below the highway bridge. Mom was a looker, and she checked us out with her binoculars as I did the same.

Jimmy came back up when I cut our engines back below the Peoria Lock and Dam. The lockman warned me about the flood of fishing boats working the channel adjacent to and immediately below the lower gates when I called. He said they do that every fall when they get a sunny day. One last trip to get some nice sauger that have the feed bag on that time of year. Jimmy called the galley on the speaker box as he slid into the captain's chair. The crew came out on the head deck and looked up at us. He keyed the microphone for the loudspeaker and said, "Need you boys out on the head soon as ya kin git there. Lots of pleasure craft here!"

Bill and Charlie nodded, grabbed their life jackets, and headed out into the sunny morning. Both had on winter Carhartts and stocking hats. Charlie was a manic Green Bay Packers fan, and he always wore some green Packer gear. Big heavy Green Bay snowmobile mittens on that morning along with his green-and-yellow stocking hat. Made me smile.

We passed all the fishing boats without issue, and Jimmy steered, negotiating the lock perfectly as he had done all the others on that trip. I went out onto the tow, and once we cleared the gates I climbed *the first ladder we came to*, grabbed the railing at the top, steadied up a bit, and headed for the pay phone. I was pleased to get through to our Lemont office. They accepted the reverse charges, and I received a loud, friendly welcome from the Lemont head dispatcher, Bud Wooster. He was a high-strung fellow. Almost always on the verge of being upset, but he and I got along very well. His counterpart, Dave, was completely the opposite. You couldn't get Dave upset no matter how hard you tried. Cool as ice all the time.

The port captain, Jack Moore, was in the office, and after a brief visit Bud transferred me over to him. "I was just getting ready to head to the airport with some guys, Captain Tom. I'm glad you caught me.

the first ladder we came to – Every 100 feet or so in a lock chamber is a recess with a ladder in it.

Photo of ladder in the lock wall.

"The way it stands right now, they want to do some engine work on that boat when you git in. Gonna ship it back up first part of next week. Everybody on there has **plenty of days**, so unless anybody wants to transfer to another boat, they can all plan on goin' home when you git here. I'll keep tabs on your progress tomorrow. Most likely you will get back down out of the city during the night, so Saturday morning I can help get everybody to transportation and headed home. I'll be sure and have cash in case anybody needs to make a draw."

I shivered in the phone booth. Early morning frost still glimmered on the damp grass near the phone booth. The sun was shining through the window facing east, and with the door closed I could see my breath. The light jacket I used to get back and forth to the pilothouse was laughable out there on the lock wall. "I would be willing to stay down here for a couple weeks if you got a spot for me," I said. "I called home from the boat store in St. Louis, and they said no snow yet. If the ground is still brown up there, I might as well be here and use my days off for snowmobiling after the first of the year."

Jack laughed and said, "That's right! You like that damn snowmobiling, don't ya! Well, sir, as it happens, I do have a spot for you. I been scrambling for a couple days to find a pilot for the *Donald O'Toole*. Ronny Nolman is captain on there. He'll be thrilled to hear you'll join him."

plenty of days – plenty of accrued days off (crews commonly earned a day off with pay for every day worked on a towboat)

I smiled, feeling good about that news. I loooooved the *Donald O'Toole*, and Ronny Nolman was one of the best guys you could ever work with. "That'll be great, Jack. I love working with Ronny. We'll figure on that and work out the details of gittin' on the *O'Toole* when we git up there."

Jack gave me a personal message to pass on to one of the deckhands on Frank's watch, and we ended our call. I walked the 400 feet back along the top of the aged concrete wall to the ladder and climbed down onto our loaded tank barge. The upper gates were just opening, so I only had a few feet to step down.

Frank was up early and doing laundry. He was getting another cribbage lesson from John in the galley when I went in to get some coffee. He and everyone on the crew were excited that the company planned to lay the boat up. The energy on our towboat went from great to extraordinary just like that. It is nearly impossible to describe the euphoria related to getting off a boat and heading home. You enjoy the work and the towboat and river environment, but you are separated from all the free choices everyone enjoys on shore every day. Looking forward to being reunited with those familiar delights, it is easy to feel genuine elation.

Up and through Peoria Lake that afternoon and past miles of backwater game refuges, we passed lots of camo-colored fishing boats heading to and from duck blinds. A massive yellow, red, or black retriever stationed still and watchful at the lookout position on the head deck of those boats, leaning precariously over the bow. A little to the west of Spring Valley the river turns and heads almost straight east for a spell. A gorgeous bright sunset greeted me directly behind our stern when I left my room to head to the galley for supper. It had been a pristine fall day in Illinois, and the blue skies and fresh country air had further buoyed everyone's spirits. Passing the engine room doors, the rumble of the two massive Caterpillar diesel engines reminded me of their faithful duty. I am as amazed today as the first day I stepped on a towboat about how those towboat engines just run and run and run. Consuming thousands of gallons of fuel each week, it is as if they have no alternative but to continue to turn those propeller shafts, nonstop and without fail.

Johnny danced a little jig as I came into the galley. No question he was excited about going home. He heaped a giant portion of fresh hot mashed potatoes alongside three modest slices of his best meatloaf and set it in front of me then slid over the bowl of fresh buns, hot beneath a white cloth. While

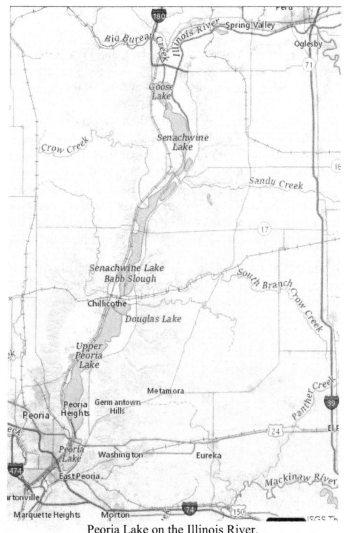

Peoria Lake on the Illinois River.

I ate, he filled me in on the details of his plans for that winter's family get-togethers and a little trip he and the missus had planned.

"Goin' to the Opry!"

"Yes, sir!" He told how the local travel agent in Jerseyville, just east of his hometown, organized charters for trips like that. "Did you know they have an exact replica of the Parthenon in Nashville?" he asked incredulously. "Full-scale replica! Same as the real one in Athens, Greece! Ain't that something?"

Pilothouse Days

I was overjoyed for him. He was such a marvelous, loving man, and it sounded like his wife kept them both young, doing things with their family and traveling with other like-minded seniors whenever they could.

Jimmy and Frank came upstairs after their supper just as we were passing under the Utica Highway Bridge, laughing and chattering. I had just finished talking with the captain of the *Sugarland*. He was departing the Starved Rock Lock with a tow of empty tank barges directly ahead of us, and we had agreed to pass on the one whistle. Both of us used our shoreside searchlights carefully, monitoring each other's location, conscious of the sheer rock faces of the riverbanks there right below the lock. Jimmy stood near me, and once we passed the *Sugarland*, I let him have the controls.

"So, yer gittin' on the *O'Toole* when we git up there, huh?" Frank asked. I poured the last cup of coffee from the pot, unplugged it, and sat down next to him. His toothpick was blue that night. John must have run out of the regular tan ones.

MV *Morgan*, previously the MV *Donald O'Toole*. 1,800 horsepower. Twin screw.

"Yep. I'm gonna enjoy that. She is such a fine boat. You been on her yet?" I asked him.

Frank shook his head and said, "Not so far. I haven't worked over here since they got her. She's sure a gorgeous boat!"

I explained a little about her. "Twin City Barge had her built just for their *lake run* a little over a year ago. Built in a shipyard in Sturgeon Bay.

lake run – working on Lake Michigan

Beautiful model hull under her. Twenty-four hundred horse. Handles like a dream. They say she's designed where she could go all the way over on her side and always come back upright. Gorgeous teak wood all over. Built like a yacht!"

Jimmy switched on his port searchlight and slowed our engines a little more as he lined us up on the lower long guide wall of the lock.

"I got a real lesson on her last winter. Scaredest I ever was! Damn near wrecked a barge and had my very own giant oil spill right on the south shore of Lake Michigan!"

Bill waved all clear as the bow of our string of empty barges passed the end of the long wall. He had his bumper ready off the corner of the barge, but Jimmy slid up on the wall so smoothly and gently that he just laid it down on the deck, unused.

I continued, "Twin City runs four or five oil tank barges back and forth across the south end of the lake. Between South Chicago and the refineries over in Gary, Indiana." Frank knew this, but I felt I needed to explain it to Jimmy. "They've had this shuttling tank barge business for years. Had two towboats just for the lake. The *Red Wing* and the *Gopher State*. Ferried barges

MV *Hannah D Hannah*, formerly the MV *Gopher State*. 1,200 hp. Twin screw. Shown pushing an oversized oil tank barge through the canal in downtown Chicago

Pilothouse Days

Jimmy reversed the engines and stopped our tow perfectly in the lock. in and out of the city just like their other towboats when not going across the lake. Both the *Red Wing* and *Gopher State* had model hulls. They were built like ocean tugs and able to deal with the big waves you git out on the lake sometimes." He placed the ship ups in neutral and turned in the chair to hear the remainder of the story.

"So, the *O'Toole* was built to replace one of them but is so much more reliable that they tied them both up, permanently, I think." I lit up a Winston, my lighter shaking a bit. Noting my sweaty palms, a little embarrassed that I was still affected so much by what happened. I picked up where I left off. "It was my first trip workin' out on the lake and I was fascinated. On there with Wayne Sibley. Super fun guy. Not a talker but great sense of humor. He helped me, explaining all the important things about ***running big water***."

Jimmy had been actively listening, nodding his head occasionally. "What do you mean, 'big water'?" he asked.

"That's a good question." I smiled at him and continued, "So a guy doesn't think about this on rivers, where you seldom get anything that is a big wave. When you git out on Lake Michigan, you get long swells sometimes and waves as high as ten or twelve feet. You can't stay faced up to a tow with those size waves. There's too much up and down movement. You'd just snap the face wires. So, you tow the barge behind on a ***hawser***."

Our young steersman continued listening intently and nodded. Frank was also actively listening and smiling, having a good idea where this was going.

"One of the things that Captain Wayne told me and was adamant about was to never take the barge out onto the lake before going out light boat and checking to see how bad the waves were. He made sure I understood that very clearly." I reached for a lit up another cigarette.

"So, it's one thirty in the morning when they finished loading our barge. We faced up, turned it loose, and I just felt my way along the canal to get out to the ***turning basin***, where we were supposed to tie the barge tempo-

running big water – navigating where large waves were common
hawser – a thick rope or cable used to tow barge(s) behind the boat
turning basin – Along the length of channels extending inland, where large ships are common, turning basins are provided so the ships can turn around and go the other direction when they need to.

rarily and go check the lake. I could see only about a barge length. Running on radar. There was not a breath of wind. I got to the turning basin and no wind, no waves, nothing. No waves in the channel going out to the lake, and it all looked still, and the fog was little thinner there."

Indiana Harbor on south shore of Lake Michigan.
Note turning basin discussed here at top center.

I looked at Frank and Jimmy and grinned. "You know what I did, right? I thought, 'To hell with it. I don't need to screw around and run out there light boat.' We were laying there all evening waiting for the barge to load, and it was foggy with no wind. It made no sense to me that there would be any waves to worry about. So, away we went. Twenty-four hundred horse. I got her hooked up. Probably going twelve, thirteen miles per hour. Still a little soupy, so running without lights. All the sudden I felt a jolt. The another, much bigger. Then, a whopper. And *bang!* There goes the starboard face wire. The next *jolt ran through the barge* and snapped the port face wire. I pulled back on the ship ups as we were thumped up and down by huge waves. My faithful old buddy Pete, our lead deckhand, took the safety line off 'cause he knew we had to get away from the barge. If we stayed there, we would have beaten the boat to pieces."

jolt ran through the barge – A barge, like a ship or an airplane wing, is constructed to allow some flexibility. In this case, the force of the huge wave striking the bow transferred through to the stern as an enormous jerk or jolt.

Even Jimmy, with his limited experience, understood the gravity of my predicament. "I could not believe the height of the waves out there. At least eight feet. Strong wind straight out of the north the day before, and the waves were still rolling. High enough that when I came up alongside the barge, there was a real danger of coming down on top of it. I had to get close enough so that we could get one of the crew on board it and hook up the **bridle** of the hawser to the tow."

I was warm all over by then, feeling clammy, just telling the story. "Wayne came up to the pilothouse through the inside passage. I kept trying to get the boat over close enough alongside the barge to get someone over onto it. My legs were shaking so bad, I was leaning against the console to keep from falling. I said to Wayne, 'Maybe you should take over.' He gave me one of his shit-eating grins and said, 'Hey, stud. You got yerself into this, yer gonna have to git yerself out of it.'

"I kept trying and trying to get close enough to the barge without coming down on top of it. By that time the headway had completely run out on the barge, and we were drifting back toward the south shore of Lake Michigan. I was imagining headlines in the *Chicago Tribune*: ALL OF CITY OF CHICAGO DRINKING WATER POLLUTED! TENS OF THOUSANDS OF GALLONS OF DIESEL FUEL LEAKING FROM OIL TANK BARGE WRECKED ON THE LAKE MICHIGAN SHORE NEAR GARY, INDIANA!"

Frank and Jimmy were caught between giggling and outright roaring with laughter. I think they were afraid to ask how it all came out. Eventually, Jimmy said, "And then?"

I explained, "Pete knew we were in serious trouble, and when I got close enough he leapt across. He landed on his face, sliding across the barge on a layer of icy water. But he got up, and in what felt like a miracle, got the bridle and the hawser on, and we were able to tow the barge across to south Chicago. He ended up **riding the barge** for two hours, soaking wet and freezing cold, alone in the dark. I was so worried about how he was doing, but he waved his flashlight at us every now and then. We got him back on the boat

riding the barge – He tucked himself into a small watertight cubbyhole designed for that purpose and stayed there until we got across.

after we got across, and once he was dried off and warmed up, I actually threatened to give him a full-mouth kiss!"

I was rewarded at the end of the story with peals of laughter from Frank and Jimmy. As uncomfortable as I was retelling that story, my feeling of relief was a sharp as it was that night aboard the *Donald O'Toole* all those years ago. Maybe it is valuable to remember how good fortune accompanies us. The errant Lake Michigan tank barge affair is at the top of my short list of events where I am certain divine intervention rescued me from a major catastrophe. I will always remember it, much wiser for the lesson.

Starved Rock Lock and Dam on the Illinois River.

The lockman sounded the horn when the upper gates were open, and Jimmy started us out of the lock. I stood, stretched, and nudged him out of the seat. "Another great day of piloting, my young friend." I moved into position and took control of the towboat.

Pilothouse Days

He was pleased with another full day of learning, and he and Frank chatted for a bit, mostly talk about how they planned to arrange transportation to get home from Lemont.

"I'll see you in about four hours, there, Mr. Struve, and I'll see you in the morning, James!" Frank said as he headed down below.

Jimmy settled in behind me and lit up one of his menthol cigarettes. "How do you usually git back and forth from down here, Tom?"

I moved our ship ups to full ahead and turned slightly in the chair so I could steer and visit at the same time. I adjusted both searchlights illuminating the many red buoys and green buoys along this stretch. Not a good place to get out of the channel. Limestone islands and outcrops on both sides.

Pilothouse view of approaching downbound tow on Illinois River.
Note the two buoys directly ahead of them.

"Most of the time I drive back and forth between Minnesota and Lemont. They got a nice safe parking area there by the shop, and I enjoy the drive. There's almost always a gas war as you cross the border between Wisconsin and Illinois around Beloit. Paid twenty-one cents a gallon last spring."

I checked out something with the binoculars then replaced them on the bath towel on the console.

"Have you ever flown standby on Northwest out of the Minneapolis airport?" Jimmy looked away, apparently a little embarrassed. "Never flown on a plane, Tom," he said, sort of under his breath. "Didn't know they would pay expenses for flying."

"When I first went to work on the river in 1970 it was common for companies to reimburse for travel expenses only on buses," I explained. "You had to take a Greyhound if you wanted the company to pay fer yer travel to and from the boat. Pilots and captains were the only ones who got expenses that included flying. Now they are OK with paying for whatever you need for all employees as long as it's not really out of proportion. They like it if ya check it out with 'em in advance.

"Maybe check with the office when we git over there. I am pretty sure they would be OK with you flying standby with Northwest. Costs twenty-five dollars. They fly ten or twelve trips a day back and forth between Minneapolis and Chicago out of O'Hare and several out of Midway. All ya do is go to the gate and tell 'em you wanna fly standby, and they put you on their list. When everybody is boarded if there's an empty seat you git it." Jimmy nodded, and I continued, "They don't take checks, so you gotta have cash or traveler's checks. Or maybe you got a credit card?"

He looked at me with a frown. "Nope. Don't got one of them. I got a hundred dollars cash though, so that should get me home. Not very excited about a bus. Is there a train?"

"Yeah, there is. Didn't think of that," I said. "You might be able to git a Milwaukee Road train that would stop and drop you off right at Hastings. I know they have a daily train between Minneapolis and Chicago. Goes to Union Station right downtown in the Loop. Maybe check the phone booths at one of the locks we make tomorrow. Git a toll-free number for Milwaukee Road in the Yellow Pages. Maybe you can call 'em and find out."

Jimmy nodded and grabbed his jacket. He slid a fresh pack of smokes out of his carton on the console and said, "Can't thank you enough, Tom. I keep learning so much, and I feel more and more comfortable with all these new things every day."

I grinned at him, gave him a pat on the shoulder, and said, "It's our pleasure, Jimmy. You're a great guy, and you learn quick. You pay attention to what we tell ya, and that's a good thing. See ya in the morning."

The night stayed mostly clear. The lights of Ottawa, Illinois, reflected off a handful of low clouds to our north. No fewer than six major marine grain terminals lined that skinny stretch of the Illinois. All still loading barges around the clock. One or two fleet boats shifting loads out and empties back in. We moved along past the *Penny of Cassville* adding four loads to their tow in the fleet on our port side. Just upstream from there I pulled into the right bank and let the *Thompson* pass downbound with fifteen empty coal hoppers. I flipped our tow back out into the channel, and we traveled the last mile upstream and onto the lower long wall of the Marseilles Lock.

Frank came up to relieve me at 11:45 as we were passing the boat docks and marina along the downtown Marseilles waterfront. No pleasure boats remained in the water at the marina. A few lighted beer signs and a marquee showing a pizza shop with a handful of cars there. Pretty quiet weekday evening.

"*I got ya*, Mr. Struve," Frank said, yawning.

I slid out of the chair, and he took control of the towboat. "I heard the *Chicago Trader* calling for upbound traffic at the Seneca railroad bridge about ten minutes ago. Not sure who else is around. Should be a quiet night for ya," I said.

Frank nodded and grinned at me, toothpick slipping in and out. "I'm gonna be home in the arms of my lovely sweet-smellin' woman Saturday night! Spend the afternoon in bed, go out get a couple cocktails, and then a nice steak at the Supper Club. Yes, sirree!"

Frank whistled a little and hummed along to a romantic ballad playing softly on the radio on the console. He was lost in thought, probably rehearsing what he might say and do upon arriving home. I put on my jacket and headed downstairs. The night air smelled of molasses and corn products. Lots of commercial corn processing nearby. Everyone said it was a record-setting year for Illinois crops. Good for the local economy. Good for the country. Good for the towboat industry.

It felt wonderful to be getting close to the end of the trip. The morning was sure to bring a busy day. Minutes after stepping into my warm, quiet quarters, I was out of my clothes and between my clean sheets. I was asleep before I could begin to count the sheep going by.

I got ya – These are the words commonly spoken when one captain takes the helm from another.

1966 Jeep Wagoner owned by author in early 1970's.

15. Brandon Road and Above

Stepping carefully out onto the guard the following morning, I could see lots of industrial lights and the glow of commerce reflecting off the low clouds of the predawn sky as I made my way to the galley. We were passing the Amoco Oil dock on our port side just coming out of the Treat's Island Cut. John had just slid Jimmy's three made-to-order sunny-side up eggs onto his plate alongside a steaming pile of sausage gravy, covering a golden baking powder biscuit.

"Just two eggs with mine, John!" I told him. "Couldn't git my belt in the right notch this morning! I gotta cut back!" The mood in the galley was almost carnival-like. Everybody was looking forward to going home.

Frank had our engines cut back, holding up for downbound traffic, so it was quiet in the galley. Seemed like a good time for a story. "I got my silly butt in a lotta trouble just up the hill from here when I was first down here deckin' on the Valley Line boats."

Jimmy and John smiled, wondering how the story was going to go. "I'd just bought the second car I ever owned. It was a used white Jeep Wagoneer. Had like a station wagon rear end, so I had my bed and everything all set in the rear. It was my version of a beginner's RV!"

Pilothouse Days

John slid my over-easy eggs onto my plate and set it in front of me. He lit a cigarette, wiped his nose on his white apron and took a long draw from his coffee cup.

"I had just enough money left after I bought the Jeep to pay for gas to git down here and **ship out** of the Union Hall. I didn't git out that first day, so I headed over just a few miles into a heavily wooded rural area southwest of Joliet, right up the hill from here. It was just gittin' dark, and I found an area that looked like a good campin' spot for the night. There was a sign saying, 'Keep Out, Natural Gas Company property.' That sign made it seem attractive. Most likely be in there by myself.

"I pulled down through the ditch and started into this wooded area. Right away the Jeep starts to bog down. Lots of short but lush grasses and bushes and countless ten-foot-tall Chinese elms. I figured, 'No problem. Got me a four-wheel-drive Jeep here.'" I paused for a mouthful of egg and a sip of coffee. "I jumped out and engaged the front hubs to put her into four-wheel. I got back in and went another hundred feet or so and came to an area where there was no clearing — trees in every direction — and I stopped. As soon as I did, I sensed it was a mistake. When I tried to move forward again the wheels started to spin, and I sank right to the frame."

John and Jimmy were bent over laughing, and after putting his breakfast plate in the sink, Jimmy rested a knee on the stool at the end of the counter, ready for the rest of the story.

"My four-wheel-drive Jeep was buried to the axles on posted private property, and I had no money. So I walked north toward the lights of Joliet, and about three miles away and across the freeway, I found an all-night truck place. I convinced them to loan me some log chains and a two-ton chain winch. I made two trips back to the Jeep to git them there. I spent all night chaining and yanking among these trees that were too small to hold an anchor once I took up the slack. It was just about daybreak when I finally got the Jeep to dry ground. Mud from head to toe and bleeding all over from tangling with the spiny thorns on those Chinese elms. I threw the chains and the winch in the Jeep and got in and put the gas to the floor. Headed straight out to the road, going right over the top of anything in front of me!"

John was laughing so hard that he spit up his coffee. Jimmy applauded a little, laughing with abandon as he and I got into our jackets to head upstairs. "You don't ever run outta stories, do ya, Tom?" John said.

As we entered the pilothouse, Frank was standing up, doing a little dance from side to side, tapping his toes and whistling. He and Jimmy looked at each other, grinned, and traded places, but not before doing a little modified waltz together.

Frank turned to me and said "I feel jist like Lucky Busbee this mornin! When he gets close to goin home he says, 'D-D-D-D-Don-n-n-n-t-t-t-t start no l-l-l-l-ong c-c-c-c-conversations!'"

Frank's imitation of Lucky's stutter had Jimmy and me in stitches. He grabbed his jacket, and danced out the door, whistling, excited to be heading home soon.

The horizon at the top of a long slope on our port side was featureless, aside from being heavily treed. A coating of frost glinted where our flanking lights shone on objects sticking out of the mud along the shore. Aging, mostly abandoned industrial buildings occasionally appeared along the shores as well as barge moorings, two elevated pipelines crossing the river, and several round chimneys spitting clouds of gray steam next to lights outlining long, low manufacturing structures. Red flashing lights decorated the guy wires of three tall radio towers. Occasional groupings of homes popped up, seeming more and more like a city than the farm country along the river downstream from there. Jimmy cut back our throttles as we made our final approach to the Brandon Road Lock. An older, ghostlike, pale gray bridge crossed between the lower lock walls in front of us and about a hundred feet below the downstream gates. One car after another going in both directions, occasional red brake lights, and mostly faint yellowish headlights highlighted the trees nearby. Each car passing over the corrugated steel *bascule bridge* decking made a loud racket.

"Do I blow for the bridge, or should I call them?" Jimmy asked.

"Shouldn't need to do anything," I said. "These bridges all through the Joliet Harbor have bridge tenders, and they do an OK job of raising them before you get there."

I'd just finished saying that when red lights started flashing on the lowering barricades on each end of the bridge. We heard a bell clanging, and then a siren blew. This was all coming through the partially open front pilothouse

---

bascule bridge – A bascule bridge is split in the middle, and both ends go up quickly and independently of each other.

Brandon Road Lock at Joliet, Illinois.

windows. The bridge decks moved upward quickly, both sides raising at once.

"So that's what a bascule bridge does," Jimmy said. "Wow. First time I ever seen that!"

We had just stopped, and the deck crew secured our tow in the lock when Bud Wooster called. "K-D-W 4-1-8 to the *Mallard*, 4-1-8 to the *Mallard*, over!" the radio barked.

"Morning, Bud," I responded. "Channel ten."

Bud was happy to hear we were so close and asked if we had an ETA for the fleet there at the Lemont office. I told him we should arrive a little after lunch without any delays. The lockman at Brandon Road said there was only one tow downbound above the Lockport Lock.

"When you git up here, we will have you drop those two empties in our fleet. We need you to run that load all the way into the city. They are screaming to git it at the chemical plant, and all our other boats are either on the way in or in the city and won't be out till late tonight. I'll make sure that whatever we have you come back out with is straightforward, so we'll have you at the office in the morning. That way everybody can get on their way."

I cleared off the marine radio and sat back in the seat as we completed our forty-seven-foot vertical ride. The lockman blew the horn, indicating we were ready to head out of the lock northbound. Jimmy got the all gone signal from both deckhands, and we moved steadily into the large pool spanned by the enormous Interstate 80 highway bridge. Now fully daylight, the first of the downtown Joliet bascule bridges carrying local street traffic was at the far horizon.

"Valley Line Fleets, here, Jimmy. Loaded tows drop on your right. Empties are fleeted on your left. That big wharf boat anchored right under the freeway bridge is Valley Line local headquarters, where you git on and off their boats and get supplies and stuff."

We passed the *Albert Heekin*, moored temporarily against a group of loaded hopper coal barges. The crew was putting out pumps and lock lines. Looked like they would be heading northbound right behind us.

"'Bout a mile that way (I pointed out the starboard pilothouse window) there's a freeway interchange, and right underneath it there is a brand-new Motel 6. Six dollars and sixty cents a night to stay. Denny's right next to it. Whenever I am down here and need to stay the night now, that is my go-to place. Used to stay at the YMCA right down the street from the Union Hall. But the new Motel 6 is only a couple dollars more."

I watched carefully to see whether Jimmy was becoming anxious about the snugness of the concrete- and limestone-lined channel. He wisely kept our engines at about three-quarters throttle, navigating along through and under each of the seven local bridges that seemed to be raised only at the very last moment. With each passing mile, the channel got narrower.

"You can get up through here three-wide, but once you leave the Lockport Lock upbound, you gotta go down to two. There's a thing called the butterfly where the shore span is reduced to ninety feet. It's an abandoned control structure in the middle of the channel that they used to use to use to divert the water over a dam near there."

I chuckled, thinking about all the times I had heard first-time captains on the marine radio, arriving at that portion of the Illinois River and whining like babies. I said. "Lotsa guys used to open rivers down below get really squirrely up here. Listening to them complain on the radio is a hoot!"

Jimmy nodded, looking around, and asked, "So, it's like this all the way up into the city?"

I nodded and said, "Pretty much. Before the river connected all the way to Lake Michigan, there was a canal, maybe sixty feet wide, along this upper end, and they towed small wooden barges back and forth with horses. Jist before the turn of the century, they dug or mined out the limestone canal we are in now and connected the lake to the river going south. Their goal was to get the sewage to flow down the river and not out into the lake where they got their drinkin' water. It was a really big deal at the time, and over the years industry and marine activities prospered here.

"Once the canal was built and the Lockport and Brandon Road Locks were up and running, Joliet was a hoppin' place. There were factories and jobs here. In the last ten or twenty years almost all the Chicago area steel mills have been boarded up. Union wages drove a stake through their hearts, and environmental issues finished the job. That triggered a massive accompanying downturn in all things industrial that spilled out this way from the city. Joliet became what it is now: a very old, mostly shuttered, and often blighted bedroom community to the city of Chicago. All along the river here, you see all sorts of buildings and rusting reminders of a time when lots of people enjoyed good jobs and a good living here. Now it's mostly mining nearby. Statesville Prison is just over there." Jimmy looked back at me, and I pointed to our left. "Lots of refineries right up ahead of us at Lockport and Lemont."

Jimmy checked our chart then pushed our throttles to full ahead now that we were in a little wider place. We shoved under a fully raised dark, stained, and rusty railroad bridge, once carrying four tracks, that looked long abandoned.

Concrete and limestone line the canal banks from Joliet upbound to Lemont, Illinois.

A twenty-foot leafless tree was anchored in the center of one of the tracks right at the edge of the open bridge. The closed downstream gates of the Lockport Lock were immediately ahead. The deckhands stepped out on the tow, doing a dance, and pretending to box. They headed out onto the tow, getting ready for the lock. Jimmy pulled back the throttles, letting our headway run out.

"Lemme tell ya a little story about something that happened here." Jimmy turned slightly in the chair, listening while steering and paying close attention to his approach to the lower lock wall. "Comin' in here one night after midnight on the old *Des Plaines*. Valley Line coal boat. A thousand eighty horse. Single screw. Had eight loaded coal barges. A ***set over single locking***. This was when I was first trip piloting. I was always in a hurry, didn't know nothin' but full ahead."

Jimmy said, "All clear," into the loudspeaker microphone as Charlie signaled the all clear as the starboard corner of our tow passed the end of the long wall. Jimmy backed our engines, stopping at the second timberhead, where Charlie caught a line. A tow was just departing northbound, and they had to dump the lock once they were clear. I continued with my story. "I musta been half asleep or something. We only had about two hundred feet to go, and I was still running three-quarters ahead. I wasn't watching my headway."

I nudged him a little from behind. "This is why I am so insistent about hammering that into you new pilots!" Jimmy nodded, chuckled, and continued listening.

"Suddenly, I realized we had way too much headway going in here. I set her to backin' full and grabbed the microphone. The mate saw what was happening. I didn't need to speak. He looked up at me, and I saw fear in his face. He raced over to the stern of our tow and got a ***double wrap of poly D lock line*** ready to drop on the floating pin in the lock wall as we came by."

Once again, I had sweaty palms, reliving the events as I told the story.

"We were gonna pile all eight of these rotten old loaded Valley Line coal barges into the wall at the end of that lock chamber and sure as hell, sink

set over single locking – A tow of eight barges is locked through, and the towboat sets over and rides in the space where the ninth barge would be.
double wrap of poly D lock line – Poly D line is thick and super strong. A double wrap is twice as strong.

'em all, right in the damn lock. As we went by the ***floating timberhead***, the mate dropped that double Poly D line over the timberhead and ran. Never seen him move that fast! I hoped it would slow us, but I felt like we were still in big trouble."

Jimmy turned, his face serious, and said, "So?"

Photo of ***floating timber head*** recessed in behind face of lock wall
It raises and lowers as the lock fills and empties.

"It was another one of those divine intervention things, Jimmy. That line stretched and banged and pinged and popped, but damn if it didn't hold. It stopped our tow. I was amazed that we didn't pull that floating timberhead right out of the dang lock wall! The mate lay down on that dirty old coal barge and just stayed there for a full minute. He got up, shook the coal dust off, and gave me a big smile. I blew him a kiss!"

The water being discharged as the lock chamber drained was churning between the head of our tow and the lock gates. The lock line fastening our tow to the wall made a loud popping noise. We had surged forward suddenly, and it startled Jimmy just a bit.

"Not an issue, Jimmy," I said. "When they dump this chamber, they don't screw around. Forty-two feet of elevation. Causes a sucking action that pulls yer tow toward the gates."

Jimmy nodded.

I pointed to where Charlie was tending his lock line. "Doesn't seem possible now, but when I was decking down here in 1970 the water was so filthy that ten or twelve feet of off-white crappy-smelling foam used to be created when they dumped the chamber. Lotsa times where Charlie is standing right now, foam would be all the way up onto your chest."

Jimmy looked astounded.

"The water was filthy back then. Didn't process sewage like they do now. And condoms everywhere. Looked like leaves on the water. They musta not screened them out at the wastewater plants." I added one more detail. "If ya fell in the river back then, they sent you to the doctor's office right away to git a tetanus shot."

Turbulent water below lock dates when water in chamber is being dumped

The lock gates swung open, and Charlie turned us loose. Once we were inside and tied off, Jack Moore from the office called.

"The *Mallard* on channel ten. Go ahead, Jack," I responded, looking back at the massive lock gates closing behind us. The aging concrete walls were wet and coated with dark green almost black moss in some spots.

Pilothouse Days

"Tom," he said, "I got a good news phone call from Jimmy Johnson's wife this morning. He's steering on there with you, correct?" Jimmy's mouth was open wide. I responded affirmatively.

"She said that his baby sister had twin babies this past Wednesday, and they are hoping to get them christened this coming Sunday. She was wondering if he would be home."

Jimmy smiled broadly and gave me a big thumbs-up. "Jimmy is right here beside me, Jack, sporting a huge smile," I said.

Jack responded, "I told her she could count on it. So I got him a plane ticket for Minneapolis leaving out of Midway at noon on Saturday. I am gonna personally see that he gets there in time for that flight."

Jimmy suppressed a squeal, jumped a bit, danced a jig, and clapped his hands.

"That is fantastic, Jack." Our vertical journey in the Lockport Lock continued. The floating timberheads moaned with the stress of the movement of the tow as the water filled the chamber.

"I'll be down at the office first thing tomorrow morning, and we'll get everybody on their way. I need a favor, though. Can you ask Morris Wilke if he can stay a few days? I need a utility deckhand on the *Windy City* just till the middle of next week. He lives right down in Pekin, and his car is here in our lot. Ask him for me, and get back to me, OK?"

"Will do, Jack. I'll get back to you." I smiled, thinking about how happy Jimmy and his family would be in a couple of days, celebrating the baptism of his sister's new babies. Bud Wooster came on the radio before they signed off and *gave me the specific orders for spotting that tanker barge*. "Then I need you to run out to *the hook*, Tommy, and there you will find two Union Mechling barges loaded with rolls of steel. Let's bring them down here to

gave me the specific orders for spotting that tanker barge – When a tank barge is offloaded, the piping on the barge is connected to a pipeline that goes ashore. The barge must be brought to a specific location that can accommodate the length of the huge flexible hose that offloads the cargo.
the hook – a mooring cable anchored to the bottom out in the deep water just behind the breakwater at the entrance to South Chicago from Lake Michigan

Lemont and drop them at Union Mechling's fleet across the channel from us here. U-M-C 2-3-3-3 and U-M-C 1-4-1-6." Bud always sound like the message was ultra-urgent.

"One other thing. You probl'y remember that sometimes the pilots for Great Lakes Towing who bring barges across from Indiana Harbor tie them off right at the very end of the *Transoceanic dock* there. Check and see it they're there as you go by. You git that done, and you can bring her in to our fleet here at the office and secure your towboat for the night."

"Ten-four, Bud. We're on it!" I made notes of the orders and hung the microphone back in its cradle. The lockman opened the upstream gates, the horn sounded, and the men cast off their lines. Jimmy sat up in the chair and clutched the engines one-quarter ahead. Once we cleared the upper gates, Jimmy brought the engines to three-quarters throttle, and we started our modest steer around the corner to starboard. I leaned on the console next to Jimmy. He looked over at me and said, "This is like a whole different world. Not like the Upper or even the Illinois River was south of Joliet. Nothin' here but destroyed concrete, bricks, and rusting metal shells of big abandoned industrial buildings. It's like going back to the turn of the century, but everybody is gone." He paused and added, "It even smells different."

His first impression was almost identical to mine when I arrived down there as a deckhand. No perfectly manicured German farmsteads. No neat as a pin public spaces and tidy residential neighborhoods. Once a thriving, tough as nails Steel Belt industrial area interspersed with tiny utilitarian houses, the only buildings remaining were sadly out of place. And the smell *was* different. Refineries, rock crushed and stacked in giant piles, and stagnant water found in pocked voids everywhere there was low spot in the miles of limestone-bottomed lowlands lining both sides of the canal.

Bill came up and asked if we were going to change the tow to get through the butterfly. I nodded, he returned downstairs, then he and Charlie headed out to catch a line on the wall up ahead.

I said to Jimmy, "There is a wide spot goin' up through here for two miles, and then you come to the Ninth Street Bridge, a high, long bridge spanning the channel. Just upstream from that is an old butterfly dam control structure that is centered between the limestone canal walls. It's like a turn-

Transoceanic dock –Transoceanic Terminal in Chicago near the lakefront. Seagoing vessels from all over the world deliver goods to the terminal that covers dozens of acres.

table for a bridge with limestone bullnoses up- and downstream. You always run the left span. The coast guard posted a warning saying something is sunk in the other side. It's eighty feet wide, so we gotta knock the width of our tow down before we git there."

"What are you thinking?" Jimmy asked. "Should we ***breast up*** the empties and put them on the head of the tank barge?"

"Probably the easiest," I replied. "Most times we just use the mooring pins all along here on your right. You can tie the load off and slide both empties up and forward and make them up that way."

Jimmy steered toward the wall, and once he had the tow sliding that way, he killed out our headway where the deck guys indicated there was a mooring pin to use. They knocked the boat out and slid the empties forward and over against the wall, positioning them side by side. Once the men completed making the coupling, we faced back up to the load, turned loose, and were again northbound.

"Take her nice and cool going through the butterfly. The wall on the left bank is smooth as can be, so favor that if you can," I said. "Right above that, you will see barges moored on the right bank for a couple of miles. Material Service has got limestone quarries and mines all along there. The canal from there up past Lemont is a hundred and sixty feet wide. One width of barges fleeted on one side or the other for most of it. So if we meet somebody southbound with two widths, one of us has to stop." He nodded and steered steadily, looking occasionally at his Illinois River chart.

I headed downstairs to check with Morris and discovered a festive group in the galley. Everybody was up, anticipating our arrival. John had a kind of picnic spread laid out for lunch. He was playing cards and taking it easy. No cook's hat or apron in sight! Made me laugh. I discussed Jack's request with Morris, and he willingly agreed to it. Frank joined me as we headed back upstairs. I called Jack Moore and told him that Morris would be happy to stay on for a week.

Jimmy made the butterfly, the tightest spot in our narrow channel, without any issue and was doing a great job splitting the distance between the sheer limestone wall to our starboard and the fleeted barges to our port. He

breast up – place barges side by side

was running along between a quarter and one-third ahead, watching carefully the movement of the loaded barges moored to the right bank as we passed. As we progressed north, a massive refinery encompassed all the area to our right. Dusty, noisy mining operations with piles of rocks on our left and a boxlike ancient-looking massive power plant on the far horizon, with three tall, rust-colored brick stacks spewing dark gray coal smoke.

"Remember when I was talkin' about those Valley Line guys laying those tows of loaded coal barges against the wall and just chugging along?" Jimmy turned and nodded. "Right here on your right is what I am talking about."

Even with the occasional cracks and seams in the limestone, there was evidence of steel rubbing against stone along the ten-foot-high wall. "See how you are steering here and splittin' the space between the rock wall and the barges on yer left?" He nodded again. "Well, they don't bother. They just let their tow lay up against the rock wall, and the suction keeps it there. Even if somebody is southbound and they gotta pass, they don't have anything to do. Nowhere to go. They just keep skidding on up the line. Jist plain lazy!"

Pilothouse view of splitting the space between the rock wall and barges alongside.

I wasn't sure Frank and Jimmy deemed that to be as big an issue as I did. Or maybe they were just preoccupied with thoughts of getting home.

Frank grinned that wonderful smile, toothpick shorter than most days, and said, "Yer gonna git to see Transoceanic, Jimmy." Jimmy looked at Frank curiously. "It's this giant international terminal just upstream from the O'Brien Lock. Ships from all over the world in and outta there. We tied off there waiting for a barge to finish loading one time. I went over and went inside. I couldn't even see the end of the building. Bet it goes for a mile. Just a huge warehouse. Pallets and stacks of pallets of anything you kin imagine from all over the world."

Pilothouse Days

Frank looked at me and said, "So, once we deliver that tank barge, we're goin' out to the hook to git two loads and come back out, huh? Outside chance we could be tied up in time to go up and get a beer at Tom's!"

I chuckled, and Jimmy looked at us puzzled. "What's the hook?" he asked before turning his attention forward of our tow and bringing the engines to neutral. A small fleet boat was wedging a barge out of a spot just ahead of us.

Frank got up and grabbed a pack of smokes from his carton and sat back down. Lighting up, he told Jimmy, "If you keep running the ship canal out through South Chicago heading for the lake, you come out into the open water. But, yer still inside this long breakwall that runs for about a mile and protects the harbor from the lake waves. They got a mooring place there where tugs drop barges that they tow over from Indiana Harbor. The call it the hook. Big floating steel tank with a shore wire on it that anchors barges there temporarily." Frank put his lighter in his pocket and continued. "Still some steel mills working over in Indiana. They load huge rolls of steel sheeting into barges, and tugs bring 'em over to the hook."

He grinned at me and asked, "Didn't you tell me you just about killed old Junior Jogurst goin' out to the hook one morning?"

I laughed, remembering that day. "Tell ya what, Jimmy, that was another time where I damn near got in trouble not watchin' my headway." Jimmy turned sideways and backed both engines for a minute, continuing to slow our headway, waiting to see what that fleet boat was doing. He was grinning, hoping for another good story.

"We were on the *Windy City*. About five thirty in the morning. Goin' out to the hook to get a barge for our downbound tow. We were light boat, almost full ahead, **light on fuel.** There was nothing around — no shore to watch. It was probably close to a mile to get out there. I got the pilothouse window open. End of a long night. Tryin' to stay awake. Goin' along good. Coming up on two loaded barges secured at the hook. Suddenly, I realized I was in trouble."

I paused dramatically, while Frank and Jimmy looked at each other and

light on fuel – fuel was loaded on Twin City's towboats weekly. It had been almost a week since fueling so the Windy City was light on fuel. She was floating higher in the water and could go faster light boat.

laughed. I lit a smoke and continued. "The ship ups on the *Windy City* are ***air over hydraulic***. They are super fussy. You got to completely stop moving from forward to reverse at neutral for a long moment. Only then can you go into reverse. Not like some boats where you kin just ***ship right through*** from full ahead to full astern. If you didn't pause long enough, the ship ups wouldn't actuate. Then you had to go through the process, pausing at neutral all over again."

I continued, "Realizing I'd waited too long before going from full ahead to neutral, I waited for the longest microsecond of my life. Finally, I shipped both controls full astern. The port engine of the fourteen-hundred horsepower, twin-screw towboat reversed. The starboard engine did not. I shouted into ***the intercom*** to warn the galley and made sure to adjust the backing rudders so at least we would hit the barge dead square. In the last second before we crashed, the port engine did a fantastic job of slowing us in that deep water. Most of our headway was gone, but we hit hard!"

My small audience roared. "Knocked a full-to-the-brim two-gallon container of orange juice forward and right into the lap of the towboat captain, Junior Jogurst. We didn't like each other before that, and he didn't become any fonder of me. He came upstairs a few minutes later, fresh change of clothes, screaming swear words I still don't think I've heard anywhere else! I was out the other door of the pilothouse and down the stairs before he got all the way up there. I thought he was going to have a stroke!"

Frank and Jimmy enjoyed a good laugh at my expense as Frank stood up, grabbed the binoculars, and checked out something over to our starboard, then he pulled the binocular case from below the console. The binoculars belonged to him and would make the journey downstairs at the end of the day. He took the bath towel that served as a soft bed for the high-powered glasses and opened the door to shake it out. Bits of dust and lots of cigarette ashes escaped into the morning breeze. The little fleet towboat in front of us was finally out of the way. Jimmy brought our engines to half ahead, and we were once again upbound. I reached for the microphone and called for downbound traffic above Romeo Bend. Two towboats responded.

"The *Des Plaines* to the *Mallard*. Downbound. Just starting to make the

---

air over hydraulic – These engine controllers required the captain to stop in neutral and let the air bleed off before going into reverse.
ship right through – On most towboats, a captain can move the levers controlling forward and reverse straight through from full ahead to full astern.
the intercom – Most towboats have a communication system where the captain can call the galley and warn of a bump.

turn up here. Got four empties. Seventy feet wide. Stoppin' down by you at the *ComEd* plant to pick up four more."

Once he stopped talking, the second boat responded. "The *Alfred Hagerty* to the *Mallard*. I'm about four barge lengths behind the *Des Plaines*. Three empties strung out, over."

"W-X 5-7-5-7, the *Mallard* back to the *Des Plaines* and the *Hagerty*. Let's go over to channel fourteen, please." Each of the boats responded and switched channels. I had a quick visit with Jimmy, and we agree that he should steer our tow over against the right bank and hold up to wait for both down-bound tows.

Pilothouse view of two tows passing near Material Service office in Romeoville, Il.

"The *Mallard* to the *Des Plaines* and the *Hagerty*. We have a loaded tank barge and two empties breasted up ahead of it. If it's OK with you two, we will pull over against the wall on the right bank right above the Material Service Fleet slip and hold up there. That'll give you time, *Des Plaines*, to back in and get your other barges and get your tow arranged. You can come on down by both of us, *Hagerty*. We'll be down here on the two whistle." Both captains agreed to my plan, and Jimmy slowed and stopped our head-way.

The offices and marine headquarters for Material Service were right out our port window. Company colors of yellow above bright red on the Quonset hut building, same as their towboats. The *Irving Crown* was tied off to the bank in their fleet area, picking up supplies and fresh water. The *Des Plaines* came around the corner ahead of us, slowed and reversed, shifting their tow

ComEd – Commonwealth Edison

into and alongside the empty barges they were picking up at the power plant. The *Hagerty* wasted no time and scurried past us, four beat-up, jumbo flat deck sand and gravel barges, with two pumps jettisoning bilgewater and two husky young deckhands on the head, who waved at us casually. Once they were clear, Jimmy pushed our ship ups to full ahead, and we backed into the center of the canal, moving past the *Des Plaines*. We had the remaining three miles to ourselves.

"When are you gonna take your license exam?" I asked Jimmy.

"I got the papers from Terry Jensen up in St. Paul before we left. He got some sample questions and answers that some guys gave him that helped him pass his test. Gonna go to the big St. Paul library when I git home and see if they got anything I can use to help for studying. Got the Rules of the Road booklet and that stuff from the Coast Guard office in St. Louis. We been mailing back and forth. I got the guy's phone number. He said in the letter to call and make an appointment. Anxious about it, but I gotta do it. Would love to pass the test and be ready for spring when they ship the boats up in St. Paul.

"You guys both got licenses?" he asked.

Frank responded first. "I never had one till last year. Didn't need one when I started out. Then they made everybody git 'em, starting last year. Wasn't as hard as I thought. I really sweated it though! I think they give all of us who were already pilots some extra leeway. The guys at the Coast Guard office in St. Louis were great. That's where I took my test."

"I took my test at the Coast Guard office in Chicago," I told them. "I found a clause in the regulations that said you could sit for a license once you had two years of service. That was back in 1973 when they required three years of working on the river. The catch was that I had to draw the map of the thirty-five miles of canal from Lockport Lock to Obrien Lock for my license exam. This very canal that we are running in. The license was harder to get at the Coast Guard office in Chicago — they didn't cut me no favors. Took me three full days to draw the maps required. All from memory. I had to do my Rules of the Road section twice. I got the license on my twenty-first birthday. They said I was the youngest First-Class Pilot ever licensed out of the Chicago office."

***

Coming up about a half mile ahead on our port side was our Chicago area home base. Twin City Barge leased a fleeting area that was a square void about 500 feet deep and 400 feet wide. A former limestone mine, now a handy stopping spot adjacent to the main canal channel. In one back corner, a tiny, white, two-story concrete block structure served as the modest headquarters and mechanics' shop for the operation.

I was standing alongside Jimmy as the guys stepped out onto the tank barge load and looked up at us. I grabbed the microphone and said, "If everything goes the way it should, we will just stick the two empties into the mouth of the fleet there, and you can catch any kind of headline temporarily. Then we'll take this load over and hang it off on the wall opposite the fleet wherever we can find a spot. Then we'll put the empties away in the fleet, grab our head gear, and head north with the tank barge."

Bill and Charlie waved their acknowledgment, and Jimmy started the steer to port and stopped the head of our tow against the barges moored there in the mouth of the Twin City Fleet. The guys grabbed a temporary line, and we dropped the load as planned. The deckhands picked up the lock lines and running gear from the bow of the empties, we cautiously crossed the canal, pulled up behind our tank barge, and faced up. The deck crew headed out and turned loose the headline, then Jimmy backed us away for the limestone wall. We headed northbound.

Lots of activity all around. Out our port windows was the *Sioux City* and New Orleans Shipyard and Fleet. A similarly sized void as next door. Home to around thirty barges moored inside the former quarry, now flooded and repurposed. Two sets of marine ways (a railroad track rising out of the water) upon which were rolling dollies supporting several barges and two towboats. Completely high and dry, their underwater surfaces were being repaired and modified by many welders working on top of lots of scaffolding. Bright flashes and sparks everywhere.

I called the office to let them know we were on the way. "W-X 5-7-5-7, the *Mallard*, to K-D-W 4-1-8. Channel ten, please."

"K-D-W 4-1-8 back, go ahead, Tom," Bud replied.

"Just dropped the empties, Bud, and heading upbound with the load," I said. "Without any delay, we should have this load at the dock at ***Bulk Terminals*** around four o'clock."

Bulk Terminals – a huge water-to-rail transshipment terminal in South Chicago at the time

Pilothouse view downbound in Chicago Sanitary Ship Canal at Lemont, Illinois.
Twin City Fleet on right and Union Mechling's fleet on left side.

16. Chicago Harbor and Canals

I was always fond of the colors of Union Mechling barges. The kept all their barges painted like new, and they were either gray with bright blue letters or a deep forest green with bright yellow letters. Union Mechling Barge Lines leased the fleeting space along there, and we were passing their barge-painting facility. Twin City's Fleet, right across the river, got their overflow. A fine brand-new high gloss paint job gleamed on a barge ready to be placed back in the water. Scattered scaffolding all around. The powerful smell of epoxy paint was thick in the air. Just ahead was a handful of very old brick buildings interspersed with tall, ancient, bare cottonwoods off to our right, making up what was left of downtown Lemont, Illinois. Directly in front of us was the Lemont Highway Bridge, and a rusty but active railroad bridge was immediately upstream from it.

Pilothouse Days

"Yer lookin' at the first of your stationary low bridges that make runnin' down here fun," I said to Jimmy. "Seventeen and a half feet of vertical clearance. This Lemont bridge is one of the lowest. They pump ballast water into some of the higher *cube empties* to get 'em under this bridge. This is where your telescopic pilothouse is important." Jimmy had pressed the *down* pedal on our pilothouse a moment before to be sure it worked prior to arriving at the bridge. Important safety practice.

"Holy cow," Jimmy said. "We sure all these tanks and hatches and ladders on this barge gonna fit under here?" He reached over and pulled back the ship ups, slowing us down.

"It's always good to be on the safe side," I responded. "As we git closer, lower our pilothouse so you are just at eye level with the very top of the highest point on your tow. Keep moving up slow, and after a while you'll be able to see if you kin make it. You git close enough, you'll be able to see the upstream bottom edge of the bridge."

He did just what I'd described, and once Jimmy was sure that the highest things on the barge would clear, he lowered our pilothouse all the way down and pushed the ship ups forward. The sound of our engines bounced off the rock walls and the bridge as we passed under, like a car going through a tunnel. Once past the adjacent railroad bridge, Jimmy raised our pilothouse back up and moved our throttles to full ahead.

"Congratulations. Yer first Chicago area low-slung stationary bridge." I gave him a poke in the back and said, "Twenty-one more road crossings and twelve railroad bridges to go before we get to the O'Brien Lock."

He grinned and let out a sigh of relief, showing that he was smart enough to have been a little anxious. That's not all bad in a cub pilot.

Frank came through the port pilothouse door and after peeling off his jacket, he nudged Jimmy out of the captain's chair. "You boys git down there and git some of Johnny's Las Vegas-style buffet. He's got all the fixin's out. Kinda like a celebration!"

"Haven't heard anybody downbound, Frank," I said. "I think we got the canal all to ourselves."

cube empties – Some barges have high vertical compartments above the waterline.

The first of many stationary bridges heading upbound into the Chicago area.
This is active railroad bridge located just north of downtown Lemont, Illinois.
Vertical clearance in 19.7 feet at normal pool level.

The sun was bright in the cloudless sky. Still plenty crisp. All in all, a nice fall day in Northern Illinois. I followed our steersman down the steps and to the stern. As we entered the galley, Johnny said, "Git in here, boys! Got some good lunch for ya!"

We feasted on the fun array of lunch meats, leftovers, and salads. It was clear Johnny was trying to clean out the industrial-sized galley fridge before getting off the boat the next morning. Another great heaping helping of his strawberries on the crisp golden shortcake, and I was once again bloated. Since it was Saturday, our supper in a little more than five hours was certain to be a thick, juicy steak. I should have planned better. Oh, well.

The mood in the galley continued to be jubilant. Lots of discussion about favorite at-home pastimes and hobbies. The deck crew members were consumed in an animated discussion about how the most recent models of the International Travelall were not just station wagons but real trucks because they were mounted on a traditional truck chassis. The cat's meow, all agreed, for pulling a camping trailer. I was unbelievably tempted to interrupt and ask if anyone knew why every man living in Illinois at that time had their name painted on the driver's door of their pickups. Decided against it. Most likely for the better.

Jimmy and I headed forward. He went up to steer for Frank, and I grabbed a life jacket and stepped out onto the barge. It had a very nice delineated and surfaced walkway around the perimeter. As I had several times since picking that barge up downriver, I fell into a nice pace, using the deck as a makeshift track. I made several circuits around the edge of the barge, and after about forty minutes, I climbed the stairs and took a seat beside Frank. He and Jimmy were discussing how close is close when lowering the pilothouse at the last minute to go under a low bridge. Jimmy slowed for the Francisco Avenue Bridge in the tight channel lined on both sides with construction barges, steel reinforce concrete forms, and various obstructions.

"Just up ahead here about two miles, I got a lesson one winter night about being sure to check your pilothouse pedal far in advance."

Frank and Jimmy turned to face me, ready for the story of another near catastrophe.

"On the *Northland*, ten thirty at night, couple years ago. Downbound with one loaded oversized tank barge, dang near exactly like this one," I said. "Colder than cold out. Snow on the ground and some slush ice in the river. Goin' along hooked up, and a little too late I hit the down pedal to check it. Nothing happened."

My listeners were open-mouthed, waiting.

"I hit the lever for the ***emergency release***. Nothing happened." Again, I recognized my hands shaking a tiny bit as I lit up a smoke. "It was far too late to stop, but I set her to backin' full and chased out the deckhand who was up there with me in the pilothouse. Had most of the headway killed out, and as we started under the bridge I slowed the engines just a little and loosened the face wires. I knew it was gonna be close. Arguing with myself. 'Do I try this or do I git out?'" I caught a breath and continued, "Loosening the face wires turned out to be a good decision. There is a long sloping roof overhang on the *Northland* shading the pilothouse windows. It acted like a ramp, and because I had the face wires loose, the boat was pushed down just enough while the roof scraped along the underside of the bridge to keep from knocking the whole pilothouse off. Tore everything on the top completely off. Running lights, whistle, antennas. It all went. Amazingly didn't bend anything. Just the damaged roof. Deep groves where the bridge bolts drug along. Another time when I had to change my drawers!"

They both laughed at my misfortune but understood how lucky I had been.

emergency release – Most telescopic pilothouses had an emergency lever for use when the pedal did not lower the pilothouse.

expansive turning basin ahead, mostly silhouettes fading into the last light of day. Lots and lots of security lights everywhere.

"A thousand-foot chamber," I noted. "Pretty new. They got some new different kind of gates. Only been here for about twelve years. Almost no elevation change. I think they put it in just to regulate the water coming out of the lake. Once yer through it upbound, you are in water that came out of Lake Michigan. The channel out to the lake is lined with elevators, boarded-up steel mills, and slips that used to moor Great Lakes ships. At least twenty-seven feet deep." Jimmy was nodding while continuing to look all around at the interesting new sights. "Even with the steelworks gone, still lots of ships. They offload coal in a couple of locations. And foreign ships getting grain for overseas. It's pretty cool."

Obrien Lock and Dam

The horn blew once. The upstream gates were open, and we traveled the last couple miles to the shoreside dolphins at the chemical plant, our destination. A shoreside *tanker man* carefully directed our positioning of the barge, and once it was tied off securely, we headed out toward the lake light boat. A clear, crisp, star-filled sky was just an hour or so away, and the heavy humid wind coming west off the lake made it seem that much cooler. I was always fascinated by all the moving parts of places like that, so I joined Jimmy and Frank, pointing and commenting about this and that.

tanker man – a person trained and licensed by the Coast Guard to handle the equipment aboard tank barges used for loading and unloading fluids.

"*Security, security, security*. The steamer *American Victory* is leaving the Interlake Coal Dock and heading outbound approaching Wisconsin Steel Bend." Lots of traffic on our marine radio. "Once again, the steamer *American Victory* is leaving the Interlake Coal Dock and heading outbound approaching Wisconsin Steel Bend. Security, security, security!"

We caught up to and passed the massive, ancient coal self-unloader lumbering along west of the 100th Street Bridge. A handful of deck lights surrounded the walkways of its fat, sagging, gray, skinned-up hull. She was escorted by two of the *classic-styled*, green-and-red Great Lakes Towing Company tugs, one on the stern and one on the bow, attached loosely to thick, off-white hawsers.

The three of us in the pilothouse continued pointing to and inquiring about the massive structures and bridges and buildings, mostly skeletons, destined to meet the wrecking ball or become the next enormous environmental catastrophe to make headlines along the shoreline. The smell of industry mixed with lake water mixed with waste of all kinds. A light skin of surface fog on the water indicated a temperature difference at the surface. Passing through each bridge, we looked both directions along skinny arterial streets to see crumbling older homes interspersed with gin mills identified by dimly lit beer signs. A final turn in the steel sheet-lined channel, and we were passing Transoceanic, the massive blue metal building extending thousands of feet behind the concrete loading docks and twisted maze of rails interconnecting loading areas and devices used to transship goods arriving from all over the world.

"Wooster said to look here at Transoceanic to see if maybe the tugs decided to bring those two loads all the way into the channel here instead of leaving them on the hook," I reminded Frank. He flipped on our starboard searchlight and sure enough, our two barges were laying alongside two others moored to shore, and they were even arranged square end to square end.

"The good news is that if we kin throw these two together and skedaddle right outta here, we might get back down to Lemont in time to go to Tom's!" Frank said, smiling and settling the boat over sideways at the coupling. The

Security, security, security – This was how most lake ships began their marine radio transmissions.
classic-styled – tugs with high front ends and model hulls

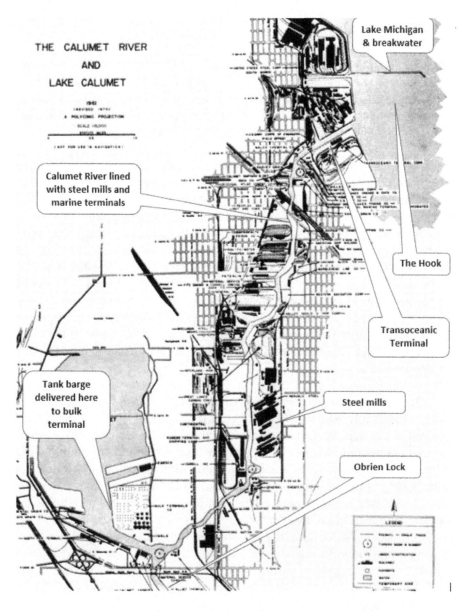

THE CALUMET RIVER
AND
LAKE CALUMET

Lake Michigan & breakwater

Calumet River lined with steel mills and marine terminals

The Hook

Transoceanic Terminal

Tank barge delivered here to bulk terminal

Steel mills

Obrien Lock

guys caught a line and quickly carried out and hooked up the rigging to fasten the two barges together in a unit.

"Bad news is you don't git to see the hook, Jimmy! Sorry, man!"

We all laughed, and Jimmy said he would make it out to the hook sometime in the future. We could see out to the lake directly in front of the boat, and it was a mostly dark and wide expanse. Too dark now to see the break-water. One or two lights on lake boats far out in the lake. Jimmy and I put on our jackets and made our way down to the galley for steaks. I was salivating, thinking about Johnny's awesome mushroom gravy layered two inches deep over my cooked-to-perfection T-bone. Suddenly I was ravenous!

Bill, the deckhand on Frank's watch, continued to tighten the rigging in the coupling, and Morris removed the line so Frank could take the boat around to the end of the tow and face up. After turning 180 degrees, Frank touched the head of the towboat against UMC 2333 and pushed the two winch buttons on the console, simultaneously taking the slack out of and tightening the face wires. Bill turned the headline loose, Morris turned the stern line loose, and after returning the waves of two crewmen leaning on the stern rail of the passing *American Victory*, Frank twisted the tow against the moored barges alongside us. Moments later we were heading downbound back toward the maze of turns and bridges in the south Chicago Harbor. By the time we approached the first sharp turn, the guys were headed back toward the boat, so he hooked her up, confident that the tow was ready for a speedy journey back to Lemont.

It was a pleasure to run a towboat like the *Mallard* in deep water with a very modest tow. She was like a fine draft horse, happy in her traces, per-forming at her very best. Almost all inland river channels are only slightly deeper than the required nine feet, and towboats struggle constantly to find efficiency without enough water for maximum thrust. With nearly thirty feet to the bottom of the channel there was no lack of water for excellent efficiency there. Frank was whistling a tune, just putting out one of his menthol ciga-rettes in the well-used ashtray when Jimmy and I walked through the pilothouse door. As we sat down, he stepped outside and emptied the over-flowing ashtray into the night.

Jimmy looked at me with raised eyebrows, and I gave him a nod. "Have at 'er there, superstud, if you still got the energy!"

Frank grinned as he and Jimmy swapped possession of the pilothouse chair. Jimmy lit up the second searchlight and focused carefully, glancing oc-casionally at our charts and noticeably enjoying this vastly stimulating stretch of the harbor. Before leaving to get his steak, Frank encouraged our student pilot. "You keep the pedal to the floor, there, young man, and we might git a beer at Tom's yet tonight!" Jimmy swung sideways and slapped Frank's hand in a high-five.

I sat behind him for the next four hours, responding to questions specific to the nuances of running the length of the **Calumet-Sag Canal** between South Chicago and Lemont. It was a quick trip. Close to eleven miles per hour in the deeper water with our nifty unit tow. He slowed perfectly approaching and making the O'Brien Lock and then against the shadows along the channel under a cold, starless night, he negotiated the cow pile perfectly. We met our only fellow southside towboat traveler of the night, the *Ida Crown* as she was dropping her three loaded aggregate barges at their dock just upstream from Ashland Avenue. Frank came back up, and he sat at the back of the pilothouse, very relaxed, tummy full of awesome steak, and a smile as big as can be.

Pilothouse view of Material Service aggregate tow passing by on Cal-Sag Canal.

"You know," I said, beginning one final story, "I had a very similar opportunity to what you just had, Jimmy, when I was first learning to steer."

Jimmy made the slight turn to port as we came out of the Calumet-Sag Canal and passed the junction with the **Chicago Sanitary and Ship Canal** just upstream from Lemont.

"Back when I was decking, you got what was called a steering letter from the office if you wanted to steer. There was only a few of us most senior deck guys that had 'em, and really, they were kind of worthless. Only a handful of captains would let you steer and then only in some boring long straight stretch where you couldn't git into any trouble."

I took a drag off my cigarette and continued. "I was the utility deckhand

Calumet-Sag Canal – Just above Lemont, Illinois, the Calumet-Sag Canal connects with the Chicago Sanitary Ship Canal and goes to the Lake Michigan port in South Chicago.
Chicago Sanitary and Ship Canal – The Chicago Sanitary and Ship Canal passes by Lemont, Illinois, and runs directly into downtown Chicago, where it terminates at the Chicago Harbor Lock. Water flows from there out of Lake Michigan and downstream, entering the Illinois River.

Pilothouse Days

on the nasty old *Pawnee*. It was February. Cold and lots of slush ice. I was on the front watch, and a pilot named Larry Hetrick was on the back watch. I asked if I could steer for him, and he said, 'Absolutely. All you want.' I was planning to take my license test in March, so the timing couldn't have been better.

"Just like you just did over the last several days, I took every opportunity. Steered all afternoon every day for sixteen days. 'Sudsy' was Larry's nickname. He was so cool. Just sat in the back of the pilothouse and never worried about anything I did. Got to do it all." I laughed at myself, thinking back at how amazed I was each time I performed another new and challenging piloting task. "One afternoon, we had four empties strung out, upbound, coming around Acme Steel Bend right below the cow pile. Pretty good wind blowing. Made that steer OK, but I really got apprehensive with the head of the tow about two barge lengths below the bridge. I told Larry I didn't think I could make it and asked if he would take the helm. He looked at me and said these words. 'OK, I'll take if her if that's what you really want. But know this. If I take her, you head your fat little ass down those stairs and don't ever ask to steer for me again. Your choice. If yer gonna do this, you gotta take the bad with the good, stud!'"

Jimmy grinned and looked at me with curiosity. "Of course, I stayed right there. And did just fine, just like you did, twice today, Jimmy." I gave him a friendly nudge, and he turned forward and lowered our pilothouse, preparing to go under the Lemont bridges. Jimmy shined our port searchlight along the wall of the Union Mechling Fleet once we raised the pilothouse back up. At least six barge lengths open for us to land and tie off our tow. He steered slightly, set us into one final perfect slide, backed us in perfectly, and the deck crew secured the barges against the limestone wall. Knocking the boat out, we landed next to the coupling, and the guys quickly stripped the rigging off and onto our head deck.

We traveled once more downbound past the Sioux City Fleet, welders on the evening shift busy under the lights, and after turning into Twin City's Fleet, Jimmy got up and slid out of the captain's chair one last time. As I took the helm, I shook his hand firmly without a word. We smiled at one another, quietly enjoying the moment, gratitude and shared admiration for all the accomplishments of that ten-day journey.

I steered the *Mallard* toward the pale-yellow rock wall and gently moved her forward, closing that last 200 feet until we bumped up against the wall in front of the office. The men placed the face wires on the mooring pins, and I pressed the buttons, snugging us in place for the night.

Those who were going uptown scrambled up the steps of the tow knee, yelling for me to join them. I waved and shouted thanks to each of them through the open front pilothouse window. I emptied the ashtray, wiped down the pilothouse console, tore off all the daily log sheets we had completed since leaving St. Paul, and after placing them in a large envelope for deposit in our office mail slot, I slipped into my jacket. The main engines shut down one by one and then there was the familiar light dim and flicker as we switched over to shore power. The generator shut down, and the *Mallard* was quiet. These final tasks complete, Morris walked out on the head deck and motioned me to follow him. He warmed up his pickup while I put the logs in the office mailbox, then I hopped in alongside him for the trip up the gravel road.

We turned right onto Stephen Street and once across the bridge, we pulled into a spot right in front of the door of Tom's Tavern. The familiar, dimly lit vintage Schlitz Beer sign cast a lovely, welcoming glow on the red-brick facade of the building. When I walked through the door, the two crew guys and Frank raised their beers and shouted a salute. Morris and I stepped up to the bar, and Tom reached out to give me a hearty, firm, long handshake.

"Great to see you, Captain Struve," Tom said. "I understand you just got in. First round's on me! What'll it be?"

I motioned a gesture of salute and accolade toward my crew and shouted, "Whiskey for me and fresh horses for my men!"

Historic Blatz Beer sign announcing, "Tom's Place" in Lemont, Illinois.
The same façade and sign today as greeted us in the 1970's.

Afterword

My heartfelt thanks to Shannon, my wife,
for the idea to frame this group of stories
amidst a towboat journey.

Writing in that way gave me such serious joy.
I was right back there, a little more than forty some years ago,
living the entire wonderful experience all over again.
I loved the river
and all the marvelous, strong lessons it taught me
about people and about living life well.

To all of my beta readers for all the books to date,
thank you very sincerely.
I am grateful for your thoughtful critique and loving feedback.
Thanks to Jan Tyree, Mary House, Robert Forbes,
Suzanne Diamond, Rich Brasch, JoAnna Foote,
Rick and Carolyn Mattern, and Tom Schuster.

Appendix

Photos Page ii- Burlington bridges- From videos, File: YouTube, Marktwained, River Captain Kyle Pfenning. Hundreds of awesome towboat videos at https://www.youtube.com/user/marktwained.com

Photo Page 11 - MV *Julie White*, sister and copy of *MV Mallard*. Used by permission of Richard Dunbar, Dick's Towboat Gallery. Photo taken by George Reichardt.

Photo Page 20 - Mississippi, From videos, File: YouTube, Marktwained, River Captain Kyle Pfenning. Hundreds of awesome towboat videos at https://www.youtube.com/user/marktwained.com

Photo Page 25 - MV *Itasca*. Used by permission of Richard Dunbar, Dick's Towboat Gallery. Thousands of towboat photos. Photo taken by Richard Dunbar.

Photo Page 29 - Couch, From videos, File: YouTube, Marktwained, River Captain Kyle Pfenning. Hundreds of awesome towboat videos at https://www.youtube.com/user/marktwained.com

Photo Page 32 – File St. Paul Union Pacific Rail Bridge in the open position.jpg. From Wikipedia Commons; Public Domain. Photo taken June 11, 2012, by McGhiever.

Photo Page 33 – Twenty-five loads, From videos, File: YouTube, Marktwained, River Captain Kyle Pfenning. Hundreds of awesome towboat videos at https://www.youtube.com/user/marktwained.com

Photo Page 34- Captain "Popyee" Tronnier, At the helm of Steamer Delta Queen. Used by permission of Jeanne Tobias from Prescott, Wisconsin.

Photo Page 35 – Fort Madison, From videos, File: YouTube, Marktwained, River Captain Kyle Pfenning. Hundreds of awesome towboat videos at https://www.youtube.com/user/marktwained.com

Photo Page 42 – File Towboat and Barges on the Mighty Mississippi.jpg. From Wikipedia Commons; Public Domain. Photo taken August 26, 2008, by Pete Markham.

Photo Page 47 – Searchlights, From videos, File: YouTube, Marktwained, River Captain Kyle Pfenning. Hundreds of awesome towboat videos at https://www.youtube.com/user/marktwained.com

Photo Page 50 - MV *Victoria*. Used by permission of Richard Dunbar, Dick's Towboat Gallery. Thousands of towboat photos. Photo taken by Mark Haury.

Photo Page 51 - Old Cedar Avenue Bridge (Long Meadow Bridge) Spanning Minnesota River, Minnesota Historical Society Photo. Used by permission. HistoricBridges.org

Pilothouse Days

Photo Page 58- MV *Viking*, downbound in Robert Street Bridges. Used by permission of Molly Isnardi @ Upper River Services, Inc.

Photo Page 62 - MV *Mary L*. Used by permission of Richard Dunbar, Dick's Towboat Gallery. Thousands of towboat photos. Photo taken by Richard Dunbar.

Photo Page 63 – Pilothouse, From videos, File: YouTube, Marktwained, River Captain Kyle Pfenning. Hundreds of awesome towboat videos at https://www.youtube.com/user/marktwained.com

Photo Page 65- MV *Sioux* at Prescott, Wisconsin. Used by permission of owner, Dallas Eggers from Prescott, Wisconsin.

Photo Page 62 - MV *Minneapolis*. Used by permission of Richard Dunbar, Dick's Towboat Gallery. Thousands of towboat photos. Photo taken by Richard Dunbar.

Photo Page 71-Pigs Eye Development, 79 \weisenberger\UAA, Richard Weingrof, http://www.dot.state.mn.us/ofrw/PDF/2013RiverTerminals.pdf Minnesota Department of Transportation.

Photo Page 73 - MV *Manco*. Used by permission of Richard Dunbar, Dick's Towboat Gallery. Thousands of towboat photos. Photo taken by Don Drot.

Photo Page 77 – Pilothouse, From videos, File: YouTube, Marktwained, River Captain Kyle Pfenning. Hundreds of awesome towboat videos at https://www.youtube.com/user/marktwained.com

Map Page 92-Locks and Dams, From Water Resources Planning for the Upper Mississippi River and Illinois Waterway, Public Domain. U.S. Army Corp of Engineers.

Photo Page 93- Confluence of Mississippi and St. Croix Rivers at Prescott, Wisconsin. Used by permission of photographer Dallas Eggers from Prescott, Wisconsin. (drone)

Photo Page 98- Milwaukee Road Rail Bridge, Spanning Mississippi River, Hastings Minnesota. Historic American Engineering Record, Creator, et al., photographer by Levy, Burt. Library of Congress

Photo Page 105- Making Lock, From videos, File: YouTube, Marktwained, River Captain Kyle Pfenning. Hundreds of awesome towboat videos at https://www.youtube.com/user/marktwained.com

Photo Pg. 108- Outdraft board, From videos, File: YouTube, Marktwained, River Captain Kyle Pfenning. Hundreds of awesome towboat videos at https://www.youtube.com/user/marktwained.com

Photo Page110 - MV *L. Wade Childress*. Used by permission of Richard Dunbar, Dick's Towboat Gallery. Thousands of towboat photos. Photo taken by Don Drot.

Photo Page 111- Tug assist, From videos, File: YouTube, Marktwained, River Captain Kyle Pfenning. Hundreds of awesome towboat videos at https://www.youtube.com/user/marktwained.com

Photo Pg. 115- Beautiful view, From videos, File: YouTube, Marktwained, River Captain Kyle Pfenning. Hundreds of awesome towboat videos at https://www.youtube.com/user/marktwained.com

Photo Page 117 - MV *Prairie Dawn*. Used by permission of Richard Dunbar, Dick's Towboat Gallery. Thousands of towboat photos. Photo taken by Mark Haury.

Photo Page 120 - MV *Pamela Dewey*. Used by permission of Richard Dunbar, Dick's Towboat Gallery. Thousands of towboat photos. Photo taken by Mark Haury.

Photo Page 121- MV *Leland Speakes*. Used by permission of Richard Dunbar, Dick's Towboat Gallery. Thousands of towboat photos. Photo taken by David L.

Photo Pg. 124- Loaded tow, From videos, File: YouTube, Marktwained, River Captain Kyle Pfenning. Hundreds of awesome towboat videos at https://www.youtube.com/user/marktwained.com

Photo Pg. 125- Coal tow, From videos, File: YouTube, Marktwained, River Captain Kyle Pfenning. Hundreds of awesome towboat videos at https://www.youtube.com/user/marktwained.com

Photo Pg. 128- Arsenal Island, From videos, File: YouTube, Marktwained, River Captain Kyle Pfenning. Hundreds of awesome towboat videos at https://www.youtube.com/user/marktwained.com

Photo Page 129- Bald Eagle. From website of National Eagle Center. Used with permission of marketing Manager, Ed Hahn.

Photo Page 135-File: Mississippi River old Lock and Dam number 26.jpg. From Wikipedia Commons; Public Domain. U.S. Army Corp of Engineers._Photographer unknown.

Photo Pg. 136- Wicket Dam, From videos, File: YouTube, Marktwained, River Captain Kyle Pfenning. Hundreds of awesome towboat videos at https://www.youtube.com/user/marktwained.com

Photo Page 139 – Wood River Refinery looking west towards the Mississippi River.jpg. From Wikipedia Commons; Public Domain. Photo taken August 25, 2006, no photographer listed.

Pilothouse Days

Photo Pg. 141- Eads Bridge, From videos, File: YouTube, Marktwained, River Captain Kyle Pfenning. Hundreds of awesome towboat videos at https://www.youtube.com/user/marktwained.com

Photo Page 144 – Joe Page Bridge, Spanning Illinois River at Harding, Illinois. BridgeHunter.com. Used by permission. Photo by John Christenson.

Photo Pg. 148- Illinois River, From videos, File: YouTube, Marktwained, River Captain Kyle Pfenning. Hundreds of awesome towboat videos at https://www.youtube.com/user/marktwained.com

Photo Page 152 – Picture of bridge from park along river in East Peoria.jpg. From Wikipedia Commons; Public Domain. Photo taken May 16, 2013, Carsonegame is photographer.

Photo Page 153- Peoria Lock and Dam, From https://www.mvr.usace.army.mil/Missions/Navigation/Lock-and-Dam-Information/Peoria-Lock-and-Dam/ Public Domain. U.S. Army Corp of Engineers.

Photo Pg. 154- Tows passing, From videos, File: YouTube, Marktwained, River Captain Kyle Pfenning. Hundreds of awesome towboat videos at https://www.youtube.com/user/marktwained.com

Photo Pg. 155- Upbound Illinois River, From videos, File: YouTube, Marktwained, River Captain Kyle Pfenning. Hundreds of awesome towboat videos at https://www.youtube.com/user/marktwained.com

Photo Pg. 159- View of Elevator, From videos, File: YouTube, Marktwained, River Captain Kyle Pfenning. Hundreds of awesome towboat videos at https://www.youtube.com/user/marktwained.com

Photo Page 164- MV *Des Plaines*. Used by permission of Richard Dunbar, Dick's Towboat Gallery. Thousands of towboat photos. Photo taken by Dan Owen.

Photo Page 167- MV *A.H. Crane*. Used by permission of Richard Dunbar, Dick's Towboat Gallery. Thousands of towboat photos. Photo taken by Dan Owen.

Photo Page 169 – Upbound tow at Pekin Railroad Bridge. BridgeHunter.com. Used by permission. Photo by Tom Winkle.

Photo Page 174 – View from train outside Chicago.jpg. From Wikipedia Commons; Public Domain. Photo taken February 10, 2010. Globalr is photographer.

Photo Page 175 – Chicago River towboat and barge 080405.jpg. From Wikipedia Commons; Public Domain. Photo taken April 5, 2008. Photographer is Jeremy Atherton.

Photo Page 177 – Aerial view of Indiana Harbor and Ship Canal.jpg. From Wikipedia Commons; Public Domain. Photo taken November 25, 2007. U.S. Corp of Engineers photograph.

Photo Page 179 – Aerial view of Starved Rock Lock and Dam on Illinois Waterway.jpg. From Wikipedia Commons; Public Domain. No photo dates. U.S. Corp of Engineers photograph.

Photo Page 186- Peoria Lock and Dam, Public Domain. U.S. Army Corp of Engineers. From https://www.mvr.usace.army.mil/Missions/Navigation/Lock-and-Dam-Information/Lockport-Lock-and-Dam-Copy/

Photo Pg. 195- Splitting space, From videos, File: YouTube, Marktwained, River Captain Kyle Pfenning. Hundreds of awesome towboat videos at https://www.youtube.com/user/marktwained.com

Photo Pg. 198- Tows passing, From videos, File: YouTube, Marktwained, River Captain Kyle Pfenning. Hundreds of awesome towboat videos at https://www.youtube.com/user/marktwained.com

Photo Pg. 201- Chicago Sanitary Ship Canal, From videos, File: YouTube, Marktwained, River Captain Kyle Pfenning. Hundreds of awesome towboat videos at https://www.youtube.com/user/marktwained.com

Map Page 205-Chicagoriversystem.jpg. From Wikipedia Commons; Public Domain. Map of Chicago Sanitary Ship Canal and Cal-Sag Canal. Source: U.S. Geological Survey.

Photo Page 207 – Aerial view of T.J. Obrien Lock and Dam on Calumet River.jpg. From Wikipedia Commons; Public Domain. Phot date; June 1, 1992. U.S. Corp of Engineers photograph.

Map Page 209- Contiguous River and Lake Sites and Their General Economic Activities, a map. From report titled *Land Use Bordering the Calumet River and Lake Calumet in Chicago, Illinois*. Authors William D Curran and Martin W Reinemann.

Photo Pg. 211- Material Service Aggregate Tow, From videos, File: YouTube, Marktwained, River Captain Kyle Pfenning. Hundreds of awesome towboat videos at https://www.youtube.com/user/marktwained.com

Pilothouse Days